MW00804422

AFFECT AND SOCIAL MEDIA

Radical Cultural Studies

Series editors: Fay Brauer, Maggie Humm, Tim Lawrence, Stephen Maddison, Ashwani Sharma and Debra Benita Shaw (Centre for Cultural Studies Research, University of East London, UK)

The Radical Cultural Studies series publishes monographs and edited collections to provide new and radical analyses of the culturopolitics, sociopolitics, aesthetics and ethics of contemporary cultures. The series is designed to stimulate debates across and within disciplines, foster new approaches to Cultural Studies and assess the radical potential of key ideas and theories.

Sewing, Fighting and Writing: Radical Practices in Work, Politics and Culture, Maria Tamboukou

Radical Space: Exploring Politics and Practice, edited by Debra Benita Shaw and Maggie Humm

Science Fiction, Fantasy and Politics: Transmedia World-Building Beyond Capitalism, Dan Hassler-Forest

EU, Europe Unfinished: Europe and the Balkans in a Time of Crisis edited by Zlatan Krajina and Nebojša Blanuša

Postcolonial Interruptions, Unauthorised Modernities, Iain Chambers

Austerity as Public Mood: Social Anxieties and Social Struggles, Kirsten Forkert

Metamodernism: Historicity, Affect, Depth edited by Robin van den Akker, Alison Gibbons and Timotheus Vermeulen

Affect and Social Media: Emotion, Mediation, Anxiety and Contagion, Edited by Tony D. Sampson, Stephen Maddison and Darren Ellis

Pornography, Materiality and Cultural Politics, Stephen Maddison (forthcoming)

Writing the Modern Family: Contemporary Literature, Motherhood and Neoliberal Culture, Roberta Garrett (forthcoming)

The Male Body in Digital Culture, Jamie Hakim (forthcoming)

Gender and Sexuality in Space Culture, Kat Deerfield (forthcoming)

AFFECT AND SOCIAL MEDIA
Emotion, Mediation, Anxiety and Contagion

Edited by
Tony D. Sampson,
Stephen Maddison
and
Darren Ellis

ROWMAN &
LITTLEFIELD
——————INTERNATIONAL
London • New York

Published by Rowman & Littlefield International Ltd
Unit A, Whitacre Mews, 26–34 Stannary Street, London SE11 4AB
www.rowmaninternational.com

Rowman & Littlefield International Ltd.is an affiliate of Rowman & Littlefield
4501 Forbes Boulevard, Suite 200, Lanham, Maryland 20706, USA
With additional offices in Boulder, New York, Toronto (Canada), and Plymouth (UK)
www.rowman.com

Selection and editorial matter © Tony D. Sampson, Stephen Maddison
and Darren Ellis 2018
Copyright in individual chapters is held by the respective chapter authors.

All rights reserved. No part of this book may be reproduced in any form or by any
electronic or mechanical means, including information storage and retrieval systems,
without written permission from the publisher, except by a reviewer who may quote
passages in a review.

British Library Cataloguing in Publication Data
A catalogue record for this book is available from the British Library

ISBN: HB 978-1-7866-0438-5
       PB 978-1-7866-0439-2
Library of Congress Cataloging-in-Publication Data

Names: Sampson, Tony D., editor. | Maddison, Stephen, 1970-editor. | Ellis,
    Darren, editor.
Title: Affect and social media : emotion, mediation, anxiety and contagion /
    edited by Tony D. Sampson, Stephen Maddison and Darren Ellis.
Description: London ; New York : Rowman & Littlefield International, [2018] |
    Series: Radical cultural studies | Includes bibliographical references and
    index.
Identifiers: LCCN 2018007129 (print) | LCCN 2018008968 (ebook) | ISBN
    9781786604408 (Electronic) | ISBN 9781786604385 (cloth : alk. paper) |
    ISBN 9781786604392 (pbk. : alk. paper)
Subjects: LCSH: Social media—Psychological aspects. | Affect (Psychology)
Classification: LCC HM742 (ebook) | LCC HM742 .A4156 2018 (print) | DDC
    302.23/1—dc23
LC record available at https://lccn.loc.gov/2018007129

Contents

A&SM3 Poster. Image by Dorota Piekorz.

Speakers, Jonas Fritsch, Camilla Møhring Reestorff and Jette Kofoed at A&SM3.
Photo by Jamie Murray.

A&SM2 audience. Photo by Jamie Murray.

Uninvited Guest at Sensorium Two (the art shows that accompany A&SM).
Art and photo by Dean Todd.

Foreword

Gregory J. Seigworth

'IT IS EASY', wrote Gilles Deleuze in his unsettlingly prescient 1990 "Postscript on Control Societies" essay, 'to set up a correspondence between any society and some kind of machine'.[1]

Wait . . . hold on a minute—"easy"? What? Did anyone alert the editors of this brilliant collection of writings? But Deleuze knew that at a certain level of abstraction, it is not especially difficult to say something like 'The contemporary era has been fundamentally reshaped and redefined by the rise of social media.' Indeed, such pithy pronouncements are sometimes so commonplace that they can feel simultaneously quasi-profound and thoroughly banal. 'Oh yes!' 'Oh, yawn'. To stake a claim, then, about a "machine"—as a highly particular and interwoven configuration of practices, materials, technologies, and sensations/sensibilities—corresponding to "any society" (this present one, that past one, some future one) must arrive not with the finality of declaratory closure but, instead, will work only if it serves to open up fresh lines of inquiry: to catalyze evocative mappings and excavations, to afford opportunities for counterclaims and inversions, to tend to the subtlest shadings of processes and events (in both their vapors and tendrils). As each of the sections and chapters of this book amply demonstrate, such an approach is at the very heart of Deleuze's belief that he was, at once, a pluralist and an empiricist. By eschewing the relative ease of sweeping abstractions in order to pursue the singularities of the concrete, Deleuze argues that 'the abstract does not explain, but must itself be explained; and the aim is not to rediscover the eternal or the universal, but to find the conditions under which something new is produced'.[2] Okay then, maybe not so easy.

Bringing affect on-board for such a critical undertaking further complicates the scenario. That's because affect doesn't track. At least not straightforwardly or cleanly. Whatever vectors, whatever blooms or decays, whatever
pilings or foldings or pealings: affect just doesn't lift up and neatly separate
from its situatedness, not without bringing along a tangle, a clot, a smudgy
impression (or an over-determined expression).

Approaching social media through the shifting prisms of affect theories
almost certainly guarantees that two things will happen: (1) the "social" of
social media will be understood as more-than-social (by encompassing the
hard-and-fast nonhuman materialities and more evanescent atmospheres
that extend through and beyond fleshy human sociality) and that (2) appris-
ing the (im-)mediations of "media" will serve as a reminder that something
like Human Computer Interaction (HCI) or digital "interface" is merely one
of our most contemporary ways of describing what continually transpires in
the rhythms and ruptures of a body's [any-body-whatever] capacities to
affect and to be affected by the moving wedge of the in-between. Given this
intertwining, the affective study of social media tends to take on the qualities
of a sort of cartographic endeavor, a plotting of coordinates—where the
latitudes of the extra-/other-than-human "social" (stretched, pulled,
extended *across*) intersect with the longitudes and deep histories of mediating
"media" (where it has only ever been interfacings intra-acting *all the way
down and back up*). Such material/conceptual intersections and affectively
attentive coordinate-capturing characterize the various chapters in this book
and are what truly set it apart so vitally from many of the previous critical
approaches to social media.

When Deleuze published his essay on "control societies" in 1990, he could
already discern the emerging contours of many of its more prominent
features—proliferating codes and passwords, surfing and undulating, continuous assessment and infinite debts, businesses with souls, cybernetic feedback mechanisms and viral marketing, gradually constrictive suppleness and
free-floating anxieties: Fully-automated affective capitalism. When added up,
Deleuze said, it all pointed to the creation of a "new monster" but rather
than 'a question of worrying or of hoping for the best' we would need to
discover "new weapons".[3] In our present age, social media—as the contribu-
tors to this volume show in their own ways—can occupy the site of "monster" and countering "weapon". That dimly emergent structure of feeling
that Deleuze intuited almost thirty years ago is now our dominant infrastructure of affective inter-relation. This gathering of writings tell us that there is
not any single machine tied to the social but a proliferation of social mediating machines and a plurality of ways of plugging into them (and/or out of
them). Does this make this book "easy"? Nope. Does this make it "affective"?

Like any machine, sometimes you won't know for sure until you pick it up and give it a whirl.

Notes

1. Deleuze, Gilles, 'Postscript on the Societies of Control', from *Negotiations* (Cambridge, MA: Columbia University Press, 1995), 180. This essay first appeared in *L'Autre journal*, (1) (May 1990).
2. Deleuze, Gilles, *Dialogues* (New York: Columbia University Press, 1987), vii.
3. Deleuze, "Postscript," 178.

Introduction

On Affect, Social Media and Criticality

Tony D. Sampson, Darren Ellis and Stephen Maddison

THE NOW NOTORIOUS 2014 publication of the research paper 'Experimental evidence of massive-scale emotional contagion through social networks' provided the initial inspiration for the first Affect and Social Media (A&SM) conference.[1] This controversial corporate-academic study, a collaboration between Facebook and Cornell University, represented to many of us working in digital media cultures just the tip of an assumed iceberg of manipulative incursions into the mostly nonconscious felt experiences of social media use. The experiment made use of over 600,000 user accounts in order to test the extent to which the manipulation of positive and negative news feeds could activate emotional contagion on Facebook. It was indeed striking to see how these efforts to emotionally trigger mass contagion related so closely to theoretical work already carried out in the areas of political affect and critical social psychology concerned with the manipulation of moods, affective atmospheres and virality.[2] The experiment also stood out as an example of a wider corporate social media strategy that could be aligned to what has since been referred to as *affective capitalism.*[3]

The validity of the perhaps overly vaunted claims to have actually triggered massive scales of emotional contagion seemed of less importance than the disquieting disclosure that corporate social media and Cornell academics were so readily engaged with unethical experiments of this kind. The notion that academic researchers can be insulated from ethical guidelines on the protection for human research subjects because they are working with a social media business that has 'no obligation to conform' to the principle of 'obtaining informed consent and allowing participants to opt out' is of course alarming in itself.[4] Indeed, although the research is of obvious socio-logical, psychological and computational interest, given that it reproduces similar responses to those already known to occur in face-to-face examples of emotional contagion, it is the political and ethical ramifications of the study, and others like it, which we felt warranted the critical attention of an academic conference.

In spite of these ethical concerns, the publication of the study provided a much needed wake up call. As follows, the negative publicity surrounding the study managed to momentarily divert attention from a prevalent and popular discursive formation, which has mostly grasped social media as a potentially problematic, yet generally rosy global village. Certainly, for a while, Facebook's superficial mantra of 'bringing the world closer together' rolled back a little to reveal a more dystopic and paradoxical underbelly. The experiment exposed a corporate social media culture that does patently *bring the world together*, but does so in order to furtively and unethically gather consumer data, and evidently, make money from carrying out large scale manipulations of this kind. If nothing else then, the brief controversy prompted by the paper's publication managed to fleetingly disrupt the cele-bratory zeal for a model of social media that brings people together for the seemingly good causes of democracy. It certainly clouded the self-congratulant role of a benevolent social media model implicated in the apparent revolutionary contagions of the Arab Spring and the spreading of Obama love, for example.

As we have since discovered, this sociable and benign model of social media needs to be grasped alongside new and widespread anxieties concern-ing the role it has played in recent populist contagions. The Brexit and Trump wins suggest that the dystopic underbelly of social media persuasion is further exploited by enigmatic behavioural data companies, like Cam-bridge Analytica, who are able to—it has been recently shown—dishonestly purchase and tap into social media derived consumer datasets from Face-book so as to undertake psychographic profiling and micro-targeting of large constituencies of voters in potentially marginal constituencies. The accusa-tion is that these data analytics firms are able to excavate behavioural datasets in order to construct massive scale appeals to voter emotions that may influ-ence election outcomes.[5] While the evidence to prove the effects of such appeals is yet to be convincingly established, at the time of writing, Cam-bridge Analytica are under investigation in the UK by the ICO (Information Commissioner's Office) and the Electoral Commission. Indeed, Facebook's complicity with the exploitation of datasets by companies like Cambridge Analytica has become an emerging international scandal.

To critically grasp the implications of these affective, emotional and feely encounters with social media we suggest that a considerable plural disciplinarity is required. For example, there is a need to draw attention to social media design strategies wherein there has been a gradual creep from ideas informed by cognitive psychology in interaction design to a seemingly universal turn toward affect, emotion and feeling. A decade before the Facebook study, influential design guru and user experience consultant, Don Norman, used his book *Emotional Design* to argue that the felt viscera of affect experienced online could override conscious cognitive decision-making processes.[6] It is significant to note that Norman was keen to stress the role positive emotions could play in influencing online consumer behaviour, brand loyalty, and as a result, drive purchase intent. In contrast, the current *modus operandi* of social media design and marketing is, it would seem, resolutely focused on negative emotions that can "hook" users by way of habit-forming interactions and the addictive checking of notifications alongside relentless anxious desires to "like" and "be liked" in return.[7]

Approaching Affect and Social Media

The first A&SM conference, and those that followed, proved that we were not alone in linking together the rise of these kinds of affective strategies to a far broader critical interest in social media. Indeed, we were initially surprised by the breadth of responses to our call for papers from across disciplinary boundaries; so much so that we found ourselves with a multifaceted series of conference programmes that were serendipitously plural in character. On one hand, this plurality clearly relates to one of the strengths of affect; that is to say, it has provided an ever expanding theoretical frame that traverses psychology, social and cultural theory, media studies, design, journalism, education, film, philosophy and fine art, to name but a few. Of course, this is not to claim that we were the first to realise the plural nature of affect. There have been much bigger and far reaching interdisciplinary conferences that have covered similar themes, such as the 2015 Affect Theory Conference hosted by Millersville University in the US.[8] On the other hand though, the inclusion of social media in the conference mix seems to have ignited a considerable spark of interest. We note here other conferences that have since gone on to specifically engage with this growing interest in affect, politics and social media.[9]

We also acknowledge other books and journals that have drawn important critical attention to social media from different theoretical and methodological perspectives, and others that have directly related affect to various kinds

of digital technology.[10] However, the aim of this book is not simply to demar-
cate a territory for a new field of study nor, indeed, endeavour to bring
disparate disciplines together to produce a kind of rapprochement. As such,
A&SM follows two guiding principles intended to set it apart from that kind
of territorializing approach. Firstly, the book endeavours to traverse the
many intersections in which affect theories arise and follow various lines of
flight, and subsequent refrains, that become manifest in these new multifaceted relations we experience with social media. This means that instead of
staking a claim for a harmonious theoretical territory, or indeed drawing out
defined battle lines that must not be crossed, our intention is to deterritoria-
lize the various debates. The reader will encounter, as such, a variety of voices
in each section that might not always fit together like a perfect jigsaw. Secondly, we want to allow for a mode of critical theory and radical thinking
that can exist in the often negotiated relations and gaps between the jagged
edges of these plural disciplinary voices. Consequently, the point is not to
expect every contributor to sing from the same song sheet. We want the
reader to embrace a variety of succinctly expressed viewpoints that will go
on to inform their critical understanding of affect and social media in novel
ways.

The Plural Disciplinarity and Politics of Affect

Affect and Social Media (A&SM) Conferences attempt to secure a commitment to disciplinary plurality: a quality of collision and creativity that has
defined the experience of the conferences on which this book draws. We
acknowledge significant approaches to affect that have characterised it as
about movement, even free fall, in the yet-ness of our bodily capacities,[11] and
we also recognise here other critical-philosophical investigations that have
ranged the theoretical and disciplinary spectrum of the neuro-, health and
social sciences approaches, as well as humanities and media and cultural
studies. Indeed, we suggest that this commitment to disciplinary plurality is
crucial to the project of apprehending the "multifaceted assemblage" that
constitutes social media.[12] As follows, we grasp the importance of Susanna
Paasonen's assertion, in her study of affect and online pornography, that
there is a need to consider assemblages of 'labor, technological innovations,
monetary exchange . . . acts and sensations, regulatory practices, verbal definitions, and interpretations' as a way to move beyond certain "simplified
dualisms" that characterised some early declarations of the affective turn.[13]

A&SM manifests the maturity of contemporary affect studies, with chapters that explore multiple intersections between the complex assemblages of

social media and the motion of affectivity. Here we note Seigworth and Gregg's assertion of a familiar articulation of this sense of motion as the capacity 'to act and be acted upon', a 'passage . . . of forces or intensities' which 'drive us toward movement, toward thought and extension'.[14] Similarly, we note Clough's sense of motion in her remarks on Deleuze's reading of Francis Bacon, whereby it is not bodies or characters that define Bacon's work, but the rhythm of his canvasses.[15] Clough further suggests that this notion of rhythm is a 'logic of sensation' that defines affect as 'time in matter', enabling a 'reformulation of methodology and presentation' appropriate to meeting the intellectual challenges of the political conjuncture. This sense of motion, which we might understand as a rhythm of time in matter, powerfully characterises the approach taken by all the authors in the book to their subjects, from questions about the potential of social media to impact on language and communication in the context of neuro-diversity, to the tensions between individuality and collectivity, or our very sense of present-ness. A&SM articulates multiple localities of flux, change and dispute, informed by intersecting refrains of affect theory, and opening up new lines of inquiry that respond to the urgent dynamics of the times. Moreover, the plurality of disciplinary approaches in A&SM reflects not only a range of social media contexts, from teen peer cultures by way of wearables, emoticons, users, selfies, supertrolls, vloggers, activists, sex parties, Ebola, newsrooms and citizen journalists, but crucially discloses a plurality of politics. If the enquiry represented by the A&SM conferences, and this book, is rhythmic, that rhythm is political, as well as being polyrhythmic, cross-rhythmic and syncopated. But more than anything else, these enquiries, in their jagged edges and pluralities, are inherently social. As Jeremy Gilbert has said, 'to think affect is to think the social, and nothing is more important right now'.[16]

Challenges Ahead

We nonetheless concede that by following our two guiding principles the book will present some readers with various challenges. To begin with, although not all of the chapters in this collection make explicit references to a particular affect theory, many are derived from some familiar and much debated plot markers, such as: Aristotle's *entelechy*; Stoic *propatheia*, Spinoza's *conatus*, Freud's *affekt*, Whitehead's "prehension", and Bergson's "virtuality", to name but a few. Indeed, whether or not these references are explicitly or implicitly made, each chapter nonetheless signals a familiar flight away from the so called "turn to language", wherein anything beyond the text might be considered unempirical, and for all intents and purposes, non-existent. This is a line of flight that certainly moves us towards a variety of disciplines that radically transcend their own often methodological and theoretical determinants. Along these lines, every chapter in the book invites, to some extent, thinking beyond the perceived, the discrete, the formulised, to offer the potential to feel, to relate, and to move. But this will be no easy task for the uninitiated or indeed the sceptical humanities reader, as affective activity is often said to occur "outside", on the jagged edges of human awareness, in a number of sometimes challenging ways.

Firstly, affect can be grasped as moving through the hardly noticed sensations, indexed in bodily rhythms that are disrupted and excited, like those considered to occur in, for example, eccrine gland secretion and cardiac ectopy. Secondly, affective activity is said to penetrate bodies fully outside of awareness through the trillions of neutrinos that pierce through us, every second, unannounced and unnoticed. Thirdly, and as the particular inspiration behind A&SM sets out, affect is also said to occur in the nonconscious manipulations of sentiment through Facebook news feeds. These various processes or movements are for many affect theorists the hidden realities of being, distorted by perception, culture and so-called consciousness. Consciousness itself is sometimes regarded as a particularised momentary assemblage, one that we attempt to actualise and stabilise to locate a "me", a "you", an "it". Affect theories encourage a thinking and feeling beyond such discursive constructs, rousing what may be termed a flirtatious dance between disciplines or what Sampson denotes as disciplinary mixtures or "interferences" between philosophy, science, art and politics.[17] This allows for a large degree of freedom of thought; a movement away from disciplinary specificity, opening creative flows and rhythms that are relatively unencumbered by too much definition. As can be seen throughout each section, it is sometimes the "ungraspability" of affect that opens up enquiry to new and radical ways of thinking.

A further challenge that some readers might face in approaching this text is that although each chapter is, as previously pointed out, "social", affectivity is often that which is unscathed by social determination. Thus, the book is caught up in the relatively impossible task of drawing attention to the multitude of processes that are constantly defying social regulation, representation and actualisation. Furthermore, some may even argue that by calling the book "Affect and Social Media" we are being somewhat misleading. It is not as if the two can be easily separated—as if affect was something that circulates and penetrates social media, rather than constituting its very being. As may be argued, the subject of the book gives way to and emerges from the affective atmospheres through which social media breathes. It is this atmosphere that infuses the user machine through contagious flows, viscerally engaging our souls, as we become social media workers, content, capital.

The Four Parts of Affect and Social Media

In order to drill down to the detail of each part of this book we have incorporated four short introductory pieces, two of which include specially invited contributions from respected colleagues Helen Powell and Jussi Parikka. So before we invite you to read on, we only need to briefly conclude our editorial introduction by setting out the general aims of these four parts.

The intention of the first part ("Digital Emotion") is to question how emotion, affect and feeling find expression in the digital. Here we find differing psychological and philosophically orientated contemplations on trigger warnings, psychophysiological measures of affect, processes and prehensions, individuation and visceral data. For example, there is a version of affect presented in this section that is theorised as existing on two psychophysiolocial dimensions: valence and arousal, while others have considered affect as constitutive of multiple dimensions.

Part II ("Mediated Connectivities, Immediacies and Intensities") draws on broadly sociological accounts of social media that connect to affective experiences of solidarity, somatic education and the temporality of feeling. In this section we encounter what Parikka calls, in his Introduction, the "affective transformations" of hashtag activism, wearable technologies and the time of affect.

Part III ("Insecurity and Anxiety") and Part IV ("Contagion: Image, Work, Politics and Control") both engage with the aforementioned dystopic underbelly of the social and cultural component of the digital. In part III, this underbelly is explored through mediated antagonistic relations with technology, anxiety branding, pornified interactions, panic and trolling. In part IV, we return to the contagion theory that inspired the first A&SM conference by way of exploring affecting violence in the work of young journalists, the emotional political chains experienced in the media during an election, the spreading of infectious images about infection and, finally, we encounter an older dystopic vision of behavioural control that seems in many ways to parallel our current social media experiences.

Notes

1. Adam D., I. Kramer, Jamie E. Guillory and Jeffrey T. Hancock, 'Experimental Evidence of Massive- Scale Emotional Contagion through Social Networks', *Proceedings of the National Academy of Sciences of the United States of America* 111(24) (2014): 8788–90, http://www.pnas .org/content/111/24/8788.full.

2. See for example, Richard Grusin, *Premediation: Affect and Mediality after 9/11*, (Basingstoke, UK: Palgrave Macmillan, 2010); Tony D. Sampson, *Virality: Contagion Theory in the Age of Networks* (Minneapolis: University of Minnesota Press, 2012); and Darren Ellis and Ian Tucker, *The Social Psychology of Emotion* (London: Sage, 2015).

3. Tero Karppi, Lotta Kähkönen, Mona Mannevuo, Mari Pajala and Tanja Sihvonen, 'Affective Capitalism: Investments and investigations', *Ephemera* 16(4), November 2016.

4. As the full statement from the publisher of the emotional contagion research, PNAS, makes clear: 'Adherence to the Common Rule [following US Federal policy on protection for human research subjects] is PNAS policy, but as a private company Facebook was under no obligation to conform to the provisions of the Common Rule when it collected the data used by the authors, and the Common Rule does not preclude their use of the data. Based on the information provided by the authors, PNAS editors deemed it appropriate to publish the paper. It is nevertheless a matter of concern that collection of the data by Facebook may have involved practices that were not fully consistent with the principles of obtaining informed consent and allowing participants to opt out.' In Adam et al. 'Experimental Evidence'.

5. Carole Cadwalladr, 'The great British Brexit robbery: how our democracy was hijacked' in *The Observer*, Sunday, May 7, 2017. https://www.theguardian.com/tech nology/2017/may/07/the-great-british-brexit-robbery-hijacked-democracy.

6. Don Norman, *Emotional Design: Why We Love (or Hate) Everyday Things* (New York: Basic Books, 2005).

7. See Nir Eyal, *Hooked: How to Build Habit Forming Products* (New York: Portfolio/Penguin, 2014).

8. Affect Theory Conference, 'Worldings, Tensions, Futures', Millersville University's Ware Center, Lancaster, Pennsylvania, October 14–17, 2015. http://wtfaffect.com/conference/about-the-2015-conference/.

9. For example, Affective Politics of Social Media Conference, University of Turku, October 12–13, 2017, https://affectivesome.wordpress.com/.

10. See for example, in the area of political economy, Christen Fuchs, *Social Media: A Critical Introduction* (London: Sage, 2014). See also the *Fibreculture Journal* Special Issue 25 on 'Apps and Affect' published in 2015, and Ganaele Langlois and Greg Elmer, 'The Research Politics of Social Media Platforms', *Culture Machine*, 14 (2013).

11. Gregory J. Seigworth, and Melissa Gregg, 'An Inventory of Shimmers', Melissa Gregg and Gregory J. Seigworth, eds., *The Affect Theory Reader* (Durham, NC: Duke University Press, 2010), 3–4.

12. Paasonen, Susanna, *Carnal Resonance: Affect and Online Pornography* (Cambridge, MA: MIT Press, 2011).

13. See also Clare Hemmings, 'Invoking Affect: Cultural Theory and the Ontological Turn', *Cultural Studies* 19(5) 2005; and Sara Ahmed, 'Imaginary Prohibitions: Some Preliminary Remarks on the Founding Gesture of "New Materialism"', *European Journal of Women's Studies*, 15(1), 2008.

14. Seigworth and Gregg, 'An Inventory of Shimmers'.

15. Patricia Ticineto Clough, 'Afterword: The Future of Affect Studies', *Body & Society* 16(2010): 227–29.

16. Jeremy Gilbert, 'Signifying Nothing: "Culture," "Discourse" and the Sociality of Affect', *Culture Machine* 6, 2004, https://www.culturemachine.net/index.php/cm/article/view/8/7.

17. Tony D. Sampson, *The Assemblage Brain: Sense Making in Neuroculture* (Minneapolis: Minnesota University Press, 2016).

Part I

Digital Emotion

EL Putnam's Digital Storge at the Third Sensorium. Photo by Dean Todd.

Introduction to Part I

Helen Powell

IN THIS PART ON DIGITAL EMOTION, the authors interrogate affective work: how it is processed online and the particular structures of feeling that digital technologies cultivate, both intended and accidental. Adopting a psycho-social approach, emoticons, forums and visceral data are positioned as both mediators and repositories of affect which leave consequential traces beyond the point of initial circulation. Examining the complex dialogic relationship between digital technologies and their embodied users in the process of meaning creation and understanding, and the emotional landscape that this cultivates, the authors recognise that once we consider communication in the context of an absent present, so we encounter the need to interrogate the management and consequences of our actions.

Taking Whitehead's *Process and Reality* (1929/1985) as his primary reference point in examining the production of meaning making, Ellis focuses on how the personal is communicated through social media. With specific reference to the use of emoticons, used for 'qualifying and fixing affect', Ellis examines how in practice the divulgence of personal information is frequently contained in its presentation and representation online. As a result, rather than functioning as anchor, emoticons now simplify how we feel to an absent present and in so doing dilute, even transgress, their intended signification. In contrast, Tucker examines affectivity through the lens of Gilbert Simondon's concept of individuation with specific reference to the affective symbiotic relationships formed between the individual and the collective as applied to social media communication and specifically "informational activity". Mapping this psycho-social activity metaphorically through Ingold's conceptualization of 'life as a line' with applied temporal dimensions and dynamics allows Tucker to examine the affective legacy of life online. In contrast, emphasis shifts to the particular in Goodings' chapter through the adoption of a case study approach of Elefriends, an online support group which centres on mental health issues. Using primary research findings, Goodings provides an alternative site for the exploration for online communication, examining specifically the affective power of the "trigger warning", a signal to other users of the potential impact of a particular posting. The embodied nature of technological engagements, and more specifically "visceral data", lies at the heart of the penultimate chapter of this section. Luke Stark deconstructs what it is and how we can identify, create and understand visceral data which captures a more longitudinal approach to affect generated in the use of technological devices. Finally, Mauri employs the Lang model of affective states to examine psychophysiological reactions to social media use. He focuses on four affective states (engagement, stress, relaxation, and boredom) which each have a unique psychophysiological signature. Mauri discusses his previous study on Facebook use and psychophysiological measures identified with affective states of "flow" and "engagement" and—for the first time—disseminates new data to identify a signature for "boredom". Including a section on psychophysiology reminds us of the manifest ways affect is theorised, its extra-discursive condition, and enables some insights into the embodied processes related to affect and social media mediation.

Several key themes, all inextricably linked, circulate this section of the book. At its heart is the examination of the psycho-social relationships of online communication, what is lost or indeed what is gained, and how this has specific temporal dimensions ranging from the affect of the immediate communication to a more enduring set of traces that evidence the legacy of online experiences. The ability to affect and be affected by others online circulates these chapters as does the tools employed to both direct, deflect and mitigate potential consequences, with the body positioned as the key processing and experiential tool. In the case of communicating mental health issues, it is recognised that mental health distress is experienced through bodily states that—once aired online—circulate in a positive cycle of action, reaction and anticipation. And indeed it is the embodied technologies that also circulate this section, how affect is shaped by and shapes future digital design and the particular experiences this has the potential to produce, intentionally and unintentionally.

Darren Ellis speaks at A&SM2. Photo by Jamie Murray.

Stephen Maddison chairs the Affect, Public and Consumption panel at A&SM3.
Photo by Jamie Murray.

Tony Sampson introduces A&SM3. Photo by Jamie Murray.

Co-curator Dean Todd and artist Bettina Fung at the Third Sensorium.
Photo by Mikey Georgeson.

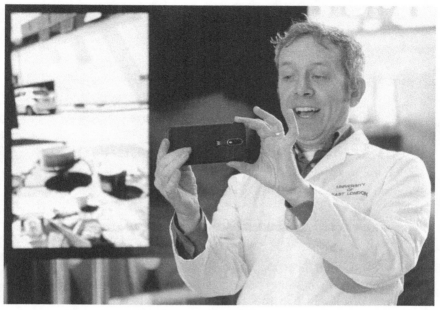

Co-curator Mikey Georgeson. Photo by Dean Todd.

1

Social Media, Emoticons and Process

Darren Ellis

I N THIS CHAPTER, I analyse notions of "personal information" and "emoti-cons" by drawing on some concepts form Whitehead's process philosophy. I will look at some of the ways that they are "prehended" through acts of "concrescence" to form as "actual entities" within the social media context. Interview data concerning everyday use of social media is drawn upon for the analysis. I conclude that personal information is often prehended as impersonal due, in part, to its marketability. Whilst emoticons may be pre-hended as more personal, these are pre-produced as universal and basic, qualities which tend to fix and strip away at emotion's affect related dynam-ics. This occurs through the multiple desires associated with social media, to simplify and qualify actual occasions.

Albert North Whitehead advocates what I refer to as a process philosophy attitude, particularly throughout his book *Process and Reality*.[1] In this work, Whitehead introduced a body of concepts which are arguably useful for the humanities and social sciences today but can appear odd when first intro-duced. For example, a relatively simple term such as "society" is defined as 'a nexus with social order and an "enduring object", or "enduring creature" . . . whose social order has taken the special form of "personal order".[2] A society for Whitehead can refer to such things as: books, rocks, and cups; in other words, things which appear to have "temporal endurance".[3] Although a society tends to be an enduring object it is additionally subject to change through an ordered series of "actual occasions". For example, Whitehead states that the life of man is a historic route of actual occasions wherein one is successively passed on to the next; for instance, the learning and forgetting of a language can be understood as an enduring object (society).[4] Any aspect of what he terms 'a person's enduring character from birth to death' can be understood as a society.

Societies, then, have some form of temporal endurance and are made up of what he terms "actual entities". Actual entities or actual occasions are central to Whitehead's metaphysics. They are moments or 'drops of experience, complex and interdependent'[5] which perish with every single instant, but unlike societies, they do not change.[6] They are rather like snapshots in time and space. They are not the material stuff, for example, of Democritus's atoms, but 'the unity to be ascribed to a particular instance of concrescense'.[7] 'A concrescence is a growing together of the remnants of a perishing past', for example the passing of aspects of an actual entity 'into the vibrant immediacy of a novel, present unity'.[8] Concrescence therefore is rather like the mechanism through which process occurs. Generation after generation of actual entities succeed one another without end, but seem to continue to exist (as a society) through the datum that they transmit. What passes from one moment of becoming (an actual entity) to the next are what Whitehead denotes as "prehensions". Prehensions are the feelings of another entity or actual occasion. 'Actual entities involve each other by reason of the prehensions of each other'.[9] In other words, prehensions are the feelings and experiences of another actual entity which are subsumed within the becoming of another actual entity, rather like a chain, or multiple matrices of chains of becomings. Prehensions, then, 'feel what is there and transform it into what is here'.[10] However, terms like feelings, experiences and prehensions are not limited to human activity, Halewood explains 'a stone feels the warmth of the sun; a tree feels the strength of the wind'.[11] Indeed "a simple feeling" for Whitehead is not to be understood in the same ways that we might understand the concept, but 'is the most primitive type of perception, devoid of consciousness'.[12] So 'actual entities involve each other by reason of their prehensions of each other'[13] within acts of concrescence. He explains that every prehension consists of three factors:

(a) 'the "subject" which is prehending; namely, the actual entity in which that prehension is a concrete element;' for example a stone or a human.

(b) 'the "datum" which is prehended;' the datum of the above example of a stone's prehension could be for instance the absorbed heat of the sun.

(c) 'the "subjective form" which is how that subject prehends that datum'.[14] It is worth noting here that the subject may have different powers (forms) of prehension. For example, although a stone may have the power to absorb heat it will not have the power to imagine heat.

The account of some of Whitehead's concepts, given above, provides a particular perspective leading to a particular process philosophy attitude, adopted here, to look at perceptions of social media, personal information and affect.

Sixteen interviews were conducted inquiring into everyday social media use. A range of people were interviewed and the only inclusion criterion was that the participants were adults and used social media daily. The interviews were concerned with how people use social media, the sorts of information they share, issues relating to security, trust and affect related activity. In the following sections, two themes of the interviews are discussed, personal information and emoticons.

According to Phelps, Nowak and Ferrell,[15] marketers tend to distinguish between two types of personal information: market level or modelled data and personal or individual specific data. Modelled data includes information about the character of the consumer group, market segment, media audience, and geographic location; while individual specific data includes more focused information (e.g. names, addresses, demographic characteristics, lifestyle interests, shopping preferences and purchase histories). Phelps and colleagues suggest that there are five general categories generally used for marketing: demographic characteristics, lifestyle characteristics (including media habits), shopping/purchasing habits, financial data, and personal identifiers (e.g. names, addresses, social security numbers).

When interviewed, participants generally tended to adhere to these marketers notions of personal information. When asked the question 'What sorts of personal information do you put up on-line?', we got responses such as:

> Participant 4: 'Personal information the only personal information I put down is where they ask you where you are from your name so me personally would say that that's probably the only personal information I put up.'
> Participant 5: 'Just like the date of birth everything like that that's already there like relationships and stuff like that that's pretty much it.'
> Participant 6: 'My name my date of birth and maybe my email will be visible.'

Personal information is relatively loosely understood here by the participants through a variety of what Whitehead would refer to as societies, for example birthplace, name, relationship status, date of birth and email address. Participant 4 suggests that the only personal information that s/he "puts down" is that which "they" ask for. The term they, here, seems to refer to the social media service provider (i.e. owners, administrators and designers etc.). The personal information that they ask for is in part driven by the desires of the marketers who will commodify this information.

The datum is abstracted and prehended by both the social media service providers and the user through processes of concrescence wherein fluid aspects of the self become frozen blocks of actual entities incorporating 'personal information'. These in turn are prehended by marketers for commodification. Participant 5 suggests that the forms of personal information that are posted are those that are "already there" or those which are predefined by the social media service providers. Participant 6 adds that it (some personal information) is made "visible" presumably for those who desire to obtain such information. Hence a relatively static data-double is formed, a datafication of the self, which is made up of societies of personal information. These "already there" societies tend to be thought of by the participants as relatively *im*personal. The "stuff like that" that they capture is almost "already there" just requiring the final forms of data that the user produces to form the actual entities which fit into the given societies of personal information. This is rather like the user completing the product on a production line, to produce what Marx would refer to as a form of alienation from the self. Thus societies of personal information denote for users that which is ironically impersonal. It is that which is abstracted from the self, and used by others as capital.

The notion that personal information is construed as impersonal is further illustrated by Participant 2. In response to the question 'What sorts of personal information do you put up on-line?' Participant 2 stated,

> Participant 2: Me I am not really one to put up personal information I would rather [pause] I don't like putting up personal information online.

Yet in response to the question 'In what ways do you communicate your emotions on-line?', the same participant stated,

> Participant 2: Well you know you can for example you know Whatsapp my status on Whatsapp usually reflects my life yeah same thing as Facebook however you feel you write it on your status because status is how you feel at the current moment so yeah definitely.

The "status" entry on social media platforms tend to be less fixed than what is considered above as personal information. One does not tend to select from such a limited set of criteria, but it affords more open and dynamic expressions that can be updated at will. It may be considered an actual entity of the current, but already passed, moment. Indeed, Participant 2 states that it 'usually reflects my life', it is 'how you feel at the current moment.' The process of actualising a particular status therefore appears to be understood as more personal than the societies of personal information. Instead, one can reflect upon life, on feelings of the current moment that are ironically considered as different from personal information. Perhaps this has something to do with such fleeting moments as not being as commodifiable as the societies of personal information due to their qualitative and open-ended capacities. However, within this study, personal information was not always considered to be impersonal, as one participant responded quite differently to the question concerning personal information.

> Participant 12: Erm the most personal stuff that gets up on-line are my emotions and thoughts and feelings at the time so it could be something like oh I'm so frustrated that I have missed the bus but then I wouldn't go deep into how I feel on Twitter or something like that.

Participant 12 portrays an understanding of personal information as similar to how Participant 2 above referred to status. Although interestingly the term personal information is not used in the response but personal stuff, not just information but "stuff", seems to imply a less formal and more transitory quality. This personal stuff includes emotions, thoughts and feelings experienced 'at the time' and hence captured in time and space through acts of concrescence of the prehensions which help produce particular kinds of actual entities 'that gets up on-line.' The actual entity that is portrayed as being concresced above is of a particularised emotion (frustration) relating to an affective activity (missing the bus). This provides an illustration of the process of concresence: a missed bus prehended, among many other affects (prehensions) producing personal stuff such as frustration—actualised on social media, in an interview, in a transcript, at a seminar, in an article—between an audience; but necessarily and purposefully lacking the complex and relatively infinite depth of the actual occasion (i.e. 'I wouldn't go deep into how I feel).' So certain prehensions are selected (which Whitehead denotes as "positive prehensions") for actualisation by Participant 12 and others deselected (which Whitehead denotes as "negative prehensions") as is always necessarily the case when humans communicate anything, but seems to be particularly so in relation to social media. The forms of actualisation afforded to users are limited by the infrastructure of the platform, among many other things. This form of actual selection is particularly illustrated through what I call 'the emoticonisation of experience'.

Emoticons can be thought of as qualifying and fixing affect, or what we refer to as an actual occasion, consisting of multiple prehensions. For example, the prehensions related to the missing of a bus can be encapsulated through an emoticon that is seen to represent "frustration". In this way, the complexity of the event is stripped, and in its place we have the seemingly stable form. In the following section I turn to look at participant's responses to questions concerning the communication of emotion on social media platforms and the use of emoticons.

> Participant 3 [I: In what ways do you communicate your emotions and feelings online?] Erm statuses—smiley faces and photos. [So emoticons are helpful?] Yes. [Are you more open to expressing emotion and feelings online than you are offline?] Yes. [Can you describe why this is?] Because if your face to face with someone and your offline you are showing your emotions more whereas when you are online it doesn't have to be taken so seriously.

In the above extract, Participant 3 explains how the emoticon creates a form of desired deception. Rather than it expressing how s/he feels, it is used as a way of masking or obscuring feelings. When face-to-face this is more difficult to achieve. This process can be understood as a form of what Goffman[16] describes as "face-work" or what Hochschild calls "emotion-work".[17] Thus the use of the emoticon here is somewhat subverted as its static nature actualises the desired affectivity.

> Participant 2: I would find it easier to express myself online reason being I get helped I've got emoticons I have phrases I have got all sorts of things to give me help in hand to explain the way I feel just in case I can't use just words.

The emoticon here, again, is used to reduce complexity. Stock phrases and emoticons are occasionally wheeled out to help "explain" feelings. A snapshot, or actual entity, here works as a visual representation of the experiences that are presently difficult to codify within the words of a language system. The prehensions are better represented in one static symbol it seems. Thus the reduced selection (negative prehensions) of basic actualised emotional expressions facilitates communication. It may not fully represent that which is prehended but it enables some form of desired effect.

> Participant 4: [OK, are emoticons helpful?] What's that sorry emoticons? [You know—the little smiley faces] Erm yeah I believe they are I mean in terms of over text because you know you won't want people on Facebook to know what you're typing to people—you could say something with a smiley face at the end and it could mean different things to different people so in that respect yeah I think they are.

Participant 4 explains how s/he uses the emoticon to reduce the ambiguity of the text. It facilitates some form of objective comprehension of the statement being expressed. Here we find the actual entity (the Facebook entry for example) in this context, enhancing the desired meaning of the text.

In the above examples, it seems that the actual entities derived through the use of emoticons on social media platforms are the result of the concrescence of prehensions actualised through multiple desires. In the three extracts we saw desires to deceive, explain and objectify experience. In each case there is a fixing and qualifying of affect. The complexity of multiple prehensions is stripped through the stable and basic form of the emoticon. The emoticon colonises the affective processes, through reducing complexity with, perhaps, the resulting increase of clicks, likes, friends, users and related economies.

The process philosophy-oriented analysis here of what can be described as the becomings of the actual entities within social media through prehensions and concrescence, moved the focus from that which is produced to the processes of production. This form of analysis led to an understanding that the so called personal information which the social media platforms often collect, tends to be prehended as static and fixed actualisations of a much more complex reality. These snapshots or slices of reality are pre-defined to fit into categories that make so called personal information easier to understand and commodify. Ironically, rather than being perceived by the social media users as personal, datafication of the self-tended to be viewed as relatively *im*personal. Additionally, phenomena which were prehended as less fixed, fluid and idiosyncratic did not tend to be considered personal information. Hence the term has taken on, for most of the participants, a different meaning, one that relates to internet economies rather than the individual. Expressions and representations of affective activity, although arguably very personal, were unlikely to be associated with the term personal information. For example, a status update, although maybe replete with emotion related information, appeared outside the realm of personal information.

Additionally, the use of affect related expressions and representations often involve processes which exonerate complexity. Emoticons can be thought of as fixing (actualising) and stripping otherwise dynamic affect related processes (prehensions), in order to simplify and qualify, for example, the relatively infinite complexity of an actual occasion and yet, they were discussed as useful signifiers of phenomena. Indeed, the emoticon incorporated multiple uses. These appeared not to be used to simply express some inner emotion or feeling in a straightforward way, but rather to reduce the complexity of affect in at least three ways by the participants, in order to facilitate deception (to manipulate how others perceive the emotional state of the user), explanation (used in place of words) and objectification (to reduce the ambiguity of a statement). The emoticon, while being produced to enhance emotional expressivity, has in some ways reduced the complexity of an expression. Ironically, this appeared to be understood by participants as bestowing advantages, as it facilitates various desired effects. The basic emotions thesis has many critics often arguing against the assumption that there are six or so hard-wired emotions that are universally expressed through the face.[18] What is interesting here is that whether these basic expressions do signify some inner reality or not may not be the point. Perhaps the emotional facial expression, like the emoticon, like the categories of personal information, indeed like all symbolic systems—but particularly those conveyed through social media—allow for reduction of that which is incessantly complex in order to undergo some form of actualised presentation, allowing the desired prehensions expression.

Notes

1. Whitehead, A. N. *Process and Reality: Corrected Edition*, David Ray Griffin and Donald W. Sherburne, eds. (New York: The Free Press, 1929/1985).

2. Ibid., 34.

3. Ibid.

4. Ibid., 89–90.

5. Ibid., 28.

6. Ibid., 35.

7. Ibid., 323.

8. Sherburne, D. *A Key to Whitehead's Process and Reality* (New York: The Macmillan Company, 1966), 206.

9. Whitehead, *Process and Reality*, 20.

10. Ibid., 133.

11. Halewood, M. *A. N. Whitehead and Social Theory: Tracing a Culture of Thought* (London: Anthem Press, 2013), 31.

12. Whitehead, *Process and Reality*, 236.

13. Ibid., 20.

14. Ibid., 23.

15. Phelps, J., G. Nowak and E. Ferrell. 'Privacy Concerns and Consumer Willingness to Provide Personal Information'. *Journal of Public Policy & Marketing*, Spring 2000, 19(1), 2000: 27–41.

16. Goffman, E. *Interaction Rituals* (New York: Garden City, 1967).

17. Hochschild, A. R. *The Managed Heart* (Berkeley: University of California Press, 1983).

18. Ellis, D. and I. Tucker. *Social Psychology of Emotion* (London: Sage Publications, 2015).

2

Anticipating Affect

Trigger Warnings in a Mental Health Social Media Site

Lewis Goodings

P OSTS TO ONLINE FORUMS AND social network sites often come with a warning. This is when the author of the post feels there is a chance that what they are about to write may *trigger* harmful reactions in other members of the community. "Trigger warnings" are statements that appear before a piece of content and feature in many online settings. This chapter will explore the social process of online trigger warnings and will consider the way that members of a social media site mediate the potential distress for others as part of the affective landscape of the site. Trigger warnings first appeared on blogs and forums where users wanted to warn others that their stories included details of abuse. This practice has been adopted by many mental health social media technologies and also been found in some offline settings (e.g. some US universities have given their course materials trigger warnings in order to warn students of potentially distressing materials therein).[1] This chapter explores the use of trigger warnings in the social media site "Elefriends" (www.elefriends.org.uk).

Elefriends is a social media site aimed at giving people a space to discuss mental health issues, encouraging people to share their own stories and experiences. The site is dedicated to peer support and there is a significant amount of people who write about distressing events and wish to avoid the possibility of encouraging stressful reactions in others. As a result, there are many conversations in Elefriends which start with a trigger warning.

Elefriends adopts a similar style to other social network sites as members can receive information from the community at large via their newsfeed or can choose to communicate in more private ways (i.e. private messaging). Elefriends was designed and developed by Mind, a UK mental health charity, and is themed around the image of the kind and helpful elephant (thus "*Ele*—friends"). The site is very user-friendly and is constructed to encourage peer support. Hence, communication in Elefriends regularly includes members discussing recent incidents relating to mental health and other members providing support or advice. Elefriends has approximately 45,000 users (August 2016) and is a space where people can speak openly and freely about their experience of mental distress. It is intentionally positioned as a peer support service and thus outside of formal care practices. This site is one of a number of sites that address the "gap" in mental health care, providing a space for people who experience mental distress to meet and talk with others.

There is a strong emphasis on the role of the community in Elefriends. However, the site is still moderated by a team at Mind from 10am to midnight through the week (Monday to Friday) and from 10 am to 2 pm/5 pm to midnight on Saturday and Sunday.). All moderation is communicated via "The Ele" and his "handlers". This might mean that a post is removed by one of the team if they feel that it does not meet the community rules (e.g. if someone is sharing personal contact details). The site is intentionally designed to avoid formal care services and Mind does not refer people directly to clinical services unless directly asked to. Mind regularly review their moderation practices and speak to the community about ways of improving this service. This space is primarily intended to be for the community members and as such the moderators try to have minimal engagement with the interactions. As such, the community has developed everyday practices for organising the way that posts are received by the community at large.

Trigger warnings are part of the way communication is *affectively* organised in Elefriends. Those who choose to post with a trigger warning are registering the affective capacity of the post to the rest of the community. There has been a growing interest in the study of affect across the humanities and social sciences (as can be attested to in this book) and it has been characterized through a variety theories and concepts.[2,3] However, it is generally accepted that affect relates to the forces at play in the patterns of motion and rest that are often delivered via an intense set of feelings, operating across both material and discursive practices.[4,5,6] In this chapter, I will be drawing on a notion of affect in order to advance some understanding of the practice of trigger warnings.

Digital Affect

Understanding the role of affect in digital communication requires consideration of the way that people process digital information. Mark Hansen encourages us to think about the way that contemporary forms of media allow the body to be continually (re)created in the act of filtering digital information.[7] This recognises how affect is directly linked to the body and, unlike some perspectives on digital spaces[8], this view does not jettison the body in order to understand digital forms of meaningful communication. Hansen's work develops ideas first put forward by Henri Bergson that argue for the role of the body in the role of perception, developing these ideas to understand the functions of digital information. A central element from Bergson explores how people come to know the body 'from within' via the process of affection. As Bergson argues:

> Yet there is one of them which is distinct from all the others, in that I do not know it only from without by perceptions, but from within by affections: it is my body.[9]

Unlike other images that are based on knowledge "from without", affect comes from within, from the body. So how do we come to know the body in digital media? Hansen develops Bergson's argument to argue that the process of engaging the digital image of the body functions via the process of "framing" digital information. Placing importance on the subtractive way in which people select images that are relevant to the body. It requires selecting from the many multiple possible images that might be available in any moment and choosing relevant information that speaks to the body. Thus the image of the body in digital spaces, and the way it moves, changes and collides with other images all contribute to how we perceive the body. Affection is the capacity to feel the body moving as it comes into contact with itself and other bodies. The physical body is heavily implicated in this practice as there is a focus on the "entire process" in which information is perceived and felt. The image requires the body to give meaning to digital information in order to transform the unbounded, limitless amount of digital information into 'concrete embodied information intrinsically imbued with (human) meaning'.[10] In support of this argument, Barad argues that bodily experiences are digitally entangled in a variety of human and non-human relations,[11] meaning that concepts commonly taken to be uniquely human (e.g. feelings, thought etc.) need to be conceptualised as products of the relationships *between* bodies and technics. Hansen captures this well when stating that 'the body's capacity to act is never simply a property it possesses in isolation; it is always a recursive and constantly modulated function of its embeddedness within a rich texture of sensation'.[12] Hansen explains how the body is continually being created anew in the process of filtering information in digital media.

In this chapter, trigger warnings are considered as part of the affective practices through which people are processing and filtering digital information about their recent experiences of distress. I argue that trigger warnings are rich with meaning and are an important part of the use of Elefriends. Through considering the role of the body in this way however, there is a danger of discarding the impact of networked subjectivity that is also important to the affective nature of posting a trigger warning, given the power of the network and the role of the other community members in Elefriends. The following section will discuss the notion of "life-space" and introduce a conceptual frame of reference for the way a person might feel about the networked affective power of the posts in Elefriends.

Feelings of Affordance

Brown and Reavey use the term "feelings of affordance" to describe the sense of the possible ways of acting that stems from the immersion of people and things in a network. These relations constitute an "affective universe" of potential affordances that are mediated by human and non-human objects.[13] In this context, the ways of feeling are directly related to the spaces we inhabit and the relationships therein. These relations are intertwined and constitute part of the ever-expanding "life-space", a notion first put forward by Kurt Lewin in his topological version of a person. Lewin identifies life-space as a *totality* of events and relations that could occur in any given moment, thereby developing a dynamic framing of person and environment where both are equally important.[14] These assemblages of relationships are continually changing (e.g. as someone new enters a friendship group), that is they are constantly "under construction".[15]

The life-space, then, unfolds in relation to particular capacities or invariances that shape the way a person can act and feel in the current moment. Therefore, posting to a social media site is a moment of action in an assemblage of relations. For the author of the trigger warning, there is a sense of what a particular action affords. Any action has the potential to impact on the overall life-space and can have wide-reaching implications for the individual and others. These actions do not determine the actions of others but contribute to the unfolding relational connections that are present in a dense network of human and non-human objects. Brown and Reavey describe feelings of affordance as 'the felt sense of the possible (what we can do and what can be done to us) that arises from our engagement with assemblies of relations'.[16] The entanglement in the assemblage of relations gives us a sense of how we can impact others and how they have the potential to impact us. These feelings are derived from being immersed in the network of relations and are part of an ever-changing life-space with continually shifting relations. The indeterminate nature of affect means that there is an intense set of feelings that are autonomous from which they are derived. Every action has potential to expand our space; Reavey and Brown further discuss this in relation to the anticipatory character of affect:

> The feeling of affordance has an anticipatory character: it stretches out and expands our sense of what we can do. Think perhaps of the experience of dancing . . . This involves a range of feelings and sensations that are bound in the collective movement of dancers. So long as the dance continues, these feelings oscillate in tone, without perhaps settling on a particular emotion. However, once the dance stops, the possibilities for movement cease, and we have to take ownership of our feelings.[17]

Posting in Elefriends is accompanied with a feeling of 'our sense of what we can do'. When someone adds a trigger warning to their content this taps into the sense of how they can affect others. These feelings and sensations are bound in the collective movement of being in Elefriends. The posts collide with a multitude of other messages that are also landing on the site in that moment. These are not posts that are somewhere in a vacuum, they are present in peoples' lives and have the power to reach people and affect them in powerful ways. The feelings of affordance allow a recognition of how we can keep experiences open and keep them in a state of anticipation. The use of a trigger warning aids the "dance" to continue, keeping the possibility for movement alive. The following section of this chapter will examine some examples of trigger warnings in Elefriends.

Data

This data was collected as part of a large-scale investigation of peer-support in Elefriends in 2014. This involved collecting actual posts from the Elefriends site over a three-month period (March to June). The study received ethical approval from the University of East London ethics committee. Participants were recruited via a post to Elefriends that could be "clicked through". As part of this study, 157 participants consented to taking part and data was coded for posts that contained references to trigger warnings and associated phrases. The first extract is a typical example of how trigger warnings might be used in Elefriends:

1. ((((Trigger Warning)))) I'm finding myself starting up again with subtle SH, which is a sure sign my anxiety is really starting to get too much. I need to find something to occupy my mind, and my hands. Did some colouring in earlier, which was actually a great help in both those respects. Too tired for it right now though, so I'm thinking the best thing would be to head to bed. Just then have to deal with the insomnia.

In the above extract, the author is opening-up to the community about their issues with self harm (SH). The trigger warning is clearly stated at the beginning of the post and the Elefriends member discloses information about their feelings of anxiety and there is an immediate sense of the affective power of this post. It is possible to imagine how someone reading this information could experience distress in relation to their own experiences of SH, anxiety or insomnia. Extract 1 shows how the author is open about their experience and is willing to share this with the rest of the community. The content of Extract 1 is most notably about movement: Movement in the hands and body (via colouring and the need to go to bed); movement in the author's current mental state (from SH to anxious); and movement in the narrative ordering of these experiences (colouring as a response to SH and that becoming "too tiring"). This movement gives meaning to digital information and frames digital information, part of the process whereby people come to know their bodies through affection (following Bergson and Hansen). The author selects images of the body that give meaning to the body.

The post provides an opportunity to organise the intense set of feelings around the recent experiences into manageable affective states. Remembering that affection is the capacity to feel the body moving as it comes into contact with itself and other bodies. When a person adds a trigger warning to a post in Elefriends, the post is laden with affective content that operates as a place where people can manage affective states through the practice of engaging with their digital bodies. In Extract 1 the recent experience is continually unfolding in relation to the affective capacity of the body in which the experience of mental distress is felt through the body (e.g. hands, mind, anxiety, tired, insomnia, etc.). This process of digitally mediating this bodily activity is reliant on our unique relationship with the body as image. The next example builds on this idea to explore how these posts contain something of the "felt sense of the possible" in the use of trigger warnings and the role of networked affect.

2. Trigger warning. Feel very ill today. . . . I hate bpd [Borderline Personality
   Disorder]! Arhhhh! This morning I was think oh I feel normal and fine
   happy but turns out that was just a manic phase and I have completely
   crashed down this evening. . . . High anxiety, suicidal thoughts. BPD takes
   over your life: (I try and be positive and feel better it's the way my brain
   processes things: (I want to be better but still long frustrating waiting lists
   on the NHS it's like they don't want us to get better!!

Extract 2 demonstrates the unfolding relation to particular invariances
that shape the way a person can act and feel in the current moment. For
example, the author speaks about the difference between "feeling normal" in
the morning through to "completely crashed" in the evening. This illustrates
how the feelings afforded by this space are both complex and ambivalent.
Communicating this experience via Elefriends displays something of the "felt
sense of the possible" in the way this post represents the opportunity to
(re)configure this experience. Here the feeling of affordance is characterised
by a sense of anticipation, movement and change. For the author in Extract
2, this means that the post to Elefriends allows them to open up the alternative ways of understanding this experience.

These possible feelings can never be predicted or determined but, in the act
of adding the post, the author is trying to make sense of the impact of the day's
events that is part of an ongoing project of gaining greater affective knowledge
of their body. Extract 2 also shows something of how feelings in a single
moment are directly related to the wider assemblage of relations that can
appear at any given moment. For example, the author describes how their
experience of NHS (National Health Service) waiting times has led them to
feel like 'they don't want us to get better,' showing how individual experiences
quickly become entangled with the desires of other beings, thereby recon-
structed in light of those relations. Elefriends offers-up potential for action in
terms of the unfolding relational connections that come from human and non-
human objects. In this case, the NHS affectively impacts on the author of this
post in this moment, illustrating how experiences are not bound to space or
time, but are relationally defined. This instills movement into the feelings surrounding this experience and means that this feeling is not finished—it is
shared with the other members and kept alive. This anticipatory function
means that the author can sense the reactions in others and creates further
opportunities for movement in relation to this experience.

Concluding Remarks

This chapter illustrates the affective universe that is bound up with a single
comment in Elefriends. Posts that carry a trigger warning are a good place to

observe the affective power of a single comment in Elefriends, as they render visible a post which is automatically laden with affective content. Therefore, they also serve as an illustration of the more complex processes that are at work in social media sites, particularly how we come to know our bodies through the process of giving meaning to digital information. The idea that trigger warnings are able to signal to others the nature of the content in the post is only the start of their affective power. As mentioned, they include something of the way that people come to know their bodies through the affective content in the posts. Following Bergson, this acknowledges the way that we know the body from within via the process of affection. This is qualitatively different to the ways we perceive other bodies as a multiplicity of colliding images. Posts that carry a trigger warning were also found to have an anticipatory nature given the way that they open-up a range of potential affordances and future ways of feeling. Therefore, a trigger warning post is a site of affective activity where members of Elefriends are able to organise their experiences and frame information into meaningful units. It also serves as a site for acting into an assemblage of digital bodies which entangle and reconfigure feelings of affordances in order to keep the dance alive.

Notes

1. Guy Boysen, Anna Wells and Kaylee Dawson, 'Instructors Use of Trigger Warnings and Behaviour Warnings in Abnormal Psychology', *Teaching in Psychology* 43(4) (2016): 334–39.

2. Steven D. Brown and Paula Reavey, *Vital Memory and Affect: Living with a Difficult Past* (New York: Routledge, 2015).

3. Margaret Wetherell, 'Trends in the Turn to Affect', *Body & Society* 43(2) (2015): 139–66.

4. Patricia Clough, *The Affective Turn: Theorising the Social* (Durham, NC: Duke University Press, 2007).

5. Melissa Gregg and Gregory J. Seigworth, *The Affect Theory Reader* (Durham, NC: Duke University Press, 2010).

6. John Cromby, *Feeling Bodies: Embodying Psychology* (Basingstoke, UK: Macmillan, 2015).

7. Mark B. N. Hansen, *New Philosophy for New Media* (London: MIT Press, 2004), 6.

8. Sherry Turkle, *Life on The Screen: Identity in The Age of the Internet* (New York: Simon & Schuster, 1995).

9. Henri Bergson, *Matter and Memory* (New York: Zone Books, 1991), 17.

10. Hansen, *New Philosophy*, 14.

11. Karen Barad, *Meeting the Universe Halfway: Quantum Physics and the Entanglement of Matter and Meaning* (Durham, NC: Duke University Press, 2007).

12. Mark N. B. Hansen, *Bodies in Code: Interfaces with Digital Media* (London: Routledge, 2006), 18.

13. Brown and Reavey, *Vital Memory*, 94.

14. Kurt Lewin, *Principles of Topological Psychology* (New York: McGraw-Hill, 1936).

15. Brown and Reavey, *Vital Memory*, 60.

16. Ibid., 219

17. Ibid., 220.

3

Digitally Mediated Emotion
Simondon, Affectivity and Individuation

Ian Tucker

THIS CHAPTER EXPLORES the potential utility of framing emotion and digital activity as two strands of "individuation" (as opposed to distinct
ontological entities). The concept of individuation is taken from the work of
Gilbert Simondon, and facilitates a non-deterministic reading of the rela-
tional/s between bodies and technologies. Core to individuation is affectivity,
which does not define an individual emotional reaction to external stimuli
but denotes a mode of being (as an individual) in relation to collectivity.
This troubles understandings of how we distinguish between the individual
and collective, with affectivity central to what Simondon defines as "psychic
individuation". The concepts of affectivity and individuation speak directly
to the reality of living in concert with a seemingly ever increasing amount of
digital media. We leave a continual informational trace, which can then
"feed-forward"[1] into future patterns of collective activity. This informational
activity has led some to define an "online self" or "data double".[2] The chapter
concludes by suggesting the concept of individuation as of greater value as it
reconfigures thinking about the processes at work in body-technology relations, as it directs us 'to know the individual through individuation rather
than individuation through the individual'.[3]

Life as Lines

At the time of writing there is a UK NHS (National Health Service) public
health campaign to promote vaccinations against the flu. The campaign takes

a hard-line stance, keenly communicating the dangers that the flu can present. Campaign posters include quotes such as 'flu can kill', and encourages all those who are able to be vaccinated for free to do so. The headline of campaign materials is 'flu can mean the end of the line', with an image of a heart rate monitor with the word flu embedded in it. Two things of interest are happening here. Firstly, there is an attempt to invoke fear amongst the general public as an act to motivate engagement with the vaccination program. Second is the utilisation of a simple yet effective metaphor for human life, namely the line. This defines life as linear and subject to continuous movement. This speaks directly to the anthropologist Tim Ingold's conceptualisation of life as "lines".[4] To think of life emerging as multiple intersecting lines is to frame it as not defined according to a set of inherent properties that remain relatively stable over time, but rather as defining a process through which transformation can occur. Ingold is very keen to move away from an idea that spatial presence should be the defining identifier for "things", towards an understanding of temporal transformation. For Ingold, things—be they humans or non human objects—can only be defined through their temporal patterns of unfolding, which he conceptualises as lines. This is the life of the line, which the flu can end.

To conceptualise life as lines is to place ourselves analytically in the midst of intersecting strands of activity and movement, made up of a range of different elements. For instance, one's social media profile can be thought of as a line that moves from body through technology to other people. This is a non-representational theory of intersectionality, in which people as located individuals are not deemed to be communicating information about themselves *through* social media; rather, digital activity forms lines of activity that intersect with other people's online behaviour. This is what Ingold would call a "meshwork", multiple lines of activity intersecting or entangling, which form the experience of our social worlds. As Ingold notes, '[W]hen everything tangles with everything else, the result is what I call a meshwork. To describe the meshwork is to start from the premise that every living being is a line or, better, a bundle of lines'.[5] Theoretically, this is a shift away from thinking of life as formed through interactions and communications between preformed entities. For Ingold, temporality is key, not spatiality. Our traditional understanding of objects situated in the world that can communicate with one another, defined according to enduring spatial properties, is replaced with one that defines things in terms of temporal lines. Movement, not stability, is of prime focus.

> The theory of the assemblage, then, will not help us. It is too static, and it fails to answer the question of how the entities of which it is composed actually fasten to each other.[6]

Ingold is keen to move away from the increasingly popular concept of assemblage, which is featured in many areas of social and cultural theory, including affect studies. The assemblage has been used to define a set of heterogenous elements coming together in a systematic way to affect a particular phenomenon. For instance, Ringrose conceptualises young people's social media activity in relation to gender and sexualized identities as an affective assemblage.[7] Whilst Ingold has sympathy with the aims of the concept of assemblage, and its use in recent social cultural theory, he feels it is too spatial in its focus, and lacks a sense of temporal transformation. Indeed, it has been pointed out that use of the English translation "assemblage" tends to lose the vitality of the original concept *agencment,* which includes a greater sense of movement and agency.[8] Instead of an assemblage, Ingold considers the "whole" as a 'correspondence, not an assemblage, the elements of which are joined not "up" but "with"'.[9] Ingold draws on the metaphor of a rope, which is constituted through the interweaving of individual intersecting threads. It is this interweaving that Ingold refers to when stating that 'knotting is the fundamental principle of coherence'.[10] Knotting, or interweaving, is what holds together lines that would otherwise be loose and formless. We can think of knowledge in this way, as much as material objects. Knotting lines are a valuable metaphor because they focus on temporal movement, rather than notions of fixity and stability. A considerable power though has developed for notions that attend to spatial, rather than temporal, metaphors. For instance, psychology has long developed into a discipline primarily concerned with conceptualising the mind as a container, within which a number of cognitive factors exist that act as the "building blocks"[11] of thought and behaviour.

Sympathy and Social Media

Ingold directs us to evaluate the ways that living "with" works (or doesn't), and how multiple lines can come to *live with* in meaningful ways. Ingold borrows from the design theorist Lars Spuybroek, the idea that to live with involves a "sympathy", a mutual feeling of how things come together as intersecting patterns of movement. The human body is a prime example of the successful development of sympathy to function effectively. This idea of sympathy, a collective awareness of how certain lines fit together as part of a meaningful whole, is a potentially novel perspective through which to consider living in contemporary digitally mediated society, in which multiple forms of data collide and entangle. This includes information largely identifiable as individual activity (e.g. social media posts), as well as other data that feed off and (re)configure online worlds of connectivity (e.g. what happens when "big" and "small" data combine). Here, the outdated demarcation between real and virtual is proven fundamentally inadequate, through its frankly ridiculous theoretical simplicity. Meshworks captures notions of entanglement, movement and connection without requiring a theoretical distinction between human and digital in advance. Moreover, it provides a way of tracking how patterns of individuality and collectivity emerge in and as "infospheres".[12] In the next section, I develop this work through Simondon's concept of affectivity, to speak directly to the experience of living in infospheres, in which one exists simultaneously as 'one and more than one'.

Simondon and Affectivity

[i]t becomes possible to think of the relation that is interior and exterior to the individual as participation, without referring to new substances.[13]

This same method may be used to explore affectivity and emotivity, which constitute the resonance of being in relation to itself, and which link the individuated being to the pre-individual reality that is linked to it. . . . [T]he psychic is made of successive individuations that allow the being to resolve the problematic states that correspond to the permanent putting into communication of that which is larger and that which is smaller than it.[14]

Simondon (1924–1989) was a key influence on philosophies of technology (e.g., Stiegler) as well as broader 20th-century post-structuralist thought (e.g., Deleuze). For Simondon, the idea of the subject is an ontogenetic one in which the role of individuality and collectivity are seen to interweave the conditions through which subjects emerge. This means that sociality emerges through processes in which "beings" are not conceived as pre-existing spatially distinct entities. This is what he means when talking of 'the individual as participation' in the quote above. Simondon's theory of affectivity defines experience as 'more than one', and as such, moves away from the traditional view of people as individual "information processors" driven and controlled by internal cognitive processes. In its place he argued for an ontogentic understanding of the formation of multiple inter-related "individuations". For Simondon, "being" precedes the individual, which is why he framed being as "pre-individual", a realm through which individual life emerges. This is akin to notions of the virtual in Deleuze's work.[15] Of import here is a need to place 'the individual into the system of reality in which the individuation occurs.'[16] This led Simondon to frame a need to 'know the individual through individuation, rather than the individuation through the individual'.[17]

The experience of being "more than one", in relation to the reality of "carrying part of future collectives", creates an affective tension which cannot be resolved solely at the individual level. The feeling of being partially collective is anxiety provoking, due to the difficulty of understanding the collective element of one's being, which has not yet emerged, it is a future happening. This means that emotional activity cannot be easily captured, identified or manipulated. We are not made to feel *by* digital technologies, we feel *with* them. Therefore, we need to consider conditions of emergence, which means not starting with a notion of actualised emotional states *within* individuals, but rather to look at the contextual conditions within which emotional activity unfolds. However, the environmental half of the experience is not easily identifiable, and as such, involves being affected by an unknown realm outside of immediate perception. Consequently, it is not possible to name or identify affectivity in a straightforward manner. Indeed, it is an experience that is not easily put into words. This though does not mean affectivity can be detached from the 'specific materiality of human bodies',[18] a theoretical move made in much affect studies work on technologies. In a sense, it follows Bergson's idea of claiming affect to have a definite human element, but without relying on reductionism to do so.[19] Moreover, the emergence of actualised emotional activity does not exhaust pre-individuation. This is because, as Simondon notes, 'that which individuation makes appear is not only the individual, but also the pair individual-environment'.[20] Even when an individual actualises from pre-individuation it does not stop being partially collective. All individual bodies (human and non-human) carry something of future collectives with them, so are always potentialised for new individuations.[21] For this reason Simondon thought of being as "more than one", because a complete individual is never fundamentally disconnected from wider collective activity, either in the present or future.

Simondon's concept of individuation does not rely on a pre-figured distinction between subject and object but rather focuses on them as parts of multi-layered processes, through which individual and collective life emerge.[22] Crucially, this means that analytic focus shifts from talking about digital media as objects encroaching on psychological life, to processes of individuation that culminate in meta-stable individuations. This resonates with Mark Hansen's point 'that media impact the general sensibility of the world prior to and as a condition for impacting human experience'.[23] Digital media play an increasingly active role in conditioning the environmental contexts of psychological life. Media act as the environmental side of the "more than one" reality of subjective life. Therefore, emotions are becoming *with* digital media rather than being controlled and dominated *by* them. This is a useful conceptual development because it provides a new perspective to digital media analysis in relation to affect and emotion. We see that living with digital media is by definition *affective*. Simondon's concept of affectivity does not lose a notion of an individual psychological emotional experience at work. Indeed, it relies on it, albeit one that does not appoint a stable internal identity as productive of emotional activity. For Simondon, affectivity is fundamentally psycho-social.

Becoming with Digital Media

The argument of this chapter is that the pre-individual realms of modern societies are increasingly digitally mediated. Affectivity defines experience as always-already individual and social. These cannot be separated, meaning that all life is social.[24] We are "leaky bodies" in relation to data with our porous bodies in continual transformation through moving in and through lines of affective individuation.[25] These form into meshworks of entangled lines of body, data and technology. Simondon's concept of affectivity captures the experience of being more than one.[26] Ingold's concept of lines focuses on movement and transformation through the *speed*[27] of meshworks of bodies and data, affectivity focuses attention on the psychological part of such events. This is not about an individual emotional cognitive process but rather a broader way of becoming as part of systems of reality that are multi-layered, spatially and temporally. No one can *see* the future lines of individuation one's data will become. Some may "feed forward"[28] into recognizable future patterns of activity. Others may contribute to information societies in ways we will never know or see. To return to the example of the NHS flu campaign stating that the illness can be the end of the line. On the face of it, this makes sense. However, in relation to living in heavily digitally mediated worlds, it is possible to think that a philosophy of individuation and affectivity opens up the idea that even when the biological body stops moving, informational activity will continue to shape future collectives and meshworks. This is an age when people have to consider their digital legacy, which in itself, will no doubt be an increasingly affecting experience.

Notes

1. Mark B. N. Hansen, *Feed Forward: On the Future of 21st Century Media* (Chicago: Chicago University Press, 2015).

2. David Lyon, *Theorizing Surveillance: The Panopticon and Beyond* (Portland, OR: Willan Publishing, 2006).

3. Alberto Toscano, *The Theatre of Production: Philosophy and Individuation between Kant and Deleuze* (Basingstoke, UK: Palgrave Macmillan, 2006), 136.

4. Tim Ingold, *The Life of Lines* (London: Routledge, 2015).

5. Ibid, 3.

6. Ibid, 6.

7. Jessica Ringrose. 'Beyond Discourse? Using Deleuze and Guattari's Schizoanalysis to Explore Affective Assemblages, Heterosexually Striated Space, and Lines of Flight Online and at School', *Educational Philosophy and Theory* 43(6) (2011): 598–618.

8. Steve Brown and Paul Stenner, *Psychology without Foundations: History, Philosophy and Psychosocial Theory* (London: Sage, 2009).

9. Ingold, *Life as Lines*, 23.

10. Ibid, 14.

11. Ibid.

12. Tiziana Terranova, *Network Culture: Politics for the Information Age* (London: Pluto Press, 2004).

13. Gilbert Simondon, 'The Position of the Problem of Ontogenesis', *Parrhesia* 7 (2009): 8.

14. Ibid, 9.

15. Brian Massumi, *Parables for the Virtual: Movement, Affect, Sensation* (Durham, NC: Duke University Press, 2002).

16. Simondon, *Parrhesia*, 4.

17. Ibid, 5.

18. Susanna Passonen, 'A Midsummer's Bonfire: Affective Intensities of Online Debate', in *Networked Affect*, Ken Hillis, Susanna Passonen and Michael Petit, eds. (Cambridge, MA: MIT Press, 2015), 27–43.

19. Lewis Goodings and Ian M. Tucker, 'Social Media and the Co-production of Bodies Online: Bergson, Serres and Facebook Timeline', *Media, Culture & Society*, 36(1) (2014): 176–83.

20. Simondon, *Parrhesia*, 5.

21. Ian M. Tucker, 'Deleuze, Sense and Life: Marking the Parameters of a Psychology of Individuation', *Theory and Psychology* 22(6) (2012): 771–85.

22. Ian M. Tucker and Lewis Goodings, 'Sensing Bodies and Digitally Mediated Distress: Serres, Simondon and Social Media', *Senses & Society*, 9(1) (2014): 55–71.

23. Mark B. N. Hansen, *Feed Forward*, 6.

24. Ingold, *The Life of Lines*.

25. Ian M. Tucker, 'Bodies and Surveillance: Simondon, Information and Affect', *Distinktion: Scandinavian Journal of Social Theory* 14(1) (2013): 31–40.

26. Darren Ellis and Ian M. Tucker, *Social Psychology of Emotion* (London: Sage, 2015).

27. Vincent Duclos, Tomas Sanchez Criado and Vinh-Kim Nguyen, 'Speed: An Introduction', *Cultural Anthropology* 32(1) (2017): 1–11.

28. Mark B. N. Hansen, *Feed Forward*.

4

Visceral Data

Luke Stark

THE WORD "visceral" means "inward feelings," stemming from the Latin words *visceralis* or "internal", or *viscera*, the 'internal organs, inner parts of the body.' Viscerality thus refers to the quality of physical, embodied sensations, "gut" feelings. We can take a visceral dislike to someone, and decide to ignore reason to "go with our gut".

In this chapter, I argue for the utility of identifying, understanding, and sometimes creating "visceral data".[1] In doing so, I urge a wider focus on the emotional, affective, and visceral aspects of human experience within digital media studies, science and technology studies (STS), and studies of human-computer interaction (HCI). The notion of visceral data has a double implication. Several years ago, I defined visceral data as the product of 'transforming a sea of disembodied information we struggle to interpret visually or aurally into [something] we see, hear, feel, breathe and even ingest'.[2] So visceral data is, on the one hand, information *visceralized*, made more materially appreciable through what Mariana Obrist and her collaborators recently dubbed "multisensory HCI".[3] Yet visceral data is also information understood or reflected on through the lens of our embodied, subjective senses of human experience, a phenomenon Katrina Höök has termed the "somaesthetic".[4] 'A key premise of the somaesthetic philosophy', Höök and her co-authors suggest, 'is the insight that all of our experiences and interactions with the world happen through our body', and learning 'to know and better use our bodies is as important as educating our minds'.[5] In other words, an attention to visceral data produces a novel epistemological lens on the empirical world. Visceral data as a category ties together both these conceptual senses of viscerality: of data made more viscerally appreciable, and of receptive humans becoming sensitive to visceral experience as a form of understanding complimentary of, not in opposition to, other epistemes of digitally mediated communication.

Exploring the domain of visceral human experience as the source of both theoretical and practical insights for scholars in media studies, HCI, and STS means taking a diversity of bodies, with the attendant diverse experiences of those bodies, seriously—not as uncomplicated objects of scholarship, but as fellow subjects to think and feel with. Moreover, a focus on the visceral also turns our probes back on ourselves: who are we, as scholars and as human beings, within the sociotechnical networks we describe and critique? Here, I briefly explore the history of the visceral as a concept; examine contemporary ideas about how to make the experience of digital media more visceral; and conclude by proposing a new avenue of research, grounded in toxicology, to apply the benefits of data visceralization. In doing so, I want readers to feel the urgency and importance of research on visceral data—right in the gut.

Viscerality and Abstraction

As a figurative adjective, "visceral" was coined during the Renaissance, but fell out of use through the Enlightenment and the Industrial Revolution, when something visceral was likely to refer specifically to the scientific or medical condition of the human gut and bowels. At the same time, emotions, passions, moods, and feelings continued to figure in philosophical and psychological debates about human ethics and values.[6,7] Before the development of formal laboratory science, human feeling was tied up with studies of perception and the senses; and from the rise of scientific medicine in the middle of the nineteenth century onward, researchers worked to sense and record physical traces of emotional states as a proxy for knowledge about these visceral sensations, including the speed at which the heart pumped blood, the electrical conductivity of the skin, and other outwards signs of inward states[8]. Yet the main currents of academic and commercial digital media have, until recently and with some notable exceptions, largely overlooked emotional and visceral experience as an element in the design, deployment and use of digital technologies. The exceptions include a number of scholars, technologists and designers working with "tangible and embodied" interfaces.[9] In the context of critical computing, work by Philip Agre and Paul Dourish on embodied interaction[10]—'the creation, manipulation, and sharing of meaning through engaged interaction with artifacts'[11]—and Lucy Suchman on situated actions,[12] have drawn attention to the embodied nature of technological engagements, and bolstered scholars in HCI considering the

nexus of human emotion and digital technologies, alongside their implications for social, technical, and cultural expression.[13]

To make data more visceral is to grapple with the injustices and inequali-
ties persisting in many of the lives mediated by digital technologies. The
concept of viscerality, of gut feelings, is not a conceptually neutral one,[14] but
is instead tied intimately to the imbrication of intersections between race,
class, gender and sexuality within hierarchies of knowledge and power. A
recent issue of *GLQ* explored the visceral as a nexus point in critical race
studies, food studies, and queer studies; as its editors point out, 'viscerality
registers those systems of meaning that have lodged in the gut, signifying the
incursion of violent intentionality into the rhythms of everyday life'—
especially around exclusionary racial hierarchies.[15] To understand digital data
as visceral—both its source and in its reception—fleshes out the observations
of legal theorists like Solon Barocas and Andrew Selbst, who note 'discrimination may be an artifact of the data mining process itself' rather than of
technical error;[16] or those of digital media scholar Wendy Chun, who suggests
the abstraction of much Big Data-driven social and behavioral science is, in
its very infrastructure, 'not designed to foster justice'.[17]

Many device designs could be improved if more attention was paid by
the designers and technologists to the holistic combination of sensory and
emotional contexts we experience while using our digital device. This much
needed attention is likely to result in an opening to the emancipatory possibilities of digital media.[18] In the aforementioned issue of *GLQ*, affect theorist
Sianne Ngai argues viscerality—a category of experience which, due to its
'specificity and corporeality seem to have made [it] resistant to theory'—
serves as an antidote to what she calls "abstraction" as a category of human
experience.[19] In the context of digital mediation I carry her argument further:
the tendency towards abstraction becomes materialized in the very mechanisms through which digital technologies work or are understood to work,
alongside the ways in which these technologies perform the schematic classi-
fication of human bodies, behaviors, and emotions into machine-legible
traits.[20] These technological schematizations interact inelegantly with the
subjective sense of human privacy most people experience as part of their
daily lives.[21]

Devices and Desires

Visceral data engages qualities of human experience impelling users to
engage with an interface or artifact over the long term on an affective level.
Thinking across aesthetic or sensory stimulation via multiple channels means

tying visceral data to a broader field of extant work on "visceral design",[22] whereby material objects or devices are designed specifically to activate allusions and associations, the sensory and physical memories of past experiences.[23] Yet far from being "instinctual", these "fast-twitch" responses are deeply implicated in human judgment and evaluation: the affective response to the visceral experience at hand engages with a user's cognitive and experiential capacities to prompt subtle and often complex emotions, thoughts and habituated actions, which then act recursively to shift or solidify an individual's evaluative judgments.

The role of visceral data in sociotechnical systems is tied tightly to what Kirsten Boehner, Lucian Leahu and Phoebe Sengers have championed as an "interactionist" model of human emotion in human-computer interaction. These authors describe emotion as 'an intersubjective phenomenon, arising in encounters between individuals or between people and society, an aspect of the socially organized life world we both inhabit and reproduce'.[24] This model stands in contrast to what Boehner et al.[25] term the "informational" model of emotion in computer science, in which feelings are understood as quantifiable inputs to be measured and analyzed through machine learning.[26] While a wholesale rejection of the computational modeling of emotion is neither possible nor perhaps desirable, I agree with Boehner and her co-authors' emphasis on visceral data as a concept grounded in human social relations. The intra-subjectivity of human visceral response enables the interactionist model of social meaning-making described by Boehner and co-authors, though it is also wholly dependent on social and communicative interactions as a context for emotions to be created and shared.

It is possible to prompt a visceral reaction through sight alone: designer Sha Hwang recently suggested designers strive to make data visualizations hit harder emotionally, by reframing the scope of their graphics and employing more explicit emotion in their products.[27] Yet visceral data is already all around us. Work in human-computer interaction on tangible and embodied interfaces (TEI), many of which exploit a variety of sensory channels, has been the topic of an official Association for Computing Machinery (ACM) conference for the last decade, producing innovative proof-of-concept examples of multisensory HCI and somaesthetic design such as the "meat book",[28] and other synesthetic user interfaces.[29] The designers of digital games like *Angry Birds* and *Candy Crush*,[30] as well as the designers of video slot machines, have used advances in gestural interfaces to exploit visceral design principles effectively—sometimes too much so, as described by Natasha Dow Schüll in *Addiction by Design*.[31]

The visceral design strategies incorporated into many of the consumer products listed above often seem to seek to make an end-run around rational thought: this instinct even extends to design in public policy contexts.[32] In contrast, a commitment to the concept of visceral data must entail focusing on how these tools and technologies can work to help make abstract information have a meaningful visceral impact on users in the interests of, to paraphrase Wendy Chun, an 'infrastructure [of] justice'.[33] This impact should be appropriate and compelling for the context and the data involved, triggering sustained reflection and evaluative self-determination, not suppress them. In other words, I advocate for a jiu-jitsu move to enlist these visceral design strategies in the service of unsettling preconceived notions, not reinforcing them. Work on "visceral notice",[34] and on the application of behavioral "nudges" in the privacy context,[35] are welcome first steps in this direction. Because value judgments possess a strong, often determinative intrasubjective component, paying attention to the visceral expression of human values via digital media is of enormous importance to scholarship on the online public sphere and the impact of emotional networked political movements on extremism and racialized nationalism.[36] Humans are better at recognizing intensity of their own visceral feelings than they are what is termed "valence"—whether the agitation you feel comes from anxiety, excitement, or a mix of both. Visceral data is one conceptual avenue for considering the impact of digital design on these contemporary political developments, as well as innovative work in the anthropology of science examining the relationship between scientists and their tools.[37]

In the future, sophisticated data visualizations—graphs, flowcharts, and infographics—which are staples of contemporary digital media products, will be increasingly insufficient to deal with what Mark Andrejevic terms the "infoglut".[38] Instead, what I call "data visceralizations"—representations of information not relying solely and primarily on sight or sound, but instead on multiple senses including touch, smell, and even taste—will be critical to designing with visceral data, and accounting for an embodied, emotional engagement with users' concerns around their digital footprints. Data represented as a visceral experience can and should work to stimulate our feelings in conjunction with our thoughts, taking advantage of the diversity of digital media's affordances.[39]

Consumers have a clear interest in taking actions to protect themselves and their data. For instance, in its September 2013 survey on "Anonymity, Privacy, and Security Online", the Pew Research Center found 86 percent of internet users had tried to 'minimize the visibility of their digital footprints' through a variety of means, ranging from the use of encryption and obfuscation techniques like providing false information, to clearing cookies and web browser histories.[40] Interfaces designed to make data sets viscerally engaging could result in a more grounded and complete process of individual decision-making around these questions, anchored in both our thoughts and our feelings. Visceral design in material products is often intended to overcome our reasoned second thoughts through the production of feelings or desires, but data visceralization in the service of protecting information privacy has the potential to level out our reactions the opposite way: as well as appreciating a problem or issue rationally, users prompted to engage viscerally will have a well-rounded sense of their own intellectual, emotional and physical stance on the matter at hand.

Towards Intuitive Data Toxicology

The impetus for my own initial focus on viscerality as an element of the experience of digital media was digital privacy, and efforts to advance "privacy by design".[41] The framework for "privacy by design" was developed in 2009 by former Ontario Privacy Commissioner Anne Cavoukian, and is an internationally recognized statement of privacy design principles.[42] The two chief technical design strategies which have predominated in attempting to provide technical answers for privacy protection, encryption and anonymization, face technical, logistical, and increasingly, legal challenges. Moreover, a focus on privacy as context makes clear neither technique is useful, appropriate,[43] or sufficient at all times or in all situations.[44]

More generally, the values inherent in the privacy by design principles, particularly the principles' commitment to usability and wide applicability, have not always succeeded translated into practice. Applying the concept of visceral data to privacy by design has the potential to give users what they claim to want[45]—a better sense of where private data is stored, how it is being used, and what steps can be taken to better understand and influence the context of these data. This insight, while novel within digital privacy scholarship, forms the basis for the concept of what statistician and risk analyst Paul Slovic terms "intuitive toxicology" in risk analysis.[46] Given that experts and lay persons often disagree regarding relative risks based on subjective perception, strong risk mitigation strategies take this fact into account and work with it instead of dismissing such perceptual judgments as automatically irrational or emotional. As Slovic observes, 'The public is not irrational. Their judgments about risk are influenced by emotion and affect in a way that is both simple and sophisticated'.[47]

The resulting literature in risk analysis acknowledges the potential of intuitive toxicology as a policy and design lever.[48] Public health interventions have leveraged subjective visceral perception of risk to warn the public (for instance, deliberate color changes of contaminated drinking water, or the addition of the smell of sulfur to otherwise odorless natural gas). This project seeks to adapt these insights, particularly those drawn from water management and safety, to the digital privacy realm, and develop systems and devices fostering a sense of "visceral privacy"—one entailing agreement between a user's subjective, embodied sense of their information privacy and the objective material conditions of their data. Privacy can be made visceral through interaction and form factor designs which adapt the extant research on intuitive toxicology to flows of data and information instead of air and water: these practices would prompt visceral responses across multiple senses, and ensuing emotional and cognitive reflection regarding a user's implicit and explicit valuation of privacy. The particular subjective experience of privacy in a given situation will condition particular privacy-related expectations, beliefs and behaviors.[49]

This line of work developing intuitive data toxicology as an example both of visceral data broadly understood, and of data visceralization more narrowly defined, suggests the potential for a wider research agenda around not only digital privacy, but also making data more visceral across digital interaction design. Novel interfaces to make data sets more viscerally engaging could result in a more grounded, complete process of individual judgment and decision making around a variety of online behaviors, with the experience of evaluating anchored in both our thoughts and our feelings. Information scholar Katie Shilton has identified what she terms "values levers": 'practices that pry open discussions about values in design and help [to] build consensus around social values as design criteria'.[50] Drawing out the ties between our private selves, our feelings, and the devices we use every day is difficult precisely because these embodied connections have often been felt, but not articulated. Yet the role of visceral experience in digital design can and should act as a central value lever in current debates around how to safeguard our autonomy and self-determination within an increasingly mediated world.

Notes

1. Luke Stark, 'The Emotional Context of Information Privacy', *The Information Society* 32(1) (2016): 14–27, doi:10.1080/01972243.2015.1107167.

2. Luke Stark, 'Come on Feel the Data (and Smell It)', *The Atlantic*, May 19, 2014, http://www.theatlantic.com/technology/archive/2014/05/data-visceralization/370899/.

3. Marianna Obrist et al., 'Sensing the Future of HCI: Touch, Taste, and Smell User Interfaces', *Interactions* 23(5) (October 2016): 40–44.

4. Kristina Höök, Anna Ståhl, Martin Jonsson, Johanna Mercurio, Anna Karlsson

and Eva-Carin Banka Johnson, 'Somaesthetic Design', *Interactions* 22(4) (August 2015): 26–33.

5. Ibid., 28.

6. Robert C. Solomon, *What Is an Emotion?: Classic and Contemporary Readings* (New York: Oxford University Press, 2003); Charles Darwin, *The Expression of the Emotions in Man and Animals*, 4th ed. (New York: Oxford University Press, 2009).

7. Thomas Dixon, *From Passions to Emotions: The Creation of a Secular Psychological Category* (Cambridge, UK: Cambridge University Press, 2003); Jesse J. Prinz, 'Introduction: Piecing Passions Apart', in *Gut Reactions: A Perceptual Theory of Emotion* (Oxford, UK: Oxford University Press, 2004), 1–11.

8. Otniel E. Dror, 'Counting the Affects: Discoursing in Numbers', *Social Research* 68(2) (July 30, 2001): 357–78; Otniel E. Dror, 'The Affect of Experiment: The Turn to Emotions in Anglo-American Physiology, 1900–1940', *Isis* 90(2) (June 1999): 205–37; Brenton Malin, *Feeling Mediated: A History of Media Technology and Emotion in America* (New York: New York University Press, 2014).

9. Katherine Isbister and Kristina Höök, 'Evaluating Affective Interactions', *International Journal of Human-Computer Studies* 65(4) (April 2007): 273–74, doi:10.1016/j.ijhcs.2006.11.004; Kristina Höök, Phoebe Sengers and Gerd Andersson, 'Sense and Sensibility: Evaluation and Interactive Art', 5 (2003): 241–48; Marianna Obrist et al., 'Temporal, Affective, and Embodied Characteristics of Taste Experiences: A Framework for Design', Chapter 14 of *Proceedings of the SIGCHI Conference on Human Factors in Computing Systems* (New York: Association for Computing Machinery, 2014), 2853–62, doi:10.1145/2556288.2557007; Aaron Levisohn et al., 'The Meatbook: Tangible and Visceral Interaction', *TEI '07: Proceedings of the 1st International Conference on Tangible and Embedded Interaction*, February 2007, 91, doi:10.1145/1226969.1226987.

10. Philip E. Agre, *Computation and Human Experience* (Cambridge, UK: Cambridge University Press, 1997).

11. Paul Dourish, *Where the Action Is: The Foundations of Embodied Interaction* (Cambridge, MA: The MIT Press, 2004), 126.

12. Lucy Suchman, *Human-Machine Reconfigurations: Plans and Situated Actions* (Cambridge, UK: Cambridge University Press, 2006).

13. Kirsten Boehner et al., Affect: From Information to Interaction (CC '05: Proceedings of the 4th Decennial Conference on Critical Computing, New York), 59–68; Lucian Leahu, Steve Schwenk and Phoebe Sengers, Subjective Objectivity: Negotiating Emotional Meaning, *Dis '08*, February 25–27 2008, 425–434; Kirsten Boehner et al., Interfaces with the Ineffable, *ACM Transactions on Computer-Human Interaction* 15, No. 3 (November 1, 2008): 1–29, doi:10.1145/1453152.1453155; Sharon Y. Tettegah and Safiya Umoja Noble, eds., *Emotions, Technology, and Design*, (London: Elsevier/Academic Press, 2016); Rosalind W Picard, *Affective Computing*, (Cambridge, MA: The MIT Press, 2000).

14. Elizabeth A. Wilson, *Gut Feminism* (Durham, NC: Duke University Press, 2015), doi:10.1215/9780822375203.

15. S. P. Holland, M. Ochoa and K. W. Tompkins, On the Visceral, *GLQ: a Journal of Lesbian and Gay Studies* 20, No. 4 (October 9, 2014): 391–406, doi:10.1215/10642684-2721339.

16. Solon Barocas and Andrew D Selbst, Big Data's Disparate Impact, *California Law Review*, 2016, 4.

17. Wendy Hui Kyong Chun, *Updating to Remain the Same: Habitual New Media* (Cambridge, MA: The MIT Press, 2016), 15.

18. Ibid.

19. Sianne Ngai, Visceral Abstractions, *GLQ: a Journal of Lesbian and Gay Studies* 21, No. 1 (January 27, 2015): 33, doi:10.1215/10642684-2818648.

20. Luke Stark and Kate Crawford, The Conservatism of Emoji: Work, Affect, and Communication, *Social Media + Society* 1, No. 2 (July 1, 2015): 2056305115604853–11, doi:10.1177/2056305115604853.

21. Irving Altman, Privacy Regulation: Culturally Universal or Culturally Specific. *Journal of Social Issues* 33(3): 66–84.

22. Stark, Come on Feel the Data (and Smell It).

23. Donald A Norman, *Emotional Design: Why We Love (or Hate) Everyday Things* (New York: Basic Books, 2005).

24. Kirsten Boehner, Rogério DePaula, Paul Dourish and Phoebe Sengers, How Emotion Is Made and Measured, *International Journal of Human-Computer Studies* 65 (2007): 280, doi:10.1016/j.ijhcs.2006.11.016.

25. Ibid.

26. Picard, *Affective Computing*.

27. Jen Christiansen, Don't Just Visualize Data—Visceralize It, *Scientific American*, February 18, 2014, http://blogs.scientificamerican.com/sa-visual/2014/02/18/dont-just-visualize-datavisceralize-it/.

28. Levisohn et al., The Meatbook: Tangible and Visceral Interaction.

29. Marianna Obrist et al., Emotions Mediated Through Mid-Air Haptics (the 33rd Annual ACM Conference, New York: ACM Press, 2015), 2053–62, doi:10.1145/2702123.2702361; Andy Wu, Tangible Visualization, November 30, 2009; Marco Spadafora et al., Designing the Behavior of Interactive Objects, The TEI '16: Tenth International Conference (New York: ACM Press, 2016), 70–77, doi:10.1145/2839462.2839502.

30. Jesper Juul, *Half-Real: Video Games Between Real Rules and Fictional Worlds* (Cambridge, MA: The MIT Press, 2005).

31. Introduction: Mapping the Machine Zone, in *Addiction by Design: Machine Gambling in Los Vegas* (Princeton, NJ: Princeton University Press, 2012), 1–27.

32. Pelle Guldborg Hansen and Andreas Maaløe Jespersen, Nudge and the Manipulation of Choice, *European Journal of Risk Regulation* 4, No. 1 (2013): 3–28.

33. Chun, *Updating to Remain the Same: Habitual New Media*, 15.

34. Ryan Calo, Against Notice Skepticism in Privacy (and Elsewhere), *Notre Dame Law Review* 87, No. 3 (2012): 1027–72.

35. Yang Wang et al., A Field Trial of Privacy Nudges for Facebook, *CHI Proceedings*, 2014, 2367–76, doi:10.1145/2556288.2557413.

36. Kate Crawford, Can an Algorithm Be Agonistic? Ten Scenes About Living in Calculated Publics, May 16, 2013; Zeynep Tufekci, Engineering the Public: Big Data, Surveillance, and Computational Politics, *First Monday* 19, No. 7 (July 7, 2014), http://firstmonday.org/article/view/4901/4097.

37. Natasha Myers and Joe Dumit, Haptic Creativity and the Mid-Embodiments

of Experimental Life, in *Companion to the Anthropology of the Body and Embodiment,* Fran Mascia-Lees, ed. (New York: Wiley-Blackwell, 2011), 239–261; Lucian Leahu, Marisa Cohn and Wendy Marsh, How Categories Come to Matter, Conference on Human Factors in Computing Systems (Paris, France, 2013), 3331–34.

38. Mark Andrejevic, *Infoglut: How Too Much Information Is Changing the Way We Think and Know* (New York: Routledge, 2013).

39. Johanna Drucker, *Graphesis: Visual Forms of Knowledge Production,* (Cambridge, MA: Harvard University Press, 2014).

40. Lee Rainie et al., Anonymity, Privacy, and Security Online (Washington, D.C.: Pew Research Center's Internet & American Life Project, September 5, 2013), http://pewinternet.org/Reports/2013/Anonymity-online.aspx.

41. Stark, The Emotional Context of Information Privacy.

42. Privacy by Design in the Age of Big Data, June 7, 2012.

43. Helen Nissenbaum, A Contextual Approach to Privacy Online, *Daedalus* 140, No. 4 (September 2011): 32–48.

44. Sarah Spiekermann and Lorrie Faith Cranor, Engineering Privacy, *IEEE Transactions on Software Engineering* 35, No. 1 (January 2009): 67–82, doi:10.1109/TSE.2008.88.

45. Mary Madden and Lee Rainie, Americans' Attitudes About Privacy, Security and Surveillance (Pew Research Center, May 20, 2015), http://www.pewinternet.org/2015/05/20/americans-attitudes-about-privacy-security-and-surveillance/.

46. Paul Slovic, Perception of Risk, *Science* 236 (April 17, 1987): 280; Nancy Neil, Torbjörn Malmfors and Paul Slovic, Intuitive Toxicology: Expert and Lay Judgments of Chemical Risks, *Toxicologic Pathology* 22, No. 2 (1994): 198–201; Paul Slovic et al., Intuitive Toxicology. II. Expert and Lay Judgments of Chemical Risks in Canada, *Risk Analysis* 15, No. 6 (1995): 661–75.

47. Paul Slovic, Trust, Emotion, Sex, Politics, and Science: Surveying the Risk-Assessment Battlefield, *Risk Analysis* 19, No. 4 (April 8, 1999): 689.

48. Vivianne H. M. Visschers and Michael Siegrist, Exploring the Triangular Relationship Between Trust, Affect, and Risk Perception: A Review of the Literature, *Risk Management* 10, No. 3 (July 2008): 156–567, doi:10.1057/rm.2008.1; Stephan Dickert et al., The Feeling of Risk: Implications for Risk Perception and Communication, in *The SAGE Handbook of Risk Communication* (Thousand Oaks, CA: Sage Publications, 2015), 41–54, doi:10.4135/9781483387918.n7.

49. Harry Surden, Structural Rights in Privacy, *SMU Law Review* 60 (2007): 101–45.

50. Katie Shilton, Values Levers: Building Ethics Into Design, *Science, Technology, & Human Values* 38, No. 3 (May 2013): 374–97, doi:10.1177/0162243912436985.

5

Psychophysiological Measures Associated with Affective States while Using Social Media

Maurizio Mauri

C URRENTLY, social media such as social networking sites (SNSs) are increasingly engaging participation. The success of SNSs like Facebook is due to, among other factors, the affective experiences generated by SNSs. In this chapter, new empirical data is presented concerning peoples' psychophysiological reactions while exposed to YouTube videos purposefully aimed to elicit boredom. This data, together with previous data from other research studies about Facebook use, support a framework to study peoples' affective states by means of psychophysiological monitoring while using social media. After detailing the model and the study, I discuss some of the implications concerned with how this model could be used to embolden understandings of social media use and human-computer interactions.

In a previous study conducted with colleagues,[1] Facebook navigation was selected as a sort of prototypical experience to elicit an affective state referred to as "engagement". The experience of using Facebook was seen to elicit the psychophysiological pattern associated with this specific affective state of engagement. In 2011, Facebook had 350 million active users, and was ranked as the second most popular SNS. At the time of writing Facebook has over 1.74 billion users, and the platform is the most popular social network platform worldwide. Reasons and explanations in the literature for its popularity differ, for instance it enables forms of information seeking strategies,[2] it incorporates a range of different use functions while navigating,[3,4] it facilitates social interactions and identity expressions[5] and it has multiple educational uses[6.] Aside from these motivations, another dimension explored was what may be considered the superordinate reason as to why people used Facebook: the *enjoyment* that engagement garners. This exploration attempted to empirically verify that, on average, the affective state experienced while using Facebook is one of the driving factors that lead people to look for that experience again. To show how the experience of engagement is associated with "Facebook use", data was collected from 30 healthy students while exposed to three different human-computer contents, namely: (1) relaxation (a 3-minute exposure to a sequence of panoramas), (2) free navigation on Facebook by means of participant's personal Facebook account (always for 3 minutes) and finally (3) the accomplishment of a mental arithmetic task (always for 3 minutes). During all conditions mentioned, skin conductance (SC), blood volume pulse (BVP), electroencephalogram (EEG), electromyography (EMG), respiratory activity (RA), and pupil dilation (PD) measurements were recorded. Results showed how, on average, Facebook use evokes a psychophysiological state of engagement characterized by positive valence (represented by a mid-low EMG contraction of *corrugator supercilii* (CS) muscles) and high arousal (represented by mid-high levels of SC). Figure 5.1 provides two-dimensional plots of Cartesian coordinates, described by Lang[7] to represent human emotions in terms of these psychophysiological indicators. However, in the above study, any experience generated by social media eliciting an affective state characterized by negative valence and mid-low arousal—situated within the fourth quadrant of the Lang model—was not considered. Thus, the fourth quadrant is where the affective states of boredom and sadness are seen to be situated. Before presenting here some preliminary data that addresses these affective states in relation to social media use, I will briefly describe the Lang model of affective states.

The Lang Model of Emotion

The Lang model of emotion was created through an experimental study where 100 participants were exposed to pictures from the International Affective Picture System (IAPS), while some of their physiological responses were monitored (e.g. SC and EMG activity from CS muscles near the eye, on the forehead). The model is represented by a Cartesian plane: on the X axis are plotted the arousal values while on Y axis, valence values. Valence and arousal are the two overarching dimensions that characterize affective states. These correlate with EMG and SC values, respectively. For example, scores on each of these dimensions work as coordinates to characterize participants' reactions to pictures in terms of psycho-physiological reactions. In addition,

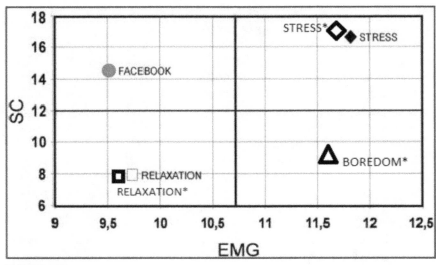

FIGURE 5.1.
Valence and arousal graph

for each picture, both valence and arousal values are expressed by participants along a pictographic scale, the so called "Self-Assessment Manikin"
(SAM), which is a 9-point scale ranging from 'I don't like it at all' to 'I like
it very much' for valence, and from 'I don't feel aroused at all' to 'I feel very
aroused.' Lang shows positive correlations (0.90) between valence values and
EMG measures, and between arousal values and SC measures (0.81). Broadly,
the concepts of affective valence and arousal are explicated in terms of specific motivational systems within the brain. According to the Lang theory,
two primary motive systems are driving all affects: on one side, the appetitive
system (for instance nurturant, sexual, consummatory, etc.) prototypically
expressed by approaching behavior and—on the other side—the aversive
system (defensive, protective, withdrawing, etc.), prototypically expressed by
escaping and avoiding behaviors. The dimension of valence correlates with
the activation/inhibition of these two motivational systems, whereas arousal
represents the intensity of activation (metabolic and neural) of either or both
motivational systems. The four quadrants in the Lang model are described
by low arousal, positive valence (relaxation); high arousal, positive valence
(excitement/engagement); high arousal, negative valence (stress); and low
arousal, negative valence (depression/boredom). These four quadrants are
quite general in comparison to the panorama of affective states that humans

can feel. Nevertheless, the model might represent the starting point for further research aimed to refine affective state detection.

Psychophysiological Patterns of Boredom
Generated by YouTube Videos

In experiments here presented for the first time, we rely again on EMG values of the CS muscle to locate the emotional reactions along the valence axis of the Lang model, and SC measures as representative of arousal dimension measurements within the same model. However, to address Lang's model in a complete way, it is important to identify its Cartesian plane and four quadrants. For this reason, three different experimental situations are selected, with the aim to identify, in terms of psychophysiological patterns, the three correspondent quadrants depicted in the Lang model, namely: relaxation, stress and boredom. The ability of relaxation and stress sessions to induce the target affective states has already been shown in other research.[8,9] Repeating the same protocol, here, that enabled identification of the pattern associated with engagement through Facebook use shows how it is possible to evaluate the reliability of the Lang model by means of physiological measures. This protocol also reveals how relaxation and stress sessions can work as points of reference in Lang Cartesian space to compare psychophysiological patterns generated by different experiences when people engage with social media. Aside from relaxation and stress, the third experience considered is generated by specific YouTube videos aimed to induce boredom, and its association with corresponding psychophysiological patterns. Comparing relaxation and stress with specific YouTube videos, aimed to induce boredom, should help the interpretation of all the psychophysiological data that emerged, not only in this study but also in the previous study about Facebook use.

The Characterization of Boredom in Terms of
Psychophysiological Measurements

In this study, we address the lack of consideration of boredom in previous kindred studies. To do so, we carried out an exploratory study where we exposed a group of students to a specific YouTube video while psychophysiological measures were monitored. We report on some preliminary univariate analyses in the results section, and refer again to Lang's framework of the

Valence-Arousal Model of affective states in discussing and interpreting results. We will try to answer the following preliminary research questions:

1) Is the experience of watching a YouTube video aimed to elicit an affective state corresponding to boredom, associated with a specific psychophysiological state? In particular, is it possible, by means of psychophysiological measures, to identify the specific pattern of participants' affective states, while experiencing YouTube content aimed to elicit boredom, approximated by measures in Valence-Arousal coordinate space. Specifically, the goal is to explore the following second research question relying on the Lang model of emotion (see figure 5.1).

2) Is the psychophysiological state of people using a specific YouTube content aimed to induce boredom characterized by negative valence and mid-low arousal?

Before looking at the results and discussions, we briefly examine a theorisation of boredom in relation to its psychophysiological correlates. As the optimal experience of flow generated by Facebook use has been described as an experience that requires "effortful attention", the prototypical experience of boredom has been described in the literature as an experience where there is a "vigilance decrement".[10] In particular, sustained attention has been understood in terms of automatic and controlled processing. This suggests that human performance can be described as due to two qualitatively different ways of information-processing.[11] On one hand, controlled processes are serial in nature, necessitating effort under an individual's direct control, and not emanating from extensive practice to provide the performance; on the other hand, automatic processing is considered parallel in nature, not limited by short-term memory capacity, necessitating little or no effort, not under the participant's direct control, and generally emanating from practice and repetition, especially for higher level cognitive functions. However, the distinction between automatic and controlled processing is induced by the characteristics of the stimuli or tasks and so has been considered an oversimplification as they enable one of the two forms of attentional control.

Posner suggests it is preferable to distinguish "endogenous" and "exogenous" attention.[12] The first kind of attention is considered to work according to a bottom-up process, not under the voluntary control of the person. The second type is described as actively and deliberately orienting attention to what is believed to be important, for instance after receiving instruction to pay attention to a certain stimulus or situation. This attention requires a top-down functioning, thus the individual has to provide effort to foster and sustain attentional orientation. There are two main theories why "attention decrement" characterizes boredom. Either it is due to the withdrawal of the supervisory attentional system caused by forms of "underarousal" reactions generated by insufficient workload generally needed to spontaneously maintain the attention,[13,14,15] or it is caused by the reduced attentional capacity while on a task for a long time, thus leading to the impossibility of maintaining attention due to high mental workload. This rationale is summarized by the so-called "boredom versus cognitive fatigue hypothesis", that considers the workload evaluation as distributed along a dimension, where on one side there is a sort of "underload" reaction, while on the other an "overload" reaction. Both of them can be related to the attention decrement that accords with the situational contexts. There are relatively recent studies supporting the existence of an "optimal level of workload" associated with an "optimal level of arousal", both in terms of cortical activity and in terms of psychophysiological reactions represented by heart rate and respiratory monitoring. For instance, the Freeman et al.[16] study suggests a correlation between the task level of difficulty with the level of arousal. This was detected through *beta* and *theta* EEG brain waves. In the present study, for the first time, the psychophysiological signature of boredom will be attempted via monitoring skin conductance and electromyography.

Experimental Protocol

Participants. Thirty healthy students from IULM University of Milan, ranging in age from 19 to 25, mean: 22 ± 2.1, volunteered to participate in the study. The only inclusion criterion was a healthy status (no cardiac or emotional pathologies). They were requested not to smoke, drink caffeine or drink alcohol—which could affect the central autonomic nervous system—for a week prior to the experiment.

Procedures. Suitable participants were contacted via email and/or telephone to plan and schedule their participation in the "Behavior and Brain Lab" experiments on IULM University campus. After arriving at the lab, they were asked to sit down in front of a computer and were informed about the relevant details of participating in the study. To collect psychophysiological data, probes were attached by the experimenter while explaining briefly the general rationale of the test. Once the participant felt comfortable, the experimental test started and participants were requested to remain still during the presentation of stimuli.

Stimuli. Three experimental situations were prepared and presented as follows: (1) the first session, aimed to induce relaxation, was conducted through the exposure of the panorama slides for three minutes (already used in a previous study[17]); (2) the second session, aimed to induce boredom, was conducted by the exposure of a specific YouTube video (a 3-minute showing of four people sitting on the same table, putting letters in envelopes); and (3) the third session, aimed to induce stress, was conducted by means of a mental arithmetic calculus task (already used in a previous study[18]). It is noteworthy that the specific YouTube video selected to induce boredom was chosen amongst a set of three YouTube videos posted and judged as 'the most boring videos' by YouTube users. The other two videos showed, respectively, a street with a traffic jam and a man reading a phone book. The three videos were introduced to and judged by a group of 100 students in a pilot study. The one with the highest score in self-reported boredom perception was selected for use in our experiment.

Results

During the relaxation sessions, the mean SC value was measured at 7.92 microOhms; during boredom sessions, mean SC was 9.21 microOhms; while the mean SC value elicited during the stress sessions was 17.65 microOhms. Thus, the lowest level of skin conductance was evidenced during the relaxation sessions, and the highest levels were produced during the stress sessions. During the viewing of the YouTube video aimed to induce boredom, SC was intermediate at 9.21 microOhms. The EMG measurements revealed that mean relaxation values were 9.64 millivolts; during boredom the mean value was 11.57 millivolts, while the mean EMG value was 11.71 millivolts during stress sessions. Thus, the ordering of EMG results is the same as for SC (from lowest to highest values: relaxation, boredom and stress), but the intermediate EMG value (produced during the boredom session) is close in value to the highest (stress session) value.

Statistical analyses (Student t tests), using SPSS software, revealed significant differences ($p < 0.05$) between SC for relaxation compared with stress and for boredom compared with stress, but there was no significant difference between relaxation and boredom. The EMG signal revealed a significant difference between relaxation and boredom and between relaxation and stress, but not for boredom compared with stress.

Discussion

Taking into account all results from SC and EMG data analyzed, it is possible to claim that the YouTube video, aimed to induce boredom, is able to elicit an affective state characterized by mid-low SC level and mid-high EMG level. None of psychophysiological signals considered can allow the detection of boredom when taken alone, however the combination of both might enable a distinction between the three affective states considered: relaxation, boredom and stress. The application of the same protocol has been able to show how it is possible to associate a specific psychophysiological pattern with relaxation, an engagement elicited when using Facebook, and stress, as reported by figure 5.1.[19] "Stress*" (in figure 5.-1) belongs to the data set here presented for the first time, as well as "Relaxation*" and "YouTube"; "Stress" without the asterisk belongs to the previous study discussed, as well as "Relaxation" without the asterisk and "Facebook" use. Considering figure 5.1, it is possible to see how the dimension of valence mentioned in the Lang model of affective states is well represented by different levels of electromyography (on the X axis). Along this axis, the level of stress is the highest, followed by boredom, then relaxation, and finally Facebook use is the lowest (the most positive experience, according to Larsen et al.[20]). On the Y axis, the dimension of intensity or arousal of affective states is also well represented, this time by SC levels: the highest values are for stress, the second is Facebook use, the third is boredom and finally we have relaxation. Moreover, considering the combination of the two axes, as represented by the diagram, it is possible to track the different affective states while participants are exposed to different social media showing different contents.

Conclusions

In this chapter, new empirical data is employed to illustrate a technique to study the emotional impact of different social media. A multidimensional psychophysiological approach is taken, enabling the assessment of human experience in terms of evidence-based methods. In addition, the data collected supports the feasibility of using SC and EMG monitoring as proficient representations of Arousal-Valence dimensions, and thus allow tracking of affective states. The results illustrate how the technique can be applied not only for engaging situations, such as navigating processes on Facebook, but also for boring situations (e.g. generated by specific YouTube videos purposely chosen to elicit prototypical affective states of boredom). Some limitations of the present study might be overcome in further research. For instance, only the average values (across a group of 30 participants) of SC and EMG that were associated with particular affective states were considered. A possible next step is to produce measurements of specific situations to identify which are the most engaging, boring, and relaxing while using social media.

Notes

1. Mauri, Maurizio, Pietro Cipresso, Anna Balgera, Marco Villamira and Giuseppe Riva. 2011. 'Why Is Facebook So Successful? Psychophysiological Measures Describe a Core Flow State While Using Facebook'. *Cyberpsychology, Behavior, and Social Networking* 14(12): 723–31. doi:10.1089/cyber.2010.0377.

2. Ramirez, Artemio, Joseph B. Walther, Judee K. Burgoon and Michael Sunnafrank. 2002. 'Information-Seeking Strategies, Uncertainty, and Computer-Mediated Communication'. *Human Communication Research* 28(2). Blackwell Publishing Ltd: 213–228. doi:10.1111/j.1468-2958.2002.tb00804.x.

3. Lampe, Cliff, Nicole Ellison and Charles Steinfield. 2006. 'A Face(book) in the Crowd'. *Proceedings of the 2006 20th Anniversary Conference on Computer Supported Cooperative Work—CSCW '06*, January: 167. doi:10.1145/1180875.1180901.

4. Joinson, Adam N. 2008. 'Looking At, Looking up or Keeping up with People?' *Proceeding of the Twenty-Sixth Annual CHI Conference on Human Factors in Computing Systems—CHI '08*, 1027. doi:10.1145/1357054.1357213.

5. Pempek, Tiffany A., Yevdokiya, A. Yermolayeva and Sandra L. Calvert. 2009. 'College Students' Social Networking Experiences on Facebook'. *Journal of Applied Developmental Psychology* 30(3). Elsevier Inc.: 227–38. doi:10.1016/j.appdev.2008.12.010.

6. Guraya, Salman Y. 2016. The Usage of Social Networking Sites by Medical Students for Educational Purposes: A Meta–analysis and Systematic Review'. *North American Journal of Medical Sciences* 8(7): 268–78. doi:10.4103/1947-2714.187131.

7. Lang, Peter J. 1995. 'The Emotion Probe: Studies of Motivation and Attention'. *American Psychologist* 50(5): 372–85. doi:10.1037/0003-066X.50.5.372.

8. Scotti, Stefano, Mauri Maurizio, Barbieri Riccardo, et al. (n.d.) 'Automatic Quantitative Evaluation of Emotions in E-Learning Applications'. http://apps.isiknowledge.com/full_record.do?product=UA&search_mode=CombineSearches&qid=18&SID=W2LKmI9F4KNekainPjF&page=2&doc=52.

9. Mauri, Maurizio, Valentina Magagnin, Pietro Cipresso, Luca Mainardi, Emery N. Brown, Sergio Cerutti, Marco Villamira and Riccardo Barbieri. 2010. 'Psychophysiological Signals Associated with Affective States'. In *2010 Annual International Conference of the IEEE Engineering in Medicine and Biology Society, EMBC'10*, 3563–3566. doi:10.1109/IEMBS.2010.5627465.

10. Pattyn, Nathalie, Xavier Neyt, David Henderickx and Eric Soetens. 2008. 'Psychophysiological Investigation of Vigilance Decrement: Boredom or Cognitive Fatigue?' *Physiology and Behavior* 93(1–2): 369–78. doi:10.1016/j.physbeh.2007.09.016.

11. Fisk, Arthur D, and Walter Schneider. 1981. 'Control and Automatic Processing during Task Requiring Sustained Attention: A New Approach to Vigilance'. *Human Factors* 23(6): 737–50. doi:10.1177/001872088102300610.

12. Posner, Michael I. 1980. 'Orienting of Attention'. *Quarterly Journal of Experimental Psychology*. doi:10.1080/00335558008248231.

13. Stuss, Donald T., Tim Shallice, Michael P Alexander and Terence W Picton. 1995. 'A Multidisciplinary Approach to Anterior Attention Functions'. *Annals of the New York Academy of Sciences* 769: 191–211.

14. Robertson, Ian H., Tom Manly, Jackie Andrade, Bart T Baddeley and Jenny Yiend. 1997. "'Oops!': Performance Correlates of Everyday Attentional Failures in Traumatic Brain Injured and Normal Subjects'. *Neuropsychologia* 35(6): 747–58. doi:10.1016/S0028-3932(97)00015-8.

15. Manly, Tom, Ian H. Robertson, Maria Galloway and Kari Hawkins. 1999. 'The Absent Mind: Further Investigations of Sustained Attention to Response'. *Neuropsychologia* 37(6): 661–70. doi:10.1016/S0028-3932(98)00127-4.

16. Freeman, Frederick G., Peter J. Mikulka, Mark W. Scerbo and Lorissa Scott. 2004. 'An Evaluation of an Adaptive Automation System Using a Cognitive Vigilance Task'. *Biological Psychology* 67(3): 283–97. doi:10.1016/j.biopsycho.2004.01.002.

17. Mauri, Maurizio, Pietro Cipresso, Anna Balgera, Marco Villamira and Giuseppe Riva. 2011. 'Why Is Facebook So Successful? Psychophysiological Measures Describe a Core Flow State While Using Facebook'. *Cyberpsychology, Behavior, and Social Networking* 14(12): 723–31. doi:10.1089/cyber.2010.0377.

18. Ibid.

19. Ibid.

20. Larsen, Jeff T., Catherine J. Norris and John T. Cacioppo. 2003. 'Effects of Positive and Negative Affect on Electromyographic Activity over *Zygomaticus Major* and *Corrugator Supercilii*'. *Psychophysiology* 40(5): 776–85. doi:10.1111/1469-8986.00078.

Part II

Mediated Connectivities, Immediacies and Intensities

Alyssa D. Niccolini's talk on the New Materialism panel at A&SM2. Photo by Jamie Murray.

Introduction to Part II

Jussi Parikka

A N AFFECT MEDIATED is an affect transformed, built up, intensified, triggered, and in search of new contexts outside its original institutional
setting. Affect is also stacked across multiple lives from persona to institutions to infrastructures of social media. In other words, mediated affect is
not merely a signal that connects A to B. Mediated affect is all about the
multiple layers where affect is one particular channel across which social
organisation, visibility, and empowerment—but also data about all those
things—flows. Moreover, social media and other digital tools like wellness
apps provide an afterlife for affect. This is a lively afterlife.

The chapters in this section offer apt case studies as to how affect behaves
in technological networks. Affect is not contained in particular personal situations but aggregates into hashtagged networks of temporary (but meaningful) contact. These are temporary attachments that provide a particular time
of affect on a network. As Rebecca Coleman points out, the time of (a)live
forms a core part of affect's vibrant impact. Building on Raymond Williams'
work, she develops this notion into a material understanding of the mediated
textures of a temporality that attaches to bodies and their relations. Where
the personal is politically characterised by a whole generation of activist,
feminist stakes, now the personal is the infrastructural is the political: an
awareness of the complexities of actual use-situations where social media
takes place in schools, in personal routines, and across the mundane and the
technical.

Alyssa D. Niccolini demonstrates how close data comes when wearable
technologies continue the work of the embodied affect as its particular
channel—educating, intensifying, guiding. Applications such as Spire (the
focus of Niccolini's chapter) are the training ground of the body: slower,

faster, focused, inhaling, exhaling, relaxing subject. Niccolini also starts to unfold a sort of infrastructural question: what assumptions are built into the guidance and governance of apps such as Spire, and what do they provide for the living social body?

Affect is also governed as a second-order affective infrastructure. In the final chapter of this section, Jessica Ringrose and Kaitlyn Mendes discuss what Twitter can do as a platform that also empowers and provides an empirically grounded feminist challenge to the often recurring misogynist discourses of social media. Building on terms such as affective publics, Ringrose offers useful case studies to 'the complex affective relationalities of solidarities' that characterise the inventive teenager's use of social media as a means to highlight institutional tensions.

The trio of articles offers us a novel set of ideas: Firstly, affect is transformative across multiple media platforms and lived experiences. Affect travels and is constantly rematerialized in different signifying and asignifying contexts. Affect mobilizes. Secondly, as it mobilizes, affect is constantly channelled, educated, intensified. We are one particular carrier of affect that becomes a motor of social actions, including politically meaningful ones. Lastly, temporary affective publics are also important to register and note as part of the cartographies of what mediated bodies can do. While constantly guided and regulated, the body becomes inventive and intensively searches for new forms of expression.

6

Social Media and the Materialisation of the Affective Present

Rebecca Coleman

A PREVALENT WAY in which social media and other digital technologies are currently framed is as hyper-connected, always on, affective and non-representational, and involved in re-working boundaries between production and consumption, and between temporalities and spatialities. For example, Twitter describes its mission as '[t]o give everyone the power to create and share ideas and information instantly, without barriers' (https://about.twit-ter.com/company), while Facebook explains its News Feed as 'a regularly updating list of stories from friends, Pages, and other connections, like groups and events' (https://newsroom.fb.com/products/). Instagram describes itself as:

> A fun and quirky way to share your life with friends through a series of pictures. Snap a photo with a mobile phone, then choose a filter to transform the image into a memory to keep around forever. We're building Instagram to allow you to experience moments in your friends' lives through pictures as they happen. We imagine a world more connected through photos' (sic). (https://www.insta-gram.com/about/faq/).

These three social media platforms self-describe as providing spatial and temporal connections, enabling links between people and events to be shared in the moment, and perhaps kept forever.

In this chapter, focus is on the ways in which social media is understood to be reworking time through its connectivity, immediacy and instantaneity. In particular, I suggest that social media may produce a particular kind of a "temporal present"[1] where bodies, technologies and the socio-cultural matrix are intertwined and experienced in terms of "aliveness",[2] and "always-on-ness".[3] I suggest these qualities of social media be understood as "pre-emergence", in the terms of Raymond Williams.[4] I draw on the materialist tradition of Williams and more recent new materialist approaches to media and culture, to consider whether and how social media constitutes an *infra*-structure of feeling, where data capture and connections between and across various platforms, devices and technologies are key, and through which practices such as linking, tagging and checking—and affects such as compulsion, frustration, anxiety and joy—are materialised.

The "Temporal Present"

One way to understand the kinds of temporality that are central to social media is in terms of the present. That is, the connectivity, instantaneity and constant availability of social media creates a present temporality; a temporality that is concerned with "the now", and is stretched and condensed in various ways. It is important to note that such a temporality does not preclude the past or the future; as noted above, present events can be archived into the future and, as I discuss below, the present is a flexible temporality, potentially incorporating other temporalities. Furthermore, such a present temporality is affective; it is fun, quirky, and involves friends sharing experiences. As a number of different scholars might put it, it is a temporality that is "(a)live".[5]

Taking up Williams' influential work on structures of feeling can help to elucidate these points. For example, in his essay "Structures of Feeling", Williams develops an account that seeks to comprehend culture not as fixed forms[6] but as an active, flexible, "temporal present"[7]. In this way, he aims to direct attention towards the dynamism of culture; rather than being analysed in terms of a "habitual past tense", culture can and should (also) be understood as 'this, here, now, alive, active'.[8] Such an approach to culture draws on the relationships between what he defines as "dominant", "residual", and "emergent" culture. Dominant culture refers to hegemonic culture[9] and residual culture to what 'has been effectively formed in the past, but is still active in the cultural process, not only, and often not at all, as an element of the past, but as an effective element of the present'.[10] Of particular salience to a concern with a present temporality is emergent culture, which Williams describes as such:

> By "emergent" I mean, first, that new meanings and values, new practices, new relationships and kinds of relationship are continually being created. But it is

exceptionally difficult to distinguish between those which are really elements of some new phase of the dominant culture (and in this sense "species-specific") and those which are substantially alternative or oppositional to it: emergent in the strict sense, rather than merely novel. Since we are always considering relations within a cultural process, definitions of the emergent, as of the residual, can be made only in relation to a full sense of the dominant.[11]

In this quotation, Williams posits emergent culture as that which is both novel and new, and which is 'substantially alternative or oppositional' to dominant culture. As such, dominant culture comes to stand for a "habitual past tense",[12] that is an understanding of culture as fixed and finished. However, dominant culture occupies an important position in Williams' schema, as it enables both emergent and residual culture to be identified and made sense of. Thus, while he emphasises an understanding of culture as (a)live, he also maintains that there is a need to attend to the past (and the future, as I will go on to discuss).

Williams (1977b: 126) goes on to offer a more complex account of emergent culture, naming what he terms "evident emergence" and that which is pre-emergent:

What matters, finally, in understanding emergent culture, as distinct from both the dominant and the residual, is that it is never only a matter of immediate practice; indeed it depends crucially on finding new forms or adaptations of form. Again and again what we have to observe is in effect a *pre-emergence*, active and pressing but not yet fully articulated, rather than the evident emergence which could be more confidently named.

Here then, Williams argues that what is most significant to an understanding of emergent culture is that which is 'active and pressing but not yet fully articulated'. It is thus not a practice that can be readily identified or that already has a form, but which is in the process of emerging. Crucially, Williams argues that:

It is to understand more closely this condition of pre-emergence, as well as the more evident forms of the emergent, the residual, and the dominant that we need to explore the concept of structures of feeling.[13]

Social Media as Pre-emergent

How might social media be understood as a 'condition of pre-emergence'? What assistance does such an understanding contribute to an exploration of a structure of feeling? Again, turning to Williams' work is productive. Published in the 1970s and 1980s, Williams focuses on how a structure of feeling is generated by textual forms. For example, in *The Welsh Industrial Novel*[14] he describes how nineteenth and twentieth century novels both capture and create a specifically "Welsh structure of feeling"[15] that comes from the physical characteristics of Welsh industrial areas and the social relations and historical events that have come to compose its working life.[16] He tracks the emergence and development of this genre of writing, explaining how it moves from the *experience* of mass industrialization in Wales to its *observation*. It is only when it is able to observe, rather than experience the situation, that it becomes a coherent genre. Drawing on the distinction made between pre-emergent and emergent culture, what Williams is pointing to here is how, in the transformation from experience to observation, a particular genre is formed. Experience may be thus conceived as pre-emergent and observation as emergent.

My suggestion is that social media is experiential, and hence is preemergent. It is a series of practices, activities, flows and events that, as Williams says, are not 'fully articulated' but hover 'at the edge of semantic availability'.[17] Consider, for example, how in the three examples introduced above, the emphasis is on what is happening. Twitter, Facebook and Instagram are platforms organised as feeds that are always updating, presenting a constant flow of images and text. These images and texts do not so much cohere as indicate the movement of data. As such, they are experienced more than they are observed.

Affect: The Pre-emergent

What is also suggested (with the understanding of social media) as preemergent is that the liveness and happening of social media is a situation that is experienced (i.e. felt) before it becomes something coherent. In this sense, the "pre" of pre-emergence becomes particularly important. Moving from the cultural materialism of Williams to the new materialisms can help shed light on this "pre". Some theorists see these two traditions as difficult to bring together. For example, Joss Hands[18] sees the new materialisms as failing to account for the social and cultural contexts in which technologies emerge, which is central to Williams' arguments. However, in terms of my focus here, in Williams' and more recent approaches, sensation and feeling are identified as key means to understand the social world. For example, while Williams concentrates on structures of feeling as essential to comprehending the dynamism and activity of the social and cultural world, Celia

Lury and Nina Wakeford propose the notion of '*the happening* of the social world—its ongoingness, relationality, contingency, and sensuousness'.[19]

Furthermore, where Williams focuses on the pre-emergent as that which helps to make sense of a structure of feeling, Patricia Ticeneto Clough argues that social and cultural theory needs to attend to the infra-empirical—that is, how the activity of our world today, to a large extent, takes place at time-space scales far finer than those of human perception, at the probabilistic scale of affect'.[20] For Clough, the social today operates not so much in terms of ideological interpellation, or subject formation, but through 'affective modulation and individuation'.[21] This is a social modulated at the edges of perception and consciousness,[22] through the "affective capacities"[23] of both humans and technologies. Taking up Clough's point, Williams' identification of the significance of the emergence of the cultural and social is amplified today: What is in a state of pre-emergence, what 'hovers at the edge of semantic availability', is increasingly not only the preserve of emergent culture, but what the dominant social and cultural "is".[24]

As I have suggested, this state of pre-emergence is especially the case with social media. Social media data is created in real time through a range of different devices, and is collected and analysed in this "same" time. While humans may be partly involved in these processes of creation, collection and analysis, they are only one aspect of it; technologies like mobile phones, swipe cards, and social media are involved in their creation, and computer technologies can analyse this data far quicker than humans. Thus, both users and analysts of social media experience rather than observe. The speed of this "real time" experience may therefore be understood in terms of the present—it is not the fixed and finished "past tense" but in Williams' terms, is the active, flexible temporal present.

A more recent work by Clough, Karen Gregory, Benjamin Haber, and R. Joshua Scannell, argues:

> Big data doesn't care about "you" so much as the bits of seemingly random information that bodies generate or that they leave as a data trail; the aim is to affect or prehend novelty.[25]

The first part of this quotation emphasises the displacement of the human within the datalogical network—a key theme in work in the new materialisms, where humans may be one part of a network or series of connections, but not necessarily most important or at its centre. The second part is productive in terms of thinking about the pre- of the present, where the aim of big data is not only to care about what "you" have done, so much as what you are doing and may do. To 'affect or prehend novelty' is for big data to 'seek to prehend incomputable data and thereby modulate the emergent forms of sociality in their emergence.'[26] Big data is concerned with the emergence, or the "pre", of the present. The present is flexible, happening, live—that is, is in the process of emerging. In this sense, it is future-oriented.

Not only is the pre-emergent important to new materialist work, it has also been theorised by those working on affect. As a force that registers in the body before it may be comprehended or made sense of, affect is understood as physical or emotional states or activities that are pre-conscious.[27] Indeed, Brian Massumi suggests that one way to understand affect is in terms of a "missing half-second"; an activity that occurs in the brain—and this also might be extended to include the body more generally—prior to that activity being made conscious.[28] Specific affects that may be produced through engagement with social media, and digital media more generally, include a compulsion to frequently check on our own or friends' Facebook posts, or our emails; the lure of the Twitter flow; an anxiety if we are away from our mobile phone; nerves about our laptop running low on battery; boredom at agreeing to terms and conditions during online shopping; frustration when internet pages take a while to load, or when updates to applications interrupt what we're doing; joy at speaking to a friend on Skype; distraction by working across different screens; or immersion in a Netflix box set. While some of these affective states might be articulable in/as language—frustration, anger, nerves, for instance—others may be vaguer, or not so easily expressed, and indeed might escape or exceed their expression in language. They hover 'at the edge of semantic availability'.[29]

Infra-structures of Feeling

Bringing together the materialist position of Williams and new materialist work on data and affect indicates that pre-emergence is a particularly significant aspect of contemporary media culture. Drawing on both Williams' definition of pre-emergence as the 'active and pressing but not yet fully articulated', and on the importance of what Clough terms the "infra-empirical" to social media and digital culture, I conclude that the concept of infra-structures of feeling is a helpful means of studying and making sense of such qualities of the present. The concept of infra-structures of feeling is intended to account for both pre-emergence and for how this pre-emergence is organised and arranged.

For Williams, a structure of feeling may be identified in a particular genre of literature or series of artworks (such as Welsh industrial novels). In terms of how the pre-emergence of social media is encountered and experienced, it is worth considering the role of, for example, various digital devices, apps, platforms, and their associated practices, as contributing to an infra-structure of feeling. That is, rather than being located in one genre, social media works across a potentially diverse range of supporting structures. In this sense, the term "infra-structures of feeling" seeks to account for the often neglected technological and institutional linkages or systems that are central to the organisation and functioning of social and cultural life.[30]

As a term that also points to the "pre"—that which cannot necessarily be articulated and is "just-before" a practice that can be clearly identified— "infra" also seeks to account for the affective dimension of the emergence of social media. Whereas Williams' analysis was largely restricted to literary texts and art, I would like to enlarge his approach to consider texts more widely, as text*ures*. In particular, it is important to note that Williams' concept of structure of feeling isn't only a means of identifying a specific culture, but is also *a methodology*—the development of a mode of analysis that doesn't split the personal and social, and convert the social to fixed forms. The term texture is then, perhaps, one way of "getting at" the infra-structures of feeling that are created through what hovers in everyday media experiences, practices, objects, devices.

As well as expanding what might count as a text, "texture" is also a means of highlighting the affectivity of social media. Williams defines a structure of feeling in terms of a:

> set, with specific internal relations, at once interlocking and in tension. Yet we are also defining a social experience which is still in process, often indeed not recognized as social but taken to be private, idiosyncratic, and even isolating, but which in analysis (though rarely otherwise) has its emerging, connecting, and dominant characteristics, indeed its specific hierarchies.[31]

There are clear connections to be made here between Williams' understanding of a structure of feeling and how Eve Kosofsky Sedgwick defines texture as 'an array of perceptual data that includes repetition' and connects and distinguishes between different scales, 'but whose organization hovers just below the level of shape or structure'.[32] Both emphasise process and emergence, and organisation and structure. In the way that I'm developing it, thinking through textures and infra-structures helps to grasp the "just-beforeness" of the present. Indeed, expanding the notion of texts to textures is to respond to Williams' argument that 'the making of art is never itself in the past tense. It is always a formative process, within a specific present'.[33] Here, it is helpful to make a connection between this definition of texture and what Kathleen Stewart terms "ordinary affects", which 'work not through "meanings" per se, but rather in the way that they pick up density and texture as they move through bodies, dreams, dramas, and social world-ings of all kinds'.[34] A texture is a becoming, a "worlding". It is, in the terms that I have been developing here, an affective experience that is temporally present.

Notes

1. Raymond Williams, 'Structures of Feeling', in *Marxism and Literature* (Oxford, UK: Oxford University Press, 1977a): 128–35.

2. Les Back and Nirmal Puwar, *Live Methods* (Malden, UK: Wiley Blackwell, 2012); Les Back, Celia Lury and Robert Zimmer, 'Doing Real Time Research: Opportunities and Challenges', Discussion Paper, National Centre for Research Methods (2013), http://eprints.ncrm.ac.uk/3157/; Williams, "Structures of Feeling".

3. Patricia Ticeneto Clough, *Autoaffection: Unconscious Thought in the Age of Teletechnology* (Minneapolis: University of Minnesota Press, 2000).

4. Williams, 'Structures of Feeling'.

5. Back and Puwar, *Live Methods*; Back, Lury and Zimmer, 'Doing Real Time Research'; Esther Weltevrede, Anne Helmond and Carolin Gerlitz, (2014) 'The Politics of Real-time: A Device Perspective on Social Media Platforms and Search Engines', *Theory, Culture and Society*, 3(6) (2014): 125–50.

6. Williams, 'Structures of Feeling', 129.

7. Ibid, 128.

8. Ibid, 128.

9. Raymond Williams, 'Dominant, Residual, and Emergent', in *Marxism and Literature* (Oxford, UK: Oxford University Press, 1977b), 121–27.

10. Ibid, 122.

11. Ibid, 123.

12. Williams, 'Structures of Feeling', 128.

13. Williams, 'Dominant, Residual, and Emergent', 126–27.

14. Raymond Williams (1980) 'The Welsh Industrial Novel', in *Culture and Materialism: Selected Essays* (London: Verso, 1980), 213–29.

15. Ibid, 221.

16. Ibid, 221–22.

17. Williams, 'Structures of Feeling', 132.

18. Joss Hands (2015) 'From Cultural to New Materialism and Back: The Enduring Legacy of Raymond Williams', *Culture, Theory and Critique*, 56(2): 133–48.

19. Celia Lury and Nina Wakeford, *Inventive Methods: The Happening of the Social* (London: Routledge, 2012), 2.

20. Patricia Ticeneto Clough, 'The New Empiricism: Affect and Sociological Method', *European Journal of Social Theory*, 12(1) (2009): 43–61.

21. Ibid, 50.

22. Ibid, 44.

23. Ibid, 50.

24. Rebecca Coleman, 'Theorising the Present: Digital Media, Pre-emergence and Infra-Structures of Feeling', under review.

25. Patricia Ticeneto Clough, Karen Gregory, Benjamin Haber and R. Joshua Scannell, 'The Datalogical Turn', in *Non-Representational Methodologies: Re-envisioning Research*, Phillip Vannini, ed. (London: Routledge, 2015), 146–64.

26. Ibid, 153.

27. Hands makes another distinction between the theorization of affect in the new materialisms and feeling in Williams' work, arguing that in the former affect is pre-conscious and in the latter feeling is sub-conscious.

28. Brian Massumi, *Parables for the Virtual: Movement. Affect, Sensation* (Durham, NC: Duke University Press, 2002). For a critique, see Margaret Wetherell, *Affect and Emotion: A New Social Science Understanding* (London: Sage, 2012) and Sara Ahmed, *The Cultural Politics of Emotion* (Edinburgh, UK: Edinburgh University Press, 2004).

29. Williams, 'Structures of Feeling', 132.

30. See, for example, Stephen Graham, *Disrupted Cities: When Infrastructures Fail* (London: Routledge, 2010); Penny Harvey and Hannah Knox, *Roads: An Anthropology of Infrastructure and Expertise* (Ithaca, NY: Cornell University Press, 2015); Andrew Lakoff and Stephen Collier, 'Infrastructure and Event: The Political Technology of Preparedness', in *Political Matter: Technoscience, Democracy and Public Life*, Bruce Braunn and Sarah Whatmore, eds. (Minneapolis: University of Minnesota Press, 210): 243–66.

31. Williams, 'Structures of Feeling', 132.

32. Eve Kosofsky Sedgwick, *Touching Feeling: Affect, Pedagogy, Performativity* (Durham, NC: Duke University Press, 2002), 16.

33. Williams, 'Structures of Feeling', 129.

34. Kathleen Stewart, *Ordinary Affects* (Durham, NC: Duke University Press, 2007), 3.

7

The Education of Feeling
Wearable Technology and Triggering Pedagogies

Alyssa D. Niccolini

Feeling Machines

ZUCKERBERG IS GOOD. Targeted ads on my Facebook feed promised me increased productivity, clarity, and 'the most calm I'd ha[ve] in 10 years'.[1] A new wearable was on the market that would prompt you to breathe when you were tense. Somehow my pre-PhD defense stress had gotten picked up by Facebook's algorithms. I now have a new technology clipped to my clothing: Spire is branded as a "Mindfulness and Activity Tracker". It promises to be 'your personal mindfulness coach' communicating through haptic prompts (vibrations) that sync with a mobile app.[2] The Amazon.com product description states:

> Spire's in-the-moment notifications makes becoming mindful more attainable throughout the day while in-app breathing exercises and guided mini-meditation sessions promote the modification of negative behaviors. Through consistent, unobtrusive, and actionable insights, Spire users take an active role in making positive, reflexive improvements towards a greater holistic health and well-being.[3]

Worn on the bra or belt, the Spire "stone", as it is called, was developed in Stanford University's Calming Technology Lab (where one of the co-founders is a researcher). Its mobile app features a "breath-wave" that undulates in real-time as you inhale and exhale. In addition, "force sensors" track respiration which is described on the website as 'an information-dense data stream [with] many components to it such as rate, depth, inhalation-to-exhalation ratio (IER), durations of inhalation, retention, exhalation, and hold, consistency, smoothness, transition, and so on'.[4]

People are feeling Spire. Amazon.com features over 1,400 reviews to date. Many fans extol it with a quasi-spiritual ecstasy. One featured on the Spire website gushes: 'I felt like frigging Buddha looking at all my glorious streaks of calm and focus'.[5] On the Spire FAQ page, marketers tap into this spiritual tone:

> Spire is a play on the Latin *spirant* which means "to breathe" and is the root of the word "respiration" as well as "spirit". It is also the root for "inspiration" and "aspire", which all come from the same root. In many diverse cultures around the world, the word "breath" and "spirit"/"life energy" are the *same* word[6].

This Zen-vibe is crafted into Spire's grey matte hardware and wood-grained charging base, evocative of the ubiquitous riverstone water features in spas, yoga studies, and therapist offices. In addition, its functionality promises '[a] beautiful and powerful mobile experience'.[7] Its body has a waterproof cover with a skin-like texture that protects its hardware. Through this intimate body-to-body contact, you touch Spire and Spire touches you—physically, emotionally, haptically, perhaps even spiritually.

Touching Education

If this wearable wants to touch you, it is in the service of *teaching* you. In this short piece, I explore how health and wellness wearables like Spire work to offer affective pedagogies. In its press kit, Spire marketers underscore the device's pedagogical function: 'the spire app *teaches* you how to use your breath to decrease this stress'.[8] Spire offers an intriguing means of studying affect in that it both demands and proffers a receptivity and responsivity of multiple bodies (human and not-human). The Spire algorithm aspires to retrain its users' sensoria, sensitizing them to their parasympathetic bodily responses (i.e. breath, tension responses), and *educating* bodies into new affective habits. We might riff on Massumi's (2002) formulation of a "shock to thought" and imagine Spire's pedagogy as offering a *vibration* to thought.[9]

Spire, then, markets itself as an affective pedagogue: a wearable that algorithmically learns from the body and in turn retrains the body to modulate affect and mood. Aligned with "getting things done" technologies[10] and a tradition of neuropedagogies, Spire dreams of technologically bridging

Cartesian splits and recircuiting the body's intelligences. Predicated on bio-feedback and the power to modulate bodily sensations and emotional responses, Spire works to retrain body-mind connectivity. Its landing page features a quote from GQ that boasts that it 'reconnects body and mind'.[11] Part of the emotional turn in brain sciences.[12] Spire links emotion and cognition, foregrounding the plasticity and retrainability of the brain. As explained on the "Science" tab of the website: '[a]dvanced algorithms in the Spire app classify your breathing patterns based on dozens of laboratory studies correlating respiration patterns with cognitive and emotional state'.[13]

What I consider here is how wearable technologies like Spire work to capture affect within a rational and individualized human subject who is able to apprehend, understand and contain sensory and affective responses. Although such wearables putatively seek to value bodily sensitivities and responsiveness, affective responses are thought of as belonging to a single, self-reflective and self-contained Cartesian subject. An Amazon.com reviewer urges potential buyers to check out Spire '[i]f you're looking to improve your well-being, [and] learn more about you'.[14] Within this "know thyself" ethos, this wearable will help you '[u]nderstand your stress by time, place, or event'.[15] Mapped within temporal, geographical, and experiential grid space, tension becomes a state to be captured as data, mitigated and interrupted. While Spire copywriters concede that tension responses are sometimes necessary 'to deal with threatening situations, store emotional memories, and prepare the body for physical exertion (exercise)',[16] the wearable acts in service of disrupting tension into what are deemed superior and more useful states (focus and calm).

As affective pedagogues (your "personal mindfulness coach"), wearables like Spire subtly collude with larger hopes, anxieties, and promises of education and implicitly position affective intensities as inimical to "productive" learning. I follow with some brief provocations to consider how wearables like Spire bear pedagogical impulses that sync with current trends within education. I contend that Spire's promises for education are in line with pushes for data-driven pedagogies, Computer Based Education (CBE), and "wired" curricula and classrooms. In addition, Spire stokes desires for learning to immediately translate to market value and, above all, for pedagogy not to be disruptive.

Productive Learning

As a community of users sharing information, the review section of Amazon-.com is itself pedagogical as reviewers seek to inform and instruct potential buyers on both their consumer choices and practices of self-styling. For instance, one reviewer shares how s/he uses Spire to be a better teacher:

> I'm a teacher, and while I can always tell at the END of the day if I've been tense, I could never tell in the moment while it was happening so I could do something about it. Enter Spire. It gently buzzes at me when I've been tense for two minutes. At that moment I plant my feet, stop taking questions, scan my classroom, and breathe slowly for a minute. Then I go back to teaching— calmer, kinder, more present.[17]

Like the teacher-reviewer above, a large number of the Amazon reviewers state that they use Spire to improve their experiences at work. For most of these reviewers, Spire helps them perform better at their jobs. While this reviewer becomes 'calmer, kinder, more present', others use it to better handle the stresses of their work environments. As one reviewer writes: 'I work in a top Internet company as a[n] executive, and it is paramount to keep mental equanimity when things go astray'.[18]

Increasing your productivity is a core promise of Spire. A featured review on the website is penned by Michael Susi, the "Global Wellness Manager" at the LinkedIn Corporation. He writes that LinkedIn 'employees use Spire to make tangible improvements to things that can seem fleeting: focus, distraction, productivity'.[19] A press release announcing Spire's first place win in a design competition, states 'Spire analyzes an individual's emotional and physical state with the goal of improving people's daily lives through greater health, balance and productivity'.[20] The power to increase productivity is made explicit by the cofounder and Chief Product Officer at Spire, who writes:

> Spire is a new kind of product. It's rooted in bringing balance and presence to life. *It can genuinely make you more productive.* More creative. Lose weight. Have work/life balance. Be a better parent. A better listener. Anything that clarity of mind, balance, and focus can give you. These are bold claims, but the truth is that Spire doesn't do these things *to* you—it helps create the conditions necessary for you to focus on achieving the things you value most in life.[21]

For whom, primarily, do health and wellness related wearables make more centered and productive? Ads for wellness wearables frequently feature able-bodied white-collar workers smiling in conference room meetings or young professionals in hip homes. With its luxury design and relatively high price tag, Spire targets consumers who are more likely able to afford stress management (or "self-care") at spas and yoga studios as well as have access to health-care and insurance-covered or even private mental health therapy. Its website features a link to its "Professionals Program", geared towards 'psychiatrists, psychologists, counselors, coaches, therapists, nutritionists and clinics',[22] many of whose services would not be covered by most US health insurances.

Triggering Pedagogies

In many ways, Spire's affective pedagogy is a retraining of speeds and intensities.[23] Spire will help you to slow down and re-center when tense, helping you to refocus on your breathing. One reviewer uses it to diminish her intensity, which she describes as 'my inner wild aggressive super absorbed motivated excited gusto'.[24] Spire works chiefly towards the suppression and diminishment of affective intensities. Tension then is positioned, in part, as inimical to learning to be productive. Through its disruption of tension states, Spire helps its wearers avoid the potentially damaging pedagogies of stress and anxiety. As it retrains wearers to address their tensions, it works to keep them in a comfortable state, free of negative affect implying that only in such a state can we achieve our best thinking and performance. We might sense similar impetuses motivating trigger warnings in higher education. Ann Pelligrini (2014) considers that:

> The admirable goal behind student initiatives for trigger warnings is to create more breathing room in the classroom and minimize students' pain. In practice, though, trigger warnings too easily become yet another disciplinary mechanism that the corporate university can use to promote consumer (and donor) satisfaction as the highest good. Forms of neoliberal values ultimately do little to nothing to look after the well-being of individual students or make structural changes that would ameliorate, let alone prevent, suffering.[25]

It's striking that Pelligrini mentions a desire for "breathing room". If wellness wearables diminish our tension and refocus us on our individual breathing rhythms, what "structural changes" might we be turning our attention away from? As more and more wearables 'impel new affective tendencies of bodies, new forms of attention, distraction, practice, and repetition',[26] what habits of thought and affective encounters might we be missing out on? Or as Sampson (2016) puts it, how do such technologies produce a "neurosubject" who is, at once, 'attentive and subdued?'[27]

The Gentle Pedagogue

On the Spire product page is stated: '*[u]nobtrusively* clipped to your belt or bra, Spire knows when you're stressed and helps you reduce tension with smart notifications and *gentle* reminders'.[28] This unobtrusiveness is frequently cited by reviewers. One reviewer gushes 'Spire is gorgeous. The back of the device is soft and I never feel it rubbing up against my skin during daily use (most of the time, I completely forget I'm wearing it)'[29]. In addition to its unobtrusiveness, Spire's *gentle* haptic prompts are also frequently celebrated in reviews: 'I have enjoyed being notified by my Spire stone with a gentle, almost a tickle (truly makes me smile when it taps me)'.[30]

If Spire is your personal mobile pedagogue, it offers a form of pedagogy that is both unobtrusive and gentle. This unobtrusive and gentleness subtly colludes with desires for non-disruptive pedagogy. In a tongue-in-cheek blog entry, a woman likens Spire to an illicit lover. After heavy sexual innuendo, she proclaims, 'Spire is totally in sync with everything I feel and even finishes my thoughts for me'.[31] In line with marketers' promises of '[a] beautiful and powerful mobile experience',[32] this feeling of being "in sync" bolsters dreams of a frictionless reciprocity with machines. It offers thinking as non-disruptive, as physically and emotionally non-taxing, as something we can outsource to the unobtrusive machines strapped to our bodies.

Tag Someone You Know

I want to end by considering what the unintended political costs might be of such a *gentle pedagogy* by turning to a video titled "Spire_Viralthread.mp4" in the Spire press kit. Ostensibly an advertisement designed to be shared on social media (or go viral on viralthread.com), the video shows people using Spire in their everyday lives, gives information about the product, and then ends with the words 'Tag someone you know who needs this'.

While the video opens with a clip of a suited man attaching Spire to his belt loop and a heterosexual couple energetically getting out of bed, it centres on the day of a woman of colour. With emotional piano tones, she rises in a glass elevator with a cityscape looming behind her. She looks a bit stressed and closes her eyes. We seem to be invited into her thoughts and are shown a series of political scenes. First, the words 'in times of intense stress and uncertainty' are printed on an image of antifascist protesters raising fists on a monument in Washington, DC. This is followed by a shot of a placard reading 'Women's Rights are Human Rights.' The final image is the backshot of a woman addressing a group of environmental activists. After we're told about Spire's different functions, we see our protagonist navigate public space. She is rushing and seems uncomfortable, if not agitated. She reaches into her handbag to check her phone and we are shown an iPhone notification: 'Your breathing suggests you are tense. Take a deep breath?'

Next, our protagonist is shown standing in front of an office window as part of a crowd. She breathes deeply and is transported into a lush field and a hip yoga outfit. She is no longer plagued by thoughts of antifascists, environmental destruction, and the fight for women's rights. The stress of being a woman of colour in both public space and in the workplace has vanished. We read: 'Because when you breathe better, you live a happier, healthier life.' The woman slowly disappears into a thickening fog as the words 'Tag someone who needs this' are seen on the screen.

In Gilles Deleuze's "Postscript on the Societies of Control" his penultimate line reads: 'Many young people strangely boast of being "motivated"; they re-request apprenticeships and permanent training. It's up to them to discover what they're being made to serve'.[33] Is this viral video suggesting we might collectively be feeling the stress motivating antifascists to protest? Is it intuiting that we might be anxious about the lack of women's rights? Could the right wearable help mitigate the microaggressions assailing women of colour? Should black bloc activists start wearing Spire so as to be better antifascists? As I sit here with my own grey-matte stone pressed against my chest, I ask myself whom am I being made to serve? What pedagogies might I be foregoing in order to be calm, focused, and more productive as I write this very chapter?

Your breathing suggests you are tense. Take a deep breath?

Notes

1. https://spire.io/.
2. https://spire.io/.
3. "Spire Mindfulness and Activity Tracker for iOS and Android," https://www.amazon.com/Spire-Mindfulness-Activity-Tracker-Android/dp/B00TH3SQOI/ref=sr_1_1?ie=UTF8&qid=1490782719&sr=8-1&keywords=spire&th=1.
4. "FAQs," https://spire.io/.
5. Gizmodo quoted on https://spire.io/.
6. "FAQs,": https://spire.io/pages/faqs.
7. "Discover Calm-App," https://spire.io/.
8. "Spire Press Kit," https://drive.google.com/drive/folders/0B07Hlwq1x6vScVo1dVYyN1JRaG8italicsadded.
9. Brian Massumi, *Parables of the Virtual: Movement, Affect, Sensation* (Durham NC: Duke University Press, 2002).
10. Melissa Gregg, 'Getting Things Done: Productivity, Self-management, and the Order of Things', in *Networked Affect*, Ken Hillis, Micheal Petit and Susanna Paasonen, eds. (Cambridge, MA: MIT Press, 2015): 187–203.
11. GQ quoted on Spire-Mindfulness & Activity Tracker, https://spire.io/.
12. Tony Sampson, *The Assemblage Brain: Sense Making in Neuroculture* (Minneapolis: University of Minnesota Press, 2016).

13. "Discover Calm-Science," https://spire.io/pages/science.

14. https://www.amazon.com/Spire-Mindfulness-Activity-Tracker-Android/dp/B00TH3SQOI?th = 1.

15. https://spire.io/pages/stress.

16. https://spire.io/pages/science.

17. https://www.amazon.com/Spire-Mindfulness-Activity-Tracker-Android/dp/B00TH3SQOI?th = 1.

18. https://www.amazon.com/Spire-Mindfulness-Activity-Tracker-Android/dp/B00TH3SQOI?th = 1.

19. https://spire.io/.

20. 'Personal Health Devise Spire Wins 2014 People's Design Award', https://www.cooperhewitt.org/2014/10/10/personal-health-device-spire-wins-2014-peoples-design-award/.

21. Neema Moraveji, 'Love, Breath, and a New Kind of Technology', http://blog.spire.io/category/science-tech/page/2/ italics added).

22. "The Spire Professionals Program," https://spire.io/pages/professionals

23. Gilles Deleuze, *Spinoza: Practical Philosophy* (San Francisco: City Lights Publishers, 2001).

24. https://www.amazon.com/Spire-Mindfulness-Activity-Tracker-Android/dp/B00TH3SQOI?th = 1.

25. Ann Pelligrini, 'Classrooms and their Dissed Contents', https://bullybloggers.wordpress.com/2014/11/27/classrooms-and-their-dissed-contents/.

26. Jasbir Puar, 'Coda: The Cost of Getting Better: Suicide, Sensation, Switchpoints', *GLQ: A Journal of Lesbian and Gay Studies* 18(1) (2012): 151.

27. Tony Sampson, *The Assemblage Brain: Sense Making in Neuroculture* (Minneapolis: University of Minnesota Press, 2016).

28. https://spire.io/, emphasis added.

29. https://www.amazon.com/Spire-Mindfulness-Activity-Tracker-Android/dp/B00TH3SQOI?th = 1.

30. https://www.amazon.com/Spire-Mindfulness-Activity-Tracker-Android/dp/B00TH3SQOI?th = 1.

31. 'Can't Help Falling in Love with You!,' https://blog.spire.io/2016/02/22/falling-love-you/.

32. 'Discover Calm-Science', https://spire.io/pages/science.

33. Gilles Deleuze, 'Postscript on the Societies of Control', *JSTOR*, October 59 (Winter, 1992): 7.

Emma Renold's 'Ruler Skirt' at the Third Sensorium. Photo by Dean Todd.

8

Mediated Affect and Feminist Solidarity

Teens using Twitter to Challenge "Rape Culture" in and Around School

Jessica Ringrose and Kaitlynn Mendes

TWITTER IS REPEATEDLY POSITIONED as a space of hostility for women[1] with research identifying women being disproportionate targets of misogynist "e-bile" and trolling.[2] Social media in general is presented largely as a space of distraction, gendered and sexualised risk, addiction, and harm for young people evident in widespread mobile phone regulation and banning at secondary schools in UK and internationally.[3] Use of Twitter amongst school aged children remains under-researched.[4] In this brief chapter, we explore how—despite the negative associations of Twitter with cyberbullying and "cyberhate"—this platform *also* offers the possibility of consciousness raising, solidarity and empowerment amongst young people. Specifically, we explore how teenaged feminist girls use the digital affordances of Twitter to connect their personal experiences of sexism and sexual harassment at school to wider cultural critiques of rape culture creating mediated affective solidarities.

Hashtag Feminism and Rape Culture

In 2016, Twitter had approximately 313 million monthly active users.[5] Twitter accounts use the @ symbol and user name as the handle and Twitter updates are limited to short bursts of content (referred to as "tweets") no longer than 140 characters (increased to 280 in 2017). Content can be strategically and thematically organized around "hashtags" (using the # sign) that hyperlink tweets in order to enable conversation between users on the hashtag topic. Thus, the platform facilitates quick moving, connected content that may be original or "retweeted" (recirculated or shared).

As use of Twitter has exploded, so has the possibility of using this medium for activism as visible in academic titles like *@ is for Activism*[6] and *Tweets and the Streets: Social Media and Contemporary Activis.*[7] The study of feminist uses of Twitter has also grown with an emerging body of literature termed "hashtag feminism".[8] Hashtag feminism explores the affordances of Twitter to mobilise campaigns around key words and slogans to raise awareness about issues such as anti-feminism, misogyny, reproductive rights and gender and sexual violence that is now popularly described as "rape culture".[9]

Rape culture is a term that originated in the 1970s, which has re-emerged within popular discourse and particularly on social media over the past five years.[10] Rape culture can broadly be defined as a socio-cultural context in which an aggressive male sexuality is eroticized and seen as a "healthy", "normal" and "desired" part of sexual relations.[11] This is because women are constructed as enjoying being aggressively pursued and, in some cases, overpowered by men. Rape culture is characterized by sexual violence and rape being culturally *legitimized*—sexual assault is not only seen as inevitable in some contexts, but desirable and excusable due to sexual double standards where women are blamed for their own victimization and understood to be at least partly responsible for rape through their behavior, clothing and reputation.[12]

Hashtag feminism has both raised the visibility of the term rape culture and created debate over its meaning and its legitimacy. For example, Carrie Rentschler[13] has documented the subversion of victim blaming rape culture myths through use of humour in the creation and use of the #SafetyTipsForLadies hashtag. In this hashtag, posters call out the victim blaming focus of most rape prevention campaigns, shifting attention from the tired trope of women simply "staying safe" and instead, humorously tweeting with the hashtag to mock the advice-giving narrative norms of traditional rape prevention discourse. Tweets that joked that women should avoid leaving the house at all costs, should wear ski masks or remove their vagina before going out, deliberately use hyperbolic exaggeration to reveal the irrational victim blaming logic behind the idea that what women wear makes them more susceptible to sexual assault. It is the digital affordances of the Twitter hashtag, however—what are termed its "platform vernacular"—that enables the viral spread of messages.[14] In the case of #SafetyTipsForLadies, parody and irony via the hashtag affectively harness outrage to alter the conditions of possibility through which rape is understood and normalised, thereby making shifts in consciousness and perhaps culture possible.

Researching Mediated Affect and Affective Solidarity

In *Life after new media: mediation as a vital process*, Sarah Kember and Joanna Zylinska[15] suggest life and liveliness is remediated by new media, enabling the possibility of generating 'unprecedented connections and unexpected events'.[16] I suggest here that these mediated connections and events on Twitter are affective. Paasonen, Hills and Petit[17] argue that theories of "networked affect" can help us to see 'how individual, collective, discursive and networked bodies both human and machine . . . are modified by one another'. Zizi Paparachisi[18] explores how "affective publics" enabled through the specific digital affordances of Twitter:

> transmit affect but also sustain affective feedback loops that generate and reproduce affective patterns of relating to others that are further reproduced as affect—that is, intensity that has not yet been cognitively processed as feeling, emotion or thought. These experiences are not separate but are integrated into congruent media practices, habits and rituals. Haptic, optic, and tactile but also the computational capabilities of media invite particular modalities of affective attunemen.[19]

Affective patterns and affective attunement work through the repetition of hashtags with key slogans and words. In relation to the *content* of feminism, Khoja-Moolji[20] argues the "affective intensities" around key feminist messages create an "intimate public" (in contrast to or in negotiation with an affective public) through the hashtag connective function. Others suggest that the collective attraction to specific sensibilities of feminism *coagulate* through affects like humour, rage or incredulity that can spread and travel through hashtag campaigns—and that is what makes consciousness raising and psychosocial transformation possible.[21]

We have settled on the notion of "mediated affect" to think about how social media intra-action enables new points of feminist connection and collectivity and political solidarity; this draws on the notion of "affective solidarity" from Clare Hemmings.[22] but digitizes it. The digital mediates energetic flows and psychical qualities of social life including physical material reality.[23] Digital technology therefore mediates material, bodily capacities to *affect or be affected.*[24] Affective flows also blur false dichotomies drawn between online and offline experiences. Our interest is in the feminist solidarity that is made possible through mass connecting up via the feminist hashtags, and receiving affirmative likes and retweets of posts and, specifically, how this is experienced and what it makes possible in an institutionalized environment such as school.

Indeed, to date, most hashtag feminist research has focused on the affordances of the hashtag, the media environment, and the media artefact.[25] But by focusing on the visible content of digital media platforms only, this mode of research is typically devoid of embodied, located, material social contexts—what scholars have called the "mediation of intimacies".[26] Here, interviews are used to explore mediated intimacies in narrative accounts of Twitter use. Also, critical to our argument is that most hashtag feminism research, including those campaigns against rape culture, has focused largely, or implicitly, on adults.[27] We seek to redress both these gaps by exploring mediated affect (both public and intimate) generated through teens' Twitter activism against rape culture.

As a sociologist of education and feminist qualitative researcher, Ringrose's work has sought to explore young peoples' lived experiences of using social media, usually starting with the social media activity of so called "produsers" (user and producer)[28] and engaging with the complex affective intra-actions between bodies, online space and school space.[29] Using an online ethnography methodology[30] that considers online posting and interviewing as key to trying to grasp the complexity of how online interactions are narrated by those who perform them, and the affective effects that can be gleaned from such interview data in relation to content posted. Here, we explore a small sub-sample of research findings from our larger Art and Humanities Research Council (AHRC) project on digital feminist activism against rape culture,[31] which included researching self-defined Twitter feminist feeds and anti-rape culture hashtags. From the wider data set, twenty-five teens between the ages of 14 and 19 who are actively using Twitter to post about feminism were interviewed. We drew upon a range of sampling strategies including research in a London school whose feminist Society used a collective Twitter handle, and utilized an online survey promoted through some of our teen feminist networks. This diverse strategy allowed us to locate moments of feminist activism within the "Twitterverse", examples which may have gone undetected by solely focusing on an analysis of trending hashtags, which has been the dominant research strategy of hashtag feminism.

Teens Calling out Rape Culture using Twitter

Teen respondents outlined a multitude of experiences that they described as sexist in and around school, including sexual harassment, as normal in peer culture. However, what is particularly significant in relation to institutional context and age is that teen girls are increasingly recognizing school policies, such as the policing of their bodies and clothing by school administrators, parents, and peers as a dimension of rape culture.[32]

In our North American data we found that teenagers were increasingly retaliating to comprehensive dress codes in many schools. For instance, in 2014, over 100 Florida students staged a mass walk-out over the use of a brightly coloured "shame suit" to publicly humiliate supposed dress code violators—most often girls who wore a skirt above the knee.[33] We interviewed Sofia, 14, from Florida, who attends a high school close to where the "shame suit" demonstrations occurred. As Sofia told us

it was on the national news . . . a nearby high school down the street where my mom went to . . . they put this girl in a shame suit . . . what happened was the girl posted it online.

The incident and the online discussions seemed to galvanise Sofia, who then also began tweeting about the dress codes at her school and about her experiences with street harassment, including tweeting: 'sick and tired of catcalling at this school' and 'whistling at me isn't a compliment it's degrading'. She also retweeted posts from girls in other schools who protested dress gender bias against girls, and noted the failure to sanction boys in dress codes through tweets such as: 'don't say dress codes are for professionalism unless you are prepared to ban sweatshirts and t-shirts too'. Twitter offered Sofia an important channel for raising her own awareness and connecting with teens outside school, but challenging the dress codes inside the school proved much more difficult. Initiatives to challenge cultural practices in her school (such as dress codes) were quickly shut down by the school administration.

In May 2015, the Twitter hashtag campaign #CropTopDay saw mass uptake in Canada when hundreds of teenage girls in Toronto went to school wearing crop tops and international headlines ensued. The protest event was spearheaded by 17-year-old Alexi Halket, who was reprimanded by her school principal for wearing a crop top to class which he noted was 'too much like a sports bra' and was "inappropriate" for school (Diblasi). Halket created a Facebook page inviting 300 people from her school to participate. The event spread throughout the teens' social media networks, including Twitter, resulting in hundreds of girls and boys across the Greater Toronto Area wearing short shirts to school the next day with over 5,000 people using the #CropTopDay Twitter hashtag to publicize the protest.[34] For example, Livia tweeted, '#STANDINSOLIDARITY #croptopday my skin never determines my consent. I'm proud of this belly!!' with an accompanying selfie in her crop top. We see the hashtag is connected to issues of activism (solidarity) around "consent", an issue which was dominant in discussions of sex education curriculum revision in Ontario in 2016,[35] and the tweet also connects to "body positivity" discourses ('proud of this belly') on Twitter.[36] Indeed, additional hashtags such as #BodyPositive #Feminism and #Rape Culture were used also demonstrating the unique affordances of the hashtags to link up discussions of bodily control in society and clothing regulations at school with feminism and sexual violence and rape culture.

The linking up of key themes enabled by joined up trending hashtags makes the tweets travel fast and spread a flow of energetic connection between online users, as has been persuasively argued in hashtag feminist research.[37] However, what we know much less about is how these public performances and digital connections are experienced by posters to Twitter, and this is what our interview methodology offers insights into.

For instance, after finding out about the Canadian #CropTopDay protests via Buzzfeed and Twitter, Adalia (19, from Oklahoma) also photographed herself wearing a crop top and tweeted the selfie alongside the hashtag #CropTopDay to show support for the movement, stating:

> I was like well I'm going to support it too! I strategically placed the picture so you didn't see a lot of my midsection because It's not part of my body I'm too happy about. But, you know in solidarity like, we have a right . . . well, we should have a right to wear crop tops. An inch of my stomach you're going to see, why does that matter to you? Why does that matter to anyone else, you know? And I think it makes more of an impact if you put an image with your words, as opposed to just, you know, I support hash tag Crop Top Day, like people might not know what you mean. So it [the image] kind of cements the message a little bit more, I feel.

Adalia's tweet image was retweeted by several of her Twitter followers and friends. Adalia's comments about the importance of putting an image of herself in a crop top up on Twitter, despite her not feeling "too happy" with her midsection, is crucial. She notes that she posts the image as a direct act of feminist "solidarity". She also argues that sharing her own image creates more "impact" than just words; indeed, she suggests the image does some affect work in "cementing" the message of this activism campaign. She also noted that she wouldn't feel comfortable posting such an image on Facebook, but that the solidarity that inheres with Twitter made her face her fears about her own midsection.

In addition to connecting with potentially largely unknown audiences via hashtags, however, many teens also established networks of support and affective solidarity inside of their schools via Twitter, through which they actively challenged school practices. For example, our UK teenage partici-pants discussed issues like street harassment in their uniforms as well as the policing of their uniform skirts in school uniform codes and teacher attitudes and practices. In our London school, the girls created a joint Twitter handle, stating Twitter was central in documenting and sharing experiences granting them some greater force and urgency due to the immediacy of the platform. For example, Kelly (16, London) told the interviewer, in response to a discus-sion of how male teachers had 'lined them up like cows' to scrutinize their outfits during a non-uniform day at school:

> So it's like, say if something sexist happened within school we can tweet about it and make people aware of it straightaway.

These girls encountered trolling from boys in their local community, but found ways to combat and cope with this, noting they had to learn to 'tweet like professionals' and find consensus within the group to Tweet effectively and learn when it was not worth it to engage with "hurtful" comments.[38] Despite setbacks then, the group also used images (albeit not selfies) as a shorthand way to communicate to the public about their experiences with uniform codes. For example, girls in the London school critiqued the sexist logic imbued in the measurement of skirt lengths by teachers by retweeting a widely circulated Tumblr image created by 18 year old Rosea Lake from Vancouver, and which has become synonymous with calling out rape culture on social media.[39] The image shows a woman's hiked up skirt with lines drawn down her leg (from highest to lowest) with the words 'whore, slut, asking for it, provocative, cheeky, flirty, proper, old fashioned, prudish and matronly' to indicate how levels of propriety align with skirt length associ-ated with victim blaming rape culture. Moving quickly from Tumblr and spreading across multiple platforms this group used the image alongside the popular hashtag #INeedFeminismBecause demonstrating again the cluster-ing of Twitter techniques including use of a hashtag, image and original tweet content used to transmit their message and generate affective responses to what made them angry and what they need to combat about rape culture.

Another participant Jamie (17, from Ohio), went further than simply publically tweeting to a largely unknown audience. She regularly tweeted her principal about sexism at school and rape culture:

> [T]hat's something that I brought up with my principal as well. Because we have a really super strict dress code. Rape culture to me is definitely something that says that men are entitled to women, and that it's women's job to protect themselves, as opposed to teaching men to not do certain things, such as catcall-ing, rape, assaults, those kinds of things.

Jamie described how her principal called a girl-only assembly to discuss dress code expectations and that this meeting became fodder for further activism amongst the girls online. Significantly, Jamie and her friends live tweeted about the discussion during the assembly, using the immediacy that social media platforms like Twitter provide to speak to and galvanise the collective in the school. Jamie tweeted 'I don't want to try have [sic] to not look at a woman's cleavage when I'm trying to talk to her. Actual quote.' She then Tweeted 'translation: Boys can't control themselves and it's the fault of girls.' Jamie's friend Theresa also tweeted 'We pay for this school and yr going to FORCE us to LEAVE because you think our FULLY COVERED legs aren't suitable for a school environment?'

The series of "back-channel" tweets and the resulting conversation show the creative use of Twitter by teens inside of school to disrupt institutionalised sexism through the immediacy of Twitter. This is methodologically significant in that they are not using a recognizable hashtag, which would make it easier to detect this activism in the Twitter network through big data Twitter hashtag harvesting and mining. Instead, we can only see this type of activism through the entry point of the social media "produser" and the interview triangulation with participants to discuss their Twitter posts. We can also see that, affectively, the teens are not simply connecting with an online affective public.[40] By joining into a trending hashtag, they are speaking to their pre-existing "intimate public" Twitter contacts.[41] The known peer group at school carries many different affective implications around visibility, privacy and voice.

We can also see a blurring of private/public space in the ways in which school happenings are incorporated into the girls' Twitter streams. After the assembly discussed above, Jamie and her friends tweeted about a humorous poster that appeared in the school corridor:

> It was like a drawing of a boy and it had one of him in normal boy attire, like, fitted t-shirt and basketball shirts. And it was pointing at problem areas where it was skin tight shirt, could see his abs, could make me really want to kiss him. Next it had him inside a fridge, keeps him cool, keeps him fresh, why don't boys wear fridges. But it had like little feminist blurb . . . It's funny and it's also like a really important issue. And I loved that poster!

In this example, which we call "Fridge-Boy" we can witness the complex affective relationalities of solidarities generated at school through social media. It shows how the resistance to the girl-only meeting on dress code during the assembly became visible and publically accessible through tweets, which later on led to the humorous drawing urging boys to wear fridges to be less "hot" to girls. Jamie eventually photographs and posts this drawing to the larger Twitterverse. In this case, the audience is her school friends, because the explanation is minimal—'protect this sign at all costs'. Whilst the post is not retweeted, it is favourited seven times, indicative that the inside intimate public appreciates the post.

Conclusion

In this brief thought piece we suggest that the connective awareness generated on Twitter is enabling discursive shifts but the means of this transformation is affective: new forms of critique of school sexism as rape culture spread virally, then enable various forms of solidarity, used publically and intimately by teen feminists. Girls are responding to school policies and practices that sanction disciplines against them for dressing in what are termed provocative or sexually "age inappropriate" ways at school (i.e. where their dress is linked to *causing* a range of behaviours from male teens and teachers in a familiar "blame the victim" of sexual harassment mentality that characterizes rape culture). Twitter enabled isolated teens like Sofia to connect with a wider feminist community on a network that critiqued dress code violation discipline (the shame suit) as part of slut-shaming. In some high-profile cases, such as #CropTopDay, girls like Alexi Halket are sparking whole new feminist activist campaigns, responded to internationally by teens like Adalia. This hashtag campaign materially manifested into wide-spread physical resistance and activism across schools; it also created international press coverage and further hashtag transmutation and uses. Likewise, Kelly and her feminist group at school used viral images and hashtags to immediately Tweet about sexism happening inside their school. In another strategy, Jamie Tweeted her principal directly, and shared the home-grown art-activism poster "Fridge-Boy", that she 'loved so much', because it was funny, which was, in turn, favourited and affirmed on Twitter. Overall we see the multiple affordances of the social media platform Twitter sparks feminist affective solidarities and enables challenges to experiences of sexism neglected or denied in official school policy and practice. What we have learned shines a light on how these practices are linked to wider institutionalised social formations of rape culture. Digital mediation enables affective flows that fold in and out of the material environment at school, activating teen feminism within and beyond this space.

Acknowledgements

This work was supported by the Arts and Humanities Research Council (UK) [grant number AH/L009587/1] 'Documenting Digital Feminist Activism:

Mapping Feminist Responses to New Media Misogyny and Rape Culture'. We would like to thank Jessalynn Keller for her comments upon this chapter, as well as the support of Editor Tony Sampson.

Notes

1. A. Shaw, 'The Internet is full of jerks, because the world is full of jerks: What feminist theory teaches us about the Internet', *Communication and Critical/Cultural Studies*, 11 (2014): 273–77.

2. E. A. Jane, *Mysogyny Online: A short (and brutish) History* (London: Sage, 2017).

3. M. Nazeer, M. and J. Ringrose. 'Adventure, intimacy, identity and knowledge: Exploring how social media are shaping and transforming youth sexuality', in J. Gilbert and S. Lamb, eds., *Handbook of Sexual Development: Childhood and Adolescence* (Cambridge, UK: Cambridge University Press, 2018).

4. For exceptions see: J. Ringrose and E. Renold, 'Cows, Cabins and Tweets: Posthuman Intra-acting Affect and Feminist Fires in Secondary School', in C. Taylor and C. Hughes, eds., *Posthuman Research Practices in Education* (London: Palgrave Macmillan, 2016); H. Retallack, J. Ringrose and E. Lawrence. 'Fuck your body image: Teen girls' Twitter and Instagram feminism in and around school', in J. Coffey Shelley Budgeon and Helen Cahill, eds., *Learning Bodies, Learning Bodies: The Body in Youth and Childhood Studies* (London: Springer, 2016).

5. Twitter, 2016.

6. Joss Hands, *@ is for Activism: Dissent, Resitance and Rebellion in a Digital Culture* (London: Pluto Press, 2010).

7. Paulo Gerbaudo, *Tweets and the Streets: Social Media and Contemporary Activism* (London: Pluto Press, 2012).

8. Susana Loza, 'Hashtag feminism, #SolidarityIsForWhiteWomen, and the other #FemFuture', *Ada: A Journal of Gender, New Media, and Technology*, 5 (2014); S. Berridge, and L. Portwood-Stacer, 'Introduction: Feminism, Hashtags and Violence Against Women and Girls', *Feminist Media Studies*, 15(2) (2015): 341–44.

9. Tanya Horeck, 'AskThicke: "Blurred Lines": Rape Culture, and the Feminist Hashtag Takeover', *Feminist Media Studies* 4(6) (2014): 1105–7; Samantha Thrift, '#YesAllWomen as a feminist meme event', *Feminist Media Studies* 14(6) (2014): 1090–92; J. Keller, K. Mendes and J. Ringrose, 'Speaking "unspeakable things": Documenting digital feminist responses to rape culture', *Journal of Gender Studies*, July 2016, http://dx.doi.org/10.1080/09589236.2016.1211511.

10. Carrie Rentschler, Carrie, 'Rape Culture and the Feminist Politics of Social Media.' *Girlhood Studies* 7(1) (2014): 65–82; A. Phipps, J. Ringrose, E. Renold and C. Jackson, 'Introduction: Rape Culture, Lad Culture and Everyday Sexism: Researching, Conceptualizing and Politicizing New Mediations of Gender and Sexual Violence', *Journal of Gender Studies*, July 2, 2017.

11. Sarah Projansky, *Watching Rape: Film and Television in Postfeminist Culture* (New York: New York University Press, 2001).

12. A. Powell and N. Henry, *Sexual Violence in a Digital Age* (London: Palgrave Macmillan, 2017).

13. C. Rentschler, '#Safetytipsforladies: Feminist Twitter Takedowns of Victim Blaming', *Feminist Media Studies* 15(2) (2015): 353–56.

14. K. Warfield, '"Reblogging someone's selfie is seen as a really nice thing to do": spatiality and emplacement within a non-dominant platform vernacular on Tumblr', paper presented at the Association of Internet Researchers Conference, Berlin, Germany, 2016; T. Sampson, *Virality: Contagion Theory in the Age of Networks* (Minneapolis: University of Minnesota Press, 2012).

15. Sarah Kember and Joanna Zylinska, *Life After New Media: Mediation as a Vital Process* (Cambridge, MA: The MIT Press, 2012), xv.

16. Ibid, 30

17. S. Paasonen, K. Hillis and M. Petit, 'Introduction: Networks of Transmission, Intensity, Sensation, Value', in K. Hills, S. Paasonen and M. Petit, eds., *Networked Affect* (Cambridge, MA: MIT Press, 2015).

18. Ziri Papacharissi, *Affective Publics: Sentiment, Technology, and Politics* (Oxford, UK: Oxford University Press, 2014).

19. Papacharissi, *Affective Publics*, ibid, 23.

20. S. Khoja-Moolji, S. 'Becoming an "Intimate Public": Exploring the Affective Intensities of Hashtag Feminism', *Feminist Media Studies*, 15(2) (2015): 347–50.

21. E. Lawrence and J. Ringrose, '@NoToFeminism, #FeministsAreUgly and Misandry Memes: How Social Media Feminist Humour is Calling out Antifeminism', in Jessalynn Keller and Maureen Ryan, eds., *Emergent Feminisms and the Challenge to Postfeminist Media Cultures* (New York: Routledge, forthcoming).

22. C. Hemmings, 'Affective Solidarity: Feminist Reflexivity and Political Transformation', *Feminist Theory,* 13 (2012): 147–61.

23. A. Kuntsmen, 'Introduction: Affect Fabrics of Digital Cultures', in E. Karatzogianni and A. Kuntsmen, eds., *Digital Cultures and the Politics of Emotion* (London: Palgrave Macmillan, 2012).

24. J. Ringrose and B. Coleman, 'Looking and Desiring Machines: A Feminist Deleuzian Mapping of Affect and Bodies', in B. Coleman and J. Ringrose, eds., *Deleuze and Research Methodologies* (Edinburgh, UK: Edinburgh University Press, 2013).

25. S. Berridge and L. Portwood-Stacer, 'Introduction: Feminism, Hashtags and Violence Against Women and Girls', *Feminist Media Studies*, 15(2) (2015): 341–44.

26. Feona Attwood, Jamie Hakim and Alison Winch, 'Mediated Intimacies: Bodies, Technologies and Relationships', *Journal of Gender Studies*, 26(3) (2017).

27. See Retallack et al. for an exception.

28. Axel Bruns, 'Blogs, Wikipedia, Second Life, and Beyond: From Production to Produsage', *Digital Formations,* 45 (2008).

29. J. Ringrose and E. Renold, 'Posthuman Intra-acting Affect and Feminist Fires in Secondary School', in C. Taylor and C. Hughes, eds., *Posthuman Research Practices in Education* (London: Palgrave Macmillan, 2016).

30. John Postill and Sarah Pink, *Social Media Ethnography: The Digital Researcher in a Messy Web*. Media International Australia, 2012; d. boyd, *It's Complicated: The Social Lives of Networked Teens* (New Haven, CT: Yale University Press, 2014).

31. Kaitlynn Mendes, Jessica Ringrose and Jessalynn Keller, *Digital Feminist Activism: Women and Girls Fight Back against Rape Culture* (Oxford, UK: Oxford University Press, 2018).

32. J. Ringrose and E. Renold, 'Posthuman Intra-acting', ibid; A. D. Niccolini, "The Rape Joke": Censorship, Affective Activisms, and Feeling Subjects', *Journal of Gender Studies* (2016): 1–12, DOI: 10.1080/09589236.2016.1202104.

33. R. Carroll, 'Students Protest "Slut Shaming" High School Dress Codes with Mass Walkouts', *The Guardian*, September 24, 2014. Retrieved from http://www.theguardian.com/education/2014/sep/24/us-high-schools-dress-codes-protest-sexism-hemline.

34. Michah Luxen, 'Crop Tops and Ripped Jeans Spark Canadian School Protests', *BBC Trending Blog*, May 31, 2015. http://www.bbc.com/news/blogs-trending-32910132.

35. Keith Leslie, 'Ontario's New Sex Ed Curriculum Will Teach Consent in Grade 2', *The Canadian Press*, February 23, 2015, https://globalnews.ca/news/1844927/ontario-revises-sex-education-curriculum/.

36. Alexandra Sastre, 'Towards a Radical Body Positive', *Feminist Media Studies*, 14(6) (2014): 929–43.

37. Tanya Horeck, 'AskThicke', ibid.

38. For a much fuller discussion of teen feminists' experiences navigating 'trolling' on Twitter see Kaitlynn Mendes, Jessica Ringrose and Jessalynn Keller, *Digital Feminist Activism: Girls and Women Fight back against Rape Culture*, ibid.

39. Sadie Whitelocks, 'Are You Prudish, Proper, Cheeky or a Slut? Artist Sparks Debate about the Message Your Skirt Length Can Send', *MailOnline*, January 16, 2013, http://www.dailymail.co.uk/femail/article-2263037/Are-prudish-proper-cheeky-slut-Artist-sparks-debate-message-skirt-length-send.html.

40. Zizi Papacharissi, *Affective Publics: Sentiment, Technology, and Politics* (Oxford, UK: Oxford University Press, 2014); S. Khoja-Moolji, 'Becoming an "Intimate Public": Exploring the Affective Intensities of Hashtag Feminism', *Feminist Media Studies*, 15(2) (2015): 347–50.

41. S. Khoja-Moolji, 'Becoming an "Intimate Public": Exploring the Affective Intensities of Hashtag Feminism', *Feminist Media Studies*, 15(2) (2015): 347–50.

Part III

Insecurity and Anxiety

Visitor to A&SM 3. Photo by Dean Todd.

Introduction to Part III

Darren Ellis and Stephen Maddison

B ECAUSE OF THE overwhelming amount of participation on social media, it is not surprising at all that it often invokes insecurity and anxiety. Our fears of a dystopian future wherein new technologies and social medias are unavoidable, and our lives are ever more determined on-line, are depicted as just a step away through recent televised science fiction (for examples see the Netflix series *Black Mirror* and the movie *The Circle*).

We are increasingly aware of how digitised affective activity can spin out in indeterminate ways, transpose through time and space and can be harnessed by and for those who know how. It is no work of science fiction that our (former) taken for granted privacy has been radically diminished as it is in persistent danger of being digitally invaded. For example, life online leads to increased fears of credit card theft, identity fraud, potential character defamation, and of course we have to not feed the trolls and beware of the bots. Additionally, our lives are increasingly at risk of being plundered through the "technosecuritisation" of everyday life, surveillance activities, hacking, and—as the final section of this book discusses—risk of being infected by our unsecure digitised social networks.

We also live with the dissatisfaction of being constantly abused online as prosumers (a term used to indicate the blurred distinction between producer and consumer in the context of the commodification of online content produced by users). Big data leads to big dollars and big institutes can obtain big power through the unacknowledged trade off of a little information from a lot of us, handed to them on a platform. For instance, our thumbs up on Facebook can be mined and tied together like a magic trick, producing "personality" profiles that can be suitably mass targeted, for instance to nudge the voter. At the other end of the scale, we are increasingly mindful of how a small ripple on social media can quickly spin out to become a giant tsunami, flooding new technologies; a mistaken tweet or a YouTube folly can be almost fatal. And yet, utility and enjoyment seem to outweigh the insecurity and anxiety that social media can provoke. The affective atmospheres of social media that contain insecurity and anxiety among many other affects do little to perturb participation. We love it! The trade-off seems worth it. Or perhaps there is so little that can be done to stop it, we might as well join in, as avoidance may be even more difficult and dangerous. In the following sections we find some novel connections between anxiety, insecurity and social media.

Greg Singh's contribution presents critical analysis of patterns of trolling and doxing in #GameGate, and offers an invaluable insight into the culture that fermented the alt-right, one where the body becomes a 'sublime reified object' subjected to affective intensities with instrumentally social effects. For Zara Dinnen, action cinema offers emotional vocabularies for negotiating the complexities of a computational reality, producing the user as subject through the figure of the hacker, a resistant and ambivalent figure. In her analysis of beauty vlogging, Sophie Bishop traces the patterns of anxiety that structure the entrepreneurial manifestation of heterosexual femininity, where anxiety comes to mark a zone of authenticity that apparently empowers consumerism. In questioning the moral panic associated with chemsex parties facilitated by geo-locational hook up apps, and frequented by gay and bisexual men, Jamie Hakim challenges the inherent simplification of those mens' affective experience, and points to a wider deficit of political discourse addressing austerity. For Stephen Maddison, gay porn blogs affect a form of entrepreneurial voyeurism, addressing lifestyle anxiety with an erotic economy of dick pics and luxury goods.

9

Wupocalypse Now

Supertrolls and Other Risk Anxieties in Social Media Interactions

Greg Singh

E MOTIONS TEND to escalate very quickly in the connected world of social media. During late 2014 and early 2015, the #GamerGate phenomenon illustrated this tendency with alarming results. #GamerGate started out as a Twitter hashtag response to a viral blog post ("The Zoe Post"), uploaded by software developer Erin Gjoni in August of 2014. In this post, Gjoni detailed his relationship with ex-partner, independent game designer Zoe Quinn. In what was something of an interminable piece, "The Zoe Post" ultimately read as an account of both a dysfunctional and narcissistic view of relationships generally, as well as a very public (and frankly, alarming) emotional melt-down. Amongst the details included allegations that she had cheated on him with colleagues working in the promotional side of the gaming industry.

This last detail is the relevant one here—people reading the post and commenting on it insinuated that her position as a designer had been made good through her relationships with gaming journalists. Subsequent commentary and responses, mainly from the crossover of gaming culture and men's rights activists on chat forums, led to allegations that Quinn had given a games journalist sexual favours in exchange for a favourable review of her free-to-play game, *Depression Quest*[1].

Only later did it transpire that the critic in question had never even reviewed the game, but by this point it was too late. That this fact came to light didn't seem to matter: during the final months of 2014, under the cover of debating ethics in videogame journalism, Quinn was subjected to widespread death and rape threats on several social media and chat fora on a daily basis from online commentators. The extremity of the response from activists involved included doxing Quinn's personal data, and the data of her family members (indeed, the doxing of friends and colleagues who publicly spoke in her defence), and the release of nude pictures of Quinn on so-called "revenge porn" websites.[2]

Whereas readers may be familiar with trolling and baiting as phenomena of social media interactions, doxing is perhaps a less familiar anti-social practice. Its usefulness as a concept is that it completely deconstructs the myth of an online-offline divide. It typically involves an escalation of disinhibited behaviours and communications in online discussions, leading to threats, intimidation, and eventually the hacking and publication of personal information (e.g. addresses, telephone numbers, family members/ages of children, place of work, social security numbers and bank details, etc.) on publicly-viewable forums. It almost always accompanies emotionally laden communications practices, and parasocial amplification of affective engagement and investment. The purpose of such actions is to create an emotionally charged climate of harassment, threats, physical retribution or sabotage in real life (IRL), against the individual in question whose information has been leaked. This tactic has been used in a number of ways for the purposes of political protest or campaigns against corruption as actions in the public interest, and so has the potential for (arguably) benign applications; but has been more notoriously utilised in toxic high profile cases involving celebrities (leaked nude photos and sex tapes, e.g. at #TheFappening) as well as the infamous #GamerGate controversy.

Such was the furore that surrounded the Gjoni/Quinn case that, where normally a story about online gaming cultures would remain resolutely niche, online and peripheral to the headlines, even the mainstream press eventually latched on to it. The reasons for such coverage almost certainly revolved around the element in the story of scrutiny surrounding ethics and journalism. However, writing retrospectively in the *Guardian* in December 2014, Keith Stuart summarised that:

> proponents of this movement say their key target is games journalism. Gamergate complains about cronyism between certain writers and developers. . . . The undercurrent, however, has always been darkly misogynistic. The victims of Gamergate's ire have mostly been female developers, academics and writers.[3]

#GamerGate has remained more than a mere Twitter hashtag, presenting a lasting effect on (especially, perhaps, but not exclusively) gender politics in social media interactions. For Shaw and Chess, #GamerGate represents a constellation of website activities—across Tumblr, subredditts, radical free speech forums such as 4chan and 8chan[4]—although evidence has shown that this whole business was initially orchestrated by a small number of 4chan activists, according to Johnston writing for *Ars Technica*:

> A set of IRC logs released Saturday appear to show that a handful of 4chan users were ultimately behind #GamerGate, the supposedly grass-roots movement aimed at exposing ethical lapses in gaming journalism. The logs show a small group of users orchestrating a "hashtag campaign" to perpetuate misogynistic attacks by wrapping them in a debate about ethics in gaming journalism.[5]

Some of the arguments made regarding anti-political correctness during the height of #GamerGate have subsequently surfaced as main planks of the so-called alt-right movement, and some of the #GamerGate movement's more vocal champions such as Milo Yiannopoulos have since become celebrity figures of the alt-right more broadly. Indeed, even when the #GamerGate controversy was in its infancy, Yiannopoulous's opportunism to use the movement for political ends was called out publicly.[6] The voracity, extremity and self-belief that #GamerGaters have displayed in their dedication to discrediting female videogame developers, critics and commentators since its height is deeply troubling in its aggression and violent imagery.[7] Well-known examples of this practice of trolling include the relentless attacks upon "Tropes vs. Women in Video Games" Youtuber and "Feminist Frequency" vlogger, Anita Sarkeesian.[8] Campaigning against Sarkeesian has been the subject of widespread memes, and has been a persistent presence across several YouTube channels. Another prominent example, and the vehicle through which I would like to outline the affective nature of risk anxieties in social media interactions, is the so-called "Operation Wupocalypse" case, which squared #GamerGate campaigners against game developer and programmer Brianna Wu.

In late January 2015, at the height of #GamerGate popularity, a video titled "Brianna Wu tried to assassinate me via street racing" was posted on ParkourDude91's YouTube channel. The video featured ParkourDude91 (aka Jace Connors) standing next to an upturned Prius on the roadside, ranting about having crashed his mother's car in suspicious circumstances. The original post had the following written description:

> On Friday, January 30 2015 I nearly died in a rollover after borrowing my mother's Prius to drive to Boston and make a video exposing Brianna Wu for her treachery in the games industry. While on the highway I was "Street Racing" by driving very quickly and challenging [sic] other drivers, in order to sneak up

on Wu un-noticed. . . . Unfortinately [sic] she saw me coming and sabotaged my vehicle. As I am typing this, I am crashing at my friend Kyle's house becuase [sic] I believe my life is in danger. I now no longer believe this was a coincidence. I am a US Retired Veteran who is also a vlogger and very interested in GamerGate and trying to root for justice, But i [sic] have been ROUTINELY Targeted by trolls from sites such as: 4chan, r/cringe, Tumblr, as well as many Feminists who ABUSIVELY falsely reported my videos for "Sexism" and nearly got my account BANNED when I tried to speak out. I am SICK and/or TIRED of this treatment and I am exposing the truth NOW.

The second half of the video explained through written captions that Connors was now launching a vendetta against Wu, revealing that he had been secretly plotting a campaign against her all along, which he named "Operation Wupocalypse". According to some reports, including Aja Ramano's piece for *The Daily Dot* the following week, this had prompted Wu to contact law enforcement.[9] However, there was at the same time widespread acknowledgement that Jace Connors was an "act"—performance, a parody.[10] Nonetheless, the threats that immediately followed in user comments on the post[11] evidenced an affective escalation of ill-feeling towards Wu, and a mob style of retribution for her perceived offences against the gaming community. As Romano has pointed out:

> Wu says that even if this incident is a satirical prank, her family is legitimately concerned by the Gamergate threats: 'We're scared and we're exhausted. I'm worried that someone is going to have to die before law enforcement takes these threats seriously. Law enforcement's reaction has been to suggest shutting off your electronic devices.'

Subsequent publicity has indeed outed ParkourDude91, aka Jace Connors, as a fictional character played by Jan Rankowski, a performance artist and comedian. Connors is Rankowski's vehicle for parodying #GamerGate, the alt-right, and men's rights activism.[12,13] This character, and other featured characters in the campaign, including friends "Kyle" and "Eli", are featured in the stunts in various posts and videos in Rankowski's on-going project "The Deagle Nation", and part of the work of comedian collective Million Dollar Extreme. Rankowski's parodic Wupocalypse campaign involved a character assassination of Wu, and a subplot to send Connors' friend Eli to Canada to blow up Tumblr's servers there in response to "Social Justice Warrior" (SJW) criticism of the campaign on that social media site. Although the original post of the car crash and viewer comments were taken down soon after the posting date, the video is still available in an alternative post, titled "Brianna Wu tried to assassinate me via street racing (January 30th, 2015)" posted by YouTube user "The Deagle Nation War Library". In an (unpublished, but YouTube-streamed) interview with *Washington Post* journalist Dave Wiegl, Deagle Nation is described by Rankowski as 'an internet performance thing that I ran, way back, when I was in high school. Basically because I thought it was funny. That was related to the whole Brianna Wu thing'.[14] As Adi Robertson noted not long after the Wupocalypse launch, 'Rankowski says that he ad-libbed the "Wupocalypse" video after getting into a real car crash, satirizing the idea of an impotently violent man who'd confused gaming with reality.[15]

It is worth mentioning here two factors about the *Washington Post* interview, and Rankowski's status as satirist, that are potentially illuminating. The first is that the interview was live streamed, and conducted with interaction from Rankowski's fans, where they were invited to suggest topics for discussion. This stunt aesthetic, familiar to consumers of *Twitch TV* and *Let's Play* gaming sites, live streaming sketches and skits, and celebrity YouTuber practices of pulling practical jokes and "challenges" for the disaffected amusement of the audience,[16] is certainly the province of YouTube-native consumers. Wiegl appeared to be unaware of this on-screen activity in Rankowski's video, and this factor adds an element of risking a live trolling experience to such straightforward traditional practices as conducting interviews via telephone. During the interview, Rankowski is seen laughing silently at live suggestions from fans, and completely deadpan in feeding information (that may or may not be factual) at his fans' suggestions. The overall effect of this is to undermine the reputation and credibility of the journalist asking questions around the topic of online cultures and trolling practices. A journalist working in this context would rely on in-depth knowledge of troll-culture, as well as a familiarity with live streaming conventions —the very mechanisms being used to subvert their credibility in a live, streamed public event.

The second factor is that, at the time of the *Washington Post* interview, Rankowski was only 22 years old. Already by this point, he had been running Deagle Nation projects for a number of years, and his working relationship with the Million Dollar Extreme collective had drawn to a close. It is worth mentioning this, because the affective properties involving the aesthetic of live streamed trolling of a professional journalist are immediately apparent to the Deagle Nation in-group fanbase—in other words the opportunity for comedy. In addition, there is something of a baseline inter-generational (or more accurately, inter-group) conflict involving digital nativism and the "fair game" ethic, that sits uncomfortably with traditional news gathering and media forms of meaning-making which seeks, at least in principle, to uphold basic codes of ethical conduct in exchange for press freedoms. It is ultimately

similar to Mizuko Ito's notion that—as well as supporting access, participation and interactive production of cultural texts (as undoubtedly Rankowski
is promoting here)—there needs to be an effort to 'support the cultivation
of a mindset of social responsibility about the sharing and circulation of
media'.[16] This mindset would clearly need to move beyond a simplistic "for
da lulz" mechanism of participation, even as it would recognise a place for
parodic interactive comedy.

This is largely because to attribute too much agency to the user's ability
(even as a professional journalist) to discern a troll when they see one is a
very real hazard. Sam Hyde, a well-known colleague of Rankowski, is the
lynchpin of the Million Dollar Extreme collective, and something of a celebrity troll. Hyde has found enough success to have landed a short run on US
cable television—Adult Swim's *Million Dollar Extreme Presents: World Peace*.
This has been covered by a number of culture-savvy online news outlets such
as *Buzzfeed*. Indeed, an article by Joseph Bernstein identifies . . . *World Peace*
as 'identity content for trolls',[17] making explicit links between Million Dollar
Extreme, the alt-right movement, and the kinds of disingenuous satirical
gesture which often end up in the popular cultural morass of fake news,
automated news feeds, and a constant flow of impact aesthetics and persistent connectivity. However, again, the pattern emerging here is that despite
the revelation that such stunts are parodic in nature, and the recognition that
the featured figure in such content is either fictional, or a troll (or both), this
doesn't get in the way of opportunities for fans and commentators to display
disinhibited mob-like behaviour. Bernstein goes on to write that:

> It's a trap just to read Sam Hyde literally—he's built a career out of making fun
> of people who take his speech too seriously. But that has not stopped Hyde's
> alt-right admirers from trying to divine his true politics, in the same way they
> scan his show for secret messages.[18]

The tension here, then, is a performative one, and familiar to students of
satire and the politics of taste. Where the critical functions of satire necessarily follow a tendency to point out folly, and to ridicule authority or rigid
institutional hierarchy, critiques of taste question value judgement, arbitra-
tion and practices of cultural gate-keeping. However, very few of these critical attributes play out in this example, and certainly seem to fall away in
everyday politics, save perhaps for the often-repeated mantra in current
affairs that ordinary people are suspicious of experts and elites. If one of the
distinguishing features of satire is that it is demonstrably witty, this is
retained in some form, but the critical content is not. The accelerated nature
of the contemporary media ecosystem, and the relatively disinhibited environments in which social media interactions occur, have led to this scenario,

where satire and "fair game" have entered an easy pact with the descendants of #GamerGate: the alt-right, and the men's rights movement. Such circles are strong on freedom of speech advocacy, but discernibly silent on the social responsibilities that are afforded through those rights. Bernstein continues:

> it's also a trap to not see the seriousness of what Hyde and co. are doing, even if they're LOLing along the way and being disingenuous. Indeed, when the consequences of a culture involve the serial harassment and illegal publication of explicit photographs of a black actress because she had the temerity to stick up for herself, does it really matter whether the people having a laugh over it are in character?[19]

The answer to this question lies in the treatment of performativity offered in any analysis of online social interactions where real-world consequences pertain. Through what might be described as a proxemics of *YouTube* and other platforms where social interaction of this kind proliferates, social psychology approaches serve to illustrate the complexities of social context cues, level of communication fidelity, non-verbal communications clarity, absence of eye-contact in non-visual communications forms, and the exaggerated effect of responsibility deferral through deindividuation.[20] It is worth noting that these psychosocial terms are descriptions of known and established internet phenomena. In online cultures, this lack of social context is known as "Poe's Law", a description for the same type of contextual framing of language to establish online etiquette, based on observations originally written on "Emily Post for Usenet" by Jerry Schwarz in 1983.[21] Therefore, there is a long-standing precedent establishing the understanding about reduced social context cues, and the kinds of responses expected towards posts where the context is not clear. Levels of trust and anxiety management[22] are made more complicated through the character of emotional investment associated with devotion to particular beliefs, ideologies, or even personalities.

It is worth noting here, as I have noted elsewhere,[23] that chat fora and other SNSs are not necessarily "safe spaces" for the kinds of encounters described in the Wupocalypse case, or any other aspect of #GamerGate. One might include here the well-worn toxic disinhibition effects of online communications described by the social psychologist John Suler.[24] These are, arguably, now part of the everyday fabric of social media communications—trolling, baiting, doxing and general use of threatening language is a problem so common that it is difficult to see a way to even begin to tackle it. Perhaps the place to begin would be in recognising the fact that whole persons with unique interests are on the other end of any interpersonal communication, and that those persons have attachments to other persons who might also be directly affected by such actions. It seems such an obvious point, but given the prevalence of content passing as satire (characterised, however, by lack of criticality) one might venture to speculate that this is best tackled from the ground up—as a question of basic ethics in digital literacy, as much as a question of moral or empathic recognition.

On this position, I draw parallels to R. D. Laing's overview of the existential equilibrium of separateness and relatedness in everyday psychopathology, as presented in his influential book *The Divided Self*. There, he argues that an existential equilibrium between a sense of separateness and a sense of relatedness is crucial to enable individuals to cope with certain lived knowledge (of both aloneness and of mutuality).[25] I argue that social media platforms, although pregnant with affirmative possibilities for political transgression, action and subversion, tend also to exacerbate the otherwise "normal" pathological split between an "inner self" and a generalized deadness of the embodied "false-self". In an accelerated media ecosystem, where interactions of the kind described above can so quickly disaggregate into moral positions of diminished recognition of others as whole persons with unique interests, this false-self is characterised by the unreal perceptions, unreal expectations and futile actions encountered in online echo chambers.

In such diminished circumstances, in failing to recognise others in this way we are also fundamentally shut off from a full recognition of ourselves. Essentially, following relational psychologists such as Aaron Balick, this is identifying with the overlying persona(e) in a false-self system as encompassing the whole thing,[26] and hence effectively sterilising lived relationships by reifying self and other. In the case of the #GamerGate phenomenon, another dimension of this falseness can be identified as an amplification of the everyday. In social media interactions where this failure to recognise whole people becomes a default position, the body itself becomes a sublime reified object: it is coded as an idealised unit of exchange, where selfies are currency for the mobilisation of identity in exchange. In the #GamerGate case, the coding was specifically sexualised and valued in gendered terms, where women especially, but also people of minority backgrounds, were systematically targeted and victimised.

In the Wupocalypse case, this general default emerged with particular characteristics. Commentators tended to position themselves forcefully as "pro-Jace", or as "anti-Jace", rarely questioning the status of Jace Connors as a real person. Commentators were also (rather abusively, and most often through homophobic and misogynistic discourse) homogenously positioned by other commentators as SJWs, feminists and anti-gamers or—on the other side—as trolls, bigots and "meatheads". Although this homogenising polarisation is interesting in itself, there are other aspects we might raise about the affective responses as a whole. It is true that Jace is, in fact a performative satire on trolling. However, there is a strong argument to be made regarding whether the intention here matters: after all, it makes little difference if the overall effect is to mobilise real hatred and IRL life-threatening actions, just as a "real" troll would do.

In this blurring of the boundaries between satricial content and outright hate-speech, identities that are inhabited and expressed through the commentary are real enough—there are trolling elements at work, certainly, but there are also factions ossifying around the support or denigration of the Deagle Nation in this instance. A discernible "tonality" of feeling emerges through consciousness of positions and groupthink, where the threshold of identities and evaluations unfold and become indeterminate as they come into being in the general field of social media interaction. The overall effect of this was for participants in Wupocalypse (on all sides) to shift, very quickly, to fixed positions (i.e. making safe their pro- or anti-#GamerGate stance) as a defence against the false-self anxieties produced by mutual distrust.

One way in which to engage distrust in general social media interactions is, in the first instance, to listen to what constituents have to say about their everyday social media interactions. In particular, one might ask how they feel about the ambiguous parasocial investments they have already made, either in everyday personal use or in professional communications. In this sense, an optimal research design would seek to find ways to actively engage sensibility and feeling about the anxieties surrounding practices of social media interaction. In short, these could be regarded as practices which, in the consequentialist terminology of Michael Sandel,[27] move beyond the instrumentally empirical and into the purposive realm of the ethical, practices that can yield pathways to meaningful and mutual engagement, rather than merely amplifying the anxieties that exist in the absence of a conciliation between separateness and mutuality.

Notes

1. Poland, B. *Haters: Harassment, Abuse, and Violence Online* (Lincoln, MA.: Potomac Books, 2016); Stuart, K. 'Zoe Quinn: "All Gamergate has done is ruin people's lives"' in *The Guardian*, December 3, 2014, https://www.theguardian.com/technology/2014/dec/03/zoe-quinn-gamergate-interview [accessed: October 1, 2017]; Kolhatkar, S. 'The Gaming Industry's Greatest Adversary Is Just Getting Started', *Bloomberg Businessweek*, November 26, 2014, https://www.bloomberg.com/news/articles/2014-11-26/anita-sarkeesian-battles-sexism-in-games-gamergate-harassment [accessed: October 1, 2017].

2. Busch, T., F. Chee, and A. Harvey, 'Corporate Responsibility and Gender in

Digital Games', in K. Grosser, L. McCarthy and Maureen A. Kilgour , eds., *Gender Equality and Responsible Business: Expanding CSR Horizons* (Sheffield, UK: Greenleaf Publishing, 2016).

3. Stuart, K., 'Zoe Quinn: "All Gamergate has done is ruin people's lives"'.

4. Shaw, A. and S. Chess, 'Afterword: Reflections on the casual games market in a post-GamerGate world', in M. Willson and T. Leaver, eds., *Social, Casual and Mobile Games: The Changing Gaming Landscape* (London: Bloomsbury, 2016).

5. Johnston, C., 'Chat logs show how 4chan users created #GamerGate controversy', *Ars Technica*, September 10, 2014. Available at: https://arstechnica.com/gaming/2014/09/new-chat-logs-show-how-4chan-users-pushed-gamergate-into-the-national-spotlight/ [accessed: October 2, 2017].

6. Jilani, Z., 'Gamergate's fickle hero: The dark opportunism of Breitbart's Milo Yiannopoulos', *Salon*, posted October 28, 2014. Available at: http://www.salon.com/2014/10/28/gamergates_fickle_hero_the_dark_opportunism_of_breitbarts_milo_yiannopoulos/ [accessed: October 3, 2017].

7. MacCallum-Stewart, E., '"Take That, Bitches!" Refiguring Lara Croft in Feminist Game Narratives', *Gamestudies* 2(14) (2014). Available at: http://gamestudies.org/1402/articles/maccallumstewart [accessed: October 1, 2017]; Poland, *Haters*.

8. Kolhatkar, 'The Gaming Industry's Greatest Adversary Is Just Getting Started'; Chess, S. and Adrienne Shaw, 'A Conspiracy of Fishes, or, How We Learned to Stop Worrying About #GamerGate and Embrace Hegemonic Masculinity', *Journal of Broadcasting & Electronic Media*, 59(1) (2015): 208–20.

9. Romano, A. 'Gamergate member threatens Brianna Wu with apparent parody video', *The Daily Dot*, posted February 2, 2015. Available at: https://www.dailydot.com/parsec/gamergate-brianna-wu-car-crash-video/ [accessed: October 3, 2017].

10. Romano, 'Gamergate member threatens Brianna Wu with apparent parody video'; Robertson, A., 'A violent, delusional Gamergate psychopath is actually a comedian's terrible hoax', *The Verge*, posted February 24, 2015. Available at: http://www.theverge.com/2015/2/24/8099531/gamergate-jace-connors-threats-comedian-hoax [accessed: October 3, 2017]; Bernstein, J., 'GamerGate's Archvillain is Really a Trolling Sketch Comedian', *BuzzFeedNews*, posted February 24, 2015. Available at: https://www.buzzfeed.com/josephbernstein/gamergates-archvillain-is-really-a-trolling-sketch-comedian?utm_term=.ngyNyOX2yQ#.ro0Q9eK49Y [accessed: October 3, 2017]; Bernstein, J., 'The Alt-Right Has Its Very Own TV Show On Adult Swim—Adult Swim's Million Dollar Extreme Presents: World Peace is identity content for trolls'. *BuzzFeedNews*, posted on August 25, 2016. Available at: https://www.buzzfeed.com/josephbernstein/the-alt-right-has-its-own-comedy-tv-show-on-a-time-warner-ne?utm_term=.tdk9e8LmeJ#.rnqOyv7ny5 [accessed: October 3, 2017].

11. Taken down shortly after initial posing due to violation of YouTube's user T&Cs.

12. Bernstein, 'GamerGate's Archvillain Is Really A Trolling Sketch Comedian'.

13. Robertson, 'A violent, delusional Gamergate psychopath is actually a comedian's terrible hoax'.

14. *Washington Post* interviews Jan Rankowski on Sam Hyde [telephone interview with Dave Wiegl—comments not published in the *Post*] streamed live on *YouTube*

December 15, 2016. Available at: https://www.youtube.com/watch?v = x_yGeiAn8rk [accessed: October 3, 2017].

15. Robertson, 'A violent, delusional Gamergate psychopath is actually a comedian's terrible hoax'.

16. Jenkins, H., M. Ito and d. boyd, *Participatory Culture in a Networked Era.* (Cambridge, UK: Polity, 2015), 104. As an aside, the recent controversy surrounding YouTube Superstar PewDiePie offers an insight into the interior conflicts between traditional news reporting, and tube-based celebrity and lifestyle culture, which are both ethical and aesthetic in nature. It also offers a secondary avenue for exploring the links between the rise of YouTube celebrity and a so-called alt-right politics. As Olivia Solon reported in the *Guardian*: 'A key part of PewDiePie's empire is a joint venture he formed with Disney's Maker Studios in 2014. This gave him co-ownership of a multi-channel network called Revelmode that produces videos, mobile apps and merchandise. Following an investigation into the anti-Semitic content by the *Wall Street Journal*, Disney has ended this joint venture.' Olivia Solon, 'Disney severs ties with YouTube star PewDiePie over antisemitic videos', *The Guardian*, February 14, 2017. Available at: https://www.theguardian.com/technology/2017/feb/13/pewdiepie -youtube-star-disney-antisemitic-videos [accessed October 3, 2017].

17. Bernstein, 'The Alt-Right Has Its Very Own TV Show on Adult Swim—Adult Swim's Million Dollar Extreme Presents: World Peace is identity content for trolls'.

18. Ibid.

19. Ibid.

20. For example, see Sproull and Kiesler 1986; Joinson 2003. Sproull, L. and S. Kiesler, 'Reducing Social Context Cues: Electronic Mail in Organizational Communications', *Management Science* 32(11) (1986), 1492–1512; Joinson, A., *Understanding the Psychology of Internet Behaviour: Virtual Worlds, Real Lives* (London: Palgrave Macmillan, 2003).

21. Poe, N., 'POE'S LAW', August 10, 2005. Schwarz's post reads: 'Avoid sarcasm and facetious remarks. Without the voice inflection and body language of personal communication these are easily misinterpreted. A sideways smile, :-), has become widely accepted on the net as an indication that "I'm only kidding". If you submit a satiric item without this symbol, no matter how obvious the satire is to you, do not be surprised if people take it seriously.' Available at: https://www.christianforums .com/threads/big-contradictions-in-the-evolution-theory.1962980/page-3#post-1760 6580 [accessed: October 3, 2017]; Schwarz, J., 'Emily Post for Usenet', originally posted November 1983. Archived version available at: https://groups.google.com/ forum/?fromgroups = #!msg/net.announce/8CsYPJuZ4Hg/8em44sgCCVYJ [accessed: October 3, 2017].

22. Gudykunst, W., 'Anxiety/Uncertainty Management (AUM) Theory: Current Status', in Wiseman, R. L., ed., *Intercultural Communication Theory* (Thousand Oaks, CA: Sage, 1995).

23. Singh, G., 'YouTubers, Online Selves and the Performance Principle: Notes from a Post-Jungian Perspective', *CM: Communication and Media Journal*, special issue on Digital Media, Psychoanalysis and the Subject, 11(38) (2017), 205–32.

24. Suler, J., 'The Online Disinhibition Effect', *International Journal of Applied Psychoanalytic Studies* 2(2) (2004), 184–88.

25. Laing, R. D., *The Divided Self: An Existential Study in Sanity and Madness* (Harmondsworth, UK: Penguin Books, 1965).

26. Balick, A., *The Psychodynamics of Social Networking: Connected-up Instantaneous Culture and the Self* (London: Karnac, 2014).

27. Sandel, M., *What Money Can't Buy: The Moral Limits of Markets* (London: Allen Lane, 2012).

10

Becoming User in Popular Culture

Zara Dinnen

THIS CHAPTER CONSIDERS the operation of mainstream cinema in enabling audiences to identify themselves as "users" of digital media rather than more radically mediational agential bodies. I consider the user of digital culture as an affective subject; and userness as affect. Actions of use are dynamic, everyday situations through which a user may identify themselves as such.[1] I turn to scenes of hacking as staged in popular culture as ways of experiencing a heightened affective encounter with everyday situations of userness. The scenes of "becoming user" that I discuss below attempt to keep legible the fantasy of an individual human subject who will benefit from the anthropocentric capitalist imaginary. Describing these scenes as staging userness is also a means of critically witnessing how little agency "individual users" have within the current political moment—these fantasies are ultimately ambivalent and offer little in terms of a way out of or alternative to userness. As a typical action hacker film, Len Wiseman's 2007 *Live Free or Die Hard*, the fourth film in the *Die Hard* franchise, attempts to render userness as proximate to a popular fantasy of antagonism between individuals and systems: the antihero versus the establishment; the good criminal in the wrong place at the wrong time; the strength of the human body against the mastery of technology.[2] In what follows I suggest that watching hackers on screen is a way of becoming user. Analysis of a series of scenes depicting hacking and control of digital media systems in *Live Free or Die Hard*, elicits a description of protracted userness and passivity which touches on the anxious condition of the individual human user of digital media in relation to planetary scale computation.[3] Which is to say, whilst purporting to be about users regaining control over a situation, *Live Free or Die Hard* is also about how human and nonhuman bodies are mediationally entangled and critically out of control.

User Affects

Cinema is an aesthetic, social, and economic coming together of bodies, narratives, affects. Following Steven Shaviro, affect is the designation of 'the fact that *every* moment of experience is qualitative and qualified'.[4] Affect troubles the distinctness of cultural and aesthetic experiences, but such experiences are also ways to apprehend affective relations. Encountering our socio-economic and political formations as an aesthetic might give us ways of registering some of the affective intensities particular to contemporary life. For Shaviro 'capitalism "itself"—however multiple and without-identity it may actually be—involves an incessant *drive towards* totalization', but 'we cannot see, feel, hear, or touch this project or process'.[5] In other words, we cannot experience capitalism as affect because everything is affective. Without fully endorsing Shaviro's position here I do take his subsequent turn to the aesthetic as a generative one. Within Shaviro's framework, the aesthetic is in fact another kind of affective scene: a way of making socio-economic and political formations 'visible, audible, and palpable'.[6] The aesthetic is both a site at which we encounter media as political or social formation, and a dynamic scene through which the political takes shape.[7] For example, in Patrick Jagoda's recent work, network aesthetics (the aesthetic manifestations of a network imaginary) are shown to 'track processes that exceed human cognition because they either fall under the threshold of perception (e.g. subconscious effects of social media) or overload an individual's real-time processing capacity (e.g. complexities of a global political system)'.[8] The turn to studies of affect is in part a reflection of the way new systems of production and control—new technologies—destabilise historically constituted social agency and "exceed" the indexicality of anthropocentric imaginaries.[9] In what follows an aesthetic scene of digital media use is interrogated for the ways it might make palpable, visible, audible the affective dimensions of life after new media.

The term "user" names a participatory figure whose action is always in relation to the medium, but here I read it as ambivalent in the sense that a user is also always in *use*. As Olia Lialina has described it, 'in times of invisible computing User is the best (the last) reminder that there are those who developed the system and those who use it, and that you are dealing with the programmed system first and foremost'.[10] In addition, the user is a mediational category of personhood, becoming with nonhuman agency (algorithmic iteration, rare minerals—multiple agents). In films featuring hackers, such as *Live Free or Die Hard*, we see the condition of userness taking shape as narrative. The hacker is an expert user, but the pitched battle between the individual hacker and the digital control system is how the anxious affect of userness is made narratable.[11] The condition of user as read here is both a generic trait of a narrative genre—action film—and a way of seeing a situation emerging. As Lauren Berlant writes, genre is not the communal manifestation of how things are, but rather 'a loose affectively invested zone of expectations about the narrative shape a situation will take'.[12] In order to discover our becoming user we need to think the social situation emerging, which is to think with and against the aesthetic (narrative and spectacle), and think with and against the affective resonance of the aesthetic. In other words, although narratologically and aesthetically *Live Free or Die Hard* favours the triumph of the individual *over* the system and is itself testimony to expert use of digital media to create a world, it affectively resonates with all the ways everyday userness is experienced as an ambivalent mode of agency.

Becoming User

About two thirds of the way through *Live Free or Die Hard*, John McClane (Bruce Willis) and Matt Farrell (Justin Long) are running out of options to prevent "bad" hacker Thomas Gabriel (Timothy Olyphant) from using Farrell's algorithm to break into various Government IT command centres. In action movies featuring hackers there are good people who hack, and bad people who hack, but there are rarely *bad* hackers; all hackers are assumed to be good at hacking and they are always a threat.[13] McClane and Farrell visit a hacker comrade of Farrell's, Freddie Kaludis, aka the "Warlock" (Kevin Smith), who will be able to get them online. In the Warlock's personal "command centre" Kaludis and Farrell attempt to work out how Farrell's algorithm is being used. Kaludis sits in swivel chair in a dug-out pit; multiple monitors rise-up in front of him. Kaludis and Farrell look at black screens filled with various pop up-windows of lines of code, blueprints, status bars, maps, and diagrams. McClane cannot parse the information on the screens and Kaludis and Farrell impatiently explain the hack they appear to be observing.

The command centre replicates the architecture of the "Control Room", 'a techno-aesthetic manifestation of the spatial and logical paradoxes of emergency jurisprudence'.[14] As the scene develops we learn Kaludis does not embody any jurisprudence; the domestic space of the command centre undermines the official authority of the control room, positioning Kaludis as a precarious user, becoming passive, ceding power to external sites of control. At the end of the scene the camera moves toward the monitor; the three men are no longer visible. The graphics switch and new windows overlay the diagrams Kaludis and Farrell have been looking at. The camera angle widens revealing more of the monitor, and then switches angle to reveal a different room, and a different computer user, sat upright at a desk; one of a row of computer operators working in what is later revealed to be a van. This computer operator is Trey (Jonathan Sadowski), a hacker in the employment of Thomas Gabriel, who is called over to look at who is looking at their hack. Trey narrates what he is doing—'calling on host server right now'—and eventually Trey and Gabriel commandeer Kaludis's web cam. In the next cut, the two distinct monitors (made one fluid image by the camera movement that passes through them) become a single window: Gabriel and Trey appear as a live feed on Kaludis's monitor; Kaludis's room as a live feed on theirs. The domestic setting that opens the scene places everyday computer use in proximity to expert professional computer use. The hack at the end of the scene, as Gabriel and Trey commandeer Kaludis's webcam, visualises the promiscuousness of networked digital computing—what Wendy Hui Kyong Chun has recently named its "leakiness"—and narrates power itself as a leaky affect.[15]

Farrell is the only hacker who can stop Gabriel; it is Farrell's algorithm that Gabriel is misusing in the first place, and so Farrell must be the one to hack the hack. As exemplified in the various narrative movements that position McClane as the only man for the job, action films are premised on the exceptional, and exceptionally heroic body.[16] Although Farrell is at first reluctant to participate in McClane's mission, he goes on to accept the uniqueness of his service. Watching the film, the audience is distinguished from the hacker on screen as we are distinguished from McClane; we are the imagined citizenry of the film to be saved by Farrell and McClane, rather than the heroes themselves. That said, the neoliberal logic of individual responsibility, so spectacularly on display in the action genre, is also the everyday reality of the audience. This situation is especially visible in scenes of computer use which position the individual user (hacker) as a sovereign entity temporarily effacing both the networked conditions of userness and the troubled sovereignty of typing into networked digital media; entering the flow of communicative capitalism, an "inversion of politics", where 'rapidly circulating differences and modulations . . . ensure nothing changes'.[17]

Drawing a distinction between the mass audience of cinema and the individuated reception and production of blogs, Jodi Dean has argued that social media must produce different kinds of affective subject to mass media such as cinema. Reading Susan Buck-Morss's *Dreamworld and Catastrophe*, Dean notes, 'cinema organizes, locates, and seats its spectators. . . . The unity of the screen produces out of the disunity of persons a singular audience that can see and recognise itself as a collective'.[18] Instead, social media, and cinema in the age of social media—what Laura Mulvey terms "the cinema of delay", watched whenever, wherever—make their subject visible to itself only as an instance of participation.[19] For Dean, 'networked information and entertainment media of communicative capitalism', "dis-place" the mass body, 'producing instead ever-accelerating circuits of images, impulses, fragments, and feelings'.[20] Hollywood action movies continue to evoke the mass of cinema; they are intended to bring people together in front of a big screen through selling a spectacle best experienced in the cinema.[21] In scenes such as *Live Free or Die Hard* the affective work of cinema as a mass medium captures the affective intensities of networked media which are always disassembling the user subject. Paradoxically then, audiences encounter their everyday userness as both the imagined collective body of mass cinema and the individual sovereign body of the hacker/user.

Once Thomas Gabriel has hacked into Kaludis's webcam he brings up an image of McClane's daughter, Lucy (Mary Elizabeth Winstead). McClane, Farrell and Kaludis watch the monitor as Lucy is shown on CCTV footage trapped in an elevator which is under the control of Gabriel. Lucy is being held hostage, although she does not know it yet. This whole sequence is a mediation on gazing as surveillance and newly "smart terror". The audience watch one set of hackers watch another set of hackers who were always passively monitoring the first set; these covert acts of watching are revealed when Gabriel acts, and introduces the additional event of watching Lucy. Each instance of looking comes loaded with impositions of how to look: at Kaludis and Farrell as amateur bodies; at McClane as a redundant body (a kind of audience-user proxy, a pawn in everyone else's spectacle); at Gabriel as a master body; at Lucy who is 'the woman as object of the combined gaze of spectator and all the male protagonists in the film'.[22] Although the audience is encouraged to identify with the omniscient narration, the digital mediation of narration here is also a mode of alienation.

In films like *Live Free or Die Hard* the computational is obfuscated, both as medium (they are digital films but not reflexively so, rather they follow the logic of digital cinema as remediation) and as narrative event (the screenplay is a series of non-sequiturs about what is happening with a hack/program).[23] Although in action hacker films the labour of the computer expert is represented, it is present in such a way so as to obfuscate the multiplex ways human and computers labour with each other. The gesture towards such work is the typing and stroking of keys seen on screen, which signifies the post-production of the film itself. The smooth transition between shots and screens in the sequence described above is enabled by animation software and cameras positioned within virtual environments. The move between rooms and between surveillance footage is aesthetically and ethically of digital media, and the particular political and social conditions it instantiates. In other words, this sequence, in its giving over agency to the screen itself—in taking it from the human subject who appears to control it—produces a scene which situates the user as becoming *with* digital media.[24] The affective resonance of this scene is to both placate the anxiety of life after new media as one of ubiquitous surveillance, and elicit an identification with the human subject of life after new media as living mediational entanglement.[25] The use of digital compositing embedded in scenes *about* digitally composed ways of being seen, and of living, give away what the film replicates about a digital society: our access to digital media beyond the screen is 'planned, mapped, orchestrated and rendered', without agency to 'penetrate or "discover" anything'.[26] In films about digital media and digital culture-as-surveillance, the anxious affect of the plot is userness made palpable, which might be both at once the acclimatising of the digital subject to their user subjectivity, and a troubling of this encounter through its reification as mass spectacle.

End User

Although this chapter has focused on *Live Free or Die Hard*, we might expand the analysis to include various scenes that similarly intensify everyday computer use by placing the action of use in proximity to the action of action cinema.[27] Such scenes appear to be narrating an instance of computation but more often represent the limits of what aspects of computation are narratologically and cinematically graspable. In mainstream action hacker/surveillance films, the consumer/viewer encounters an affect of userness. The passive mode of watching cinematic spectacle becomes the passive mode of social media; not the total experience of social media as an individual, but the total effect in terms of the economics of production. That is communicative capitalism, in which, as Jodi Dean describes it, 'we confront a multiplication of resistances and assertions so extensive that it hinders the formation of strong counter-hegemonies'.[28] Registering the affective ambivalence of user sovereignty in the domain of communicative capitalism through scenes of hacking in a *Die Hard* movie is possible in part because action cinema, as a definitive genre of mass market capitalism, has always depicted ambivalent modes of sovereignty. In action cinema we watch the spectacle, space and bodies, but not always in ways contained by a legible plot. More specifically, the visual spectacle of action cinema often registers precisely at the limits of what a human body is able to endure and withstand, at the limits of an anthropocentric capitalist imaginary.[29]

Action cinema is a historically dynamic site in which an audience encounters the affective dimensions of new flows, intensities, and networks of capitalism. Steven Shaviro argues that cinematic affect itself has been incorporated into our small screen culture, as a process of attunement, of enduring and negotiating 'the "unthinkable complexity"—of cyberspace and the unrepresentable immensity and intensity of "the world space of multinational capital'".[30] *Live Free or Die Hard* is an example of the genre of mainstream action hacker/surveillance cinema that operates as an affectively invested zone where narratives of our userness are taking shape. I have argued here that we can describe watching hackers as a way of becoming user. In other words, such ambivalent scenes as described above are an affective transmission, an experience of userness through popular fantasy, and a situation in which users are becoming.

Notes

1. Here "situation" does not describe a fixed event or arrangement, but rather an arrangement in process. As Lauren Berlant has it, 'a situation is a state of things in which something that will perhaps matter is unfolding amidst the usual activity of life.' Lauren Berlant, "Thinking about Feeling Historical", *Emotion, Space and Society*, 1 (2008): 5.

2. To name some: *Tron* (Lisberger 1982); *WarGames* (Badham 1983); *Lawnmower Man* (Leonard 1992); *Hackers* (Softley 1995); *The Matrix* (Wachowski and Wachowski 1999); *Swordfish* (Sena 2001); *Transformers* (Bay 2007); *The Social Network* (Fincher 2010); *The Girl with the Dragon Tattoo* (Fincher 2011); *Skyfall* (Mendes 2012); *The Fifth Estate* (Condon 2013); *Avengers: Age of Ultron* (Whedon 2015); *Blackhat* (Mann 2015); *Furious 7* (Wan 2015).

3. Here I am thinking of planetary scale computation in the sense Benjamin Bratton refers to it in his formulation of "The Stack": a scenario in which "*Users*, human or nonhuman, are cohered in relation to *Interfaces*, which provide synthetic total images of the *Addressed* landscapes and networks of the whole, from the physical and virtual envelopes of the *City*, to the geographic archipelagos of the *Cloud* and the autophagic consumption of *Earth's* minerals, electrons, and climates that power all of the above". B. H. Bratton, *The Stack: On Software and Sovereignty* (Cambridge, MA: MIT Press, 2015).

4. Steven Shaviro, "A Response: Steven Shaviro's Post-Cinematic Affect", *in media res*, September 2, 2011, accessed March 11, 2017, http://mediacommons.futureofthebook.org/imr/2011/09/02/response.

5. Ibid. Italics in original.

6. Ibid.

7. For more on this formulation of contemporary aesthetics and its relation to

affect theory see Patrick Jagoda, *Network Aesthetics* (Chicago: University of Chicago Press, 2016); and Sianne Ngai, *Our Aesthetic Categories: Zany, Cute, Interesting* (Cambridge, MA: Harvard University Press, 2012).

8. Jagoda, *Network Aesthetics*, 32–33.

9. As Gregory J. Seigworth and Melissa Gregg put it in their introduction to *The Affect Theory Reader*, Gregg and Seigworth, eds. (Durham, NC: Duke University Press, 2010), 2: 'At once intimate and impersonal, affect *accumulates* across both relatedness and interruptions in relatedness, becoming a palimpsest of force encounters traversing the ebbs and swells of intensities that pass between 'bodies' (bodies defined not by an outer skin-envelope or other surface boundary but by their potential to reciprocate or co-participate in the passages of affect)'.

10. Olia Lialina, 'Re: Digital Citizenship: from liberal privilege to democratic', *nettime*, March 23, 2015. Accessed March 23, 2015, http://nettime.org/Lists-Archives/ nettime-l-1503/msg00034.html.

11. For more on the narratability of digital media in narrative cinema see forthcoming Zara Dinnen, 'Cinema and the Unnarratability of Computation', *Edinburgh Companion to Contemporary Narrative Theories* (Edinburgh, UK: Edinburgh University Press, 2018).

12. Lauren Berlant, 'Austerity, Precarity, Awkwardness', *supervalentthought.com*, November 2011, accessed March 11, 2017 https://supervalentthought.files.word press.com/2011/12/berlant-aaa-2011final.pdf.

13. Some exceptions here could be Richard Pryor's character, Gus Gorman, in *Superman III* (1983) and Jesse Bradford's character Joey Pardella in *Hackers* (1995). That said, in both cases the klutz hacker unwittingly pulls off a great hack. So perhaps there are no truly *bad* hackers in movies.

14. Cormac Deane, 'The Control Room: A Media Archaeology', *Culture Machine*, 16 (2015): 1–34, accessed http://culturemachine.net/index.php/cm/article/view/590/ 597.

15. See Wendy Hui Kyong Chun, *Updating to Remain the Same: Habitual New Media* (Cambridge, MA: MIT Press, 2016), especially the third chapter.

16. See Yvonne Tasker, *Spectacular Bodies: Gender, Genre and the Action Cinema* (London: Routledge, 1993); and *The Hollywood Action and Adventure Film*, Yvonne Tasker, ed. (West Sussex, UK: Wiley-Blackwell, 2015).

17. Jodi Dean, 'Whatever Blogging', in *Digital Labor: The Internet as Playground and Factory*, Trebor Scholz, ed. (New York: Routledge, 2013), 135. On the performance of user sovereignty through hackers in film see Dinnen, 'Cinema and the Unnarratability of Computation'.

18. Dean, "Whatever", 132.

19. Laura Mulvey, *Death 24x a Second: Stillness and the Moving Image* (London: Reaktion, 2006), 190.

20. Dean, 'Whatever', 134.

21. Lisa Purse, *Contemporary Action Cinema* (Edinburgh, UK: Edinburgh University Press, 2011).

22. Laura Mulvey, 'Visual Pleasure in Narrative Cinema', *Screen* 16(3) (1875): 13.

23. For work on remediation see David Bolter and Richard Grusin, *Remediation:*

Understanding New Media (Cambridge, MA: MIT Press, 1999); Alexander R. Galloway, *The Interface Effect* (Cambridge, UK: Polity, 2012); for commentary on remediation and filmic interfaces see Aylish Wood, *Digital Encounters* (Oxon, UK: Routledge, 2007); and Dinnen *The Digital Banal: New Media and American Literature and Culture* (New York: Columbia University Press, 2018).

24. Here "becoming-with" media is taken from Kember and Zylinska's work on mediation in *Life After New Media*: 'media need to be perceived as particular enactments of *tekhnē*, or as temporary "fixings" of technological and other forms of becoming. This is why it is impossible to speak about media in isolation without considering the process of mediation that enables such "fixings"'. See Sarah Kember and Joanna Zylinska., *Life after New Media: Mediation as a Vital Process* (Cambridge, MA: MIT Press, 2012). 21.

25. Ibid.

26. Nick Jones, 'Expanding the Esper: Virtualised Spaces of Surveillance in sf Film', *Science Fiction Film and Television*, 9(1) (2016), 6, accessed March 11, 2017, http://online.liverpooluniversitypress.co.uk.ezproxye.bham.ac.uk/doi/pdf/10.3828/sfftv.2016.

27. See note 2.

28. Jodi Dean, 'Communicative Capitalism: Circulation and the Foreclosure of Politics', *Cultural Politics* 1(1) (2005): 53, accessed June 12, 2016, DOI: 10.2752/174321905778054845.

29. See Purse, *Contemporary Action Cinema*, 21–28.

30. Steven Shaviro, *Post-Cinematic Affect* (Hants: 0-Books, 2010), 138.

11

#YouTubeanxiety

Affect and Anxiety Performance in UK Beauty vlogging

Sophie Bishop

B EAUTY VLOGGERS (video bloggers) individually operate cosmetic and fashion themed YouTube channels, often supported by a textual blog and a heavy social media presence. They parse a performance of girl-next-door likeability into makeup tutorials and an amalgamation of highly feminized video content, reminiscent of conventional teen magazines.[1] This chapter will focus on a faction of highly visible beauty vloggers that I have termed the vlogging "A List" in the UK. These young women are successful, eloquent, poised and meticulously groomed 'subjects *par excellence* and also subjects of excellence'.[2] The "A List" vloggers are overwhelmingly white, young, conventionally attractive and middle class. They have successfully negotiated the YouTube algorithm and gained millions of loyal subscribers on the video sharing platform. They are the visible girls: luminescent on the YouTube platform, on billboards paid for by YouTube, in magazines and L'Oreal commercials.[3] For them, vlogging is a lucrative full time job as they earn advertising revenue through the YouTube Partnership Program and valuable sponsorship deals with brands. Although the majority of beauty vlogging content is comprised of beauty tutorials, fashion "lookbooks", lifestyle guidance, and healthy eating and baking demonstrations, one common beauty vlogging genre can be described as the "anxiety video". In the anxiety video, the beauty vlogger discusses their personal experiences of generalized anxiety disorder, social anxiety or depression. Some videos clearly signpost their content by featuring "anxiety" in the title; examples include "Dealing with Panic Attacks and Anxiety"[4] and "Anxiety Chat!".[5] Other vloggers reveal their anxiety disorder under more cryptic titles including "STUFF YOU DON'T KNOW ABOUT ME"[6] and "The Big Chat".[7] The anxiety video typically opens with the beauty vlogger speaking directly to camera within domestic space, often their bedroom. They disclose to their audience they are about to reveal the "real" side of themselves they have been hiding for a long time. Often videos are filmed using natural light, beside an open window to generate background noise, pets or boyfriends audible in the background. These stylistic choices are sutured together to signal a genuine performance, or authenticity, within the commercial noise of the platform.

The anxiety video that sparked the genre on YouTube in the UK was produced by the most followed UK based beauty vlogger Zoella, in 2012. Zoella is a white beauty vlogger, based in the seaside town of Brighton. Anxiety has become an important cornerstone of her self-brand; dominant themes within Zoella's series of anxiety videos now make up a majority of her channel remit. Symptoms of anxiety disorder discussed in these videos are evocative of an ideology that links femininity with domesticity; Zoella is frightened of public spaces and rarely goes out unaccompanied. Indeed, the symptoms of anxiety disorder cited in the video speak to ideals of patriarchal society, the retreat to the home, to the domestic, to the limitation of participation in public life, the constant re-application of cosmetics in pursuit of "self-confidence" and emphasizing self-care.

Zoella's first anxiety video was published in 2012, and coincided with her meteoric rise to vlogging stardom. When she made the video, Zoella had a total of 150,000 subscribers on YouTube, now she has amassed over 11 million. In her first anxiety video, "Dealing with Panic Attacks and Anxiety", Zoella opens with the affirmation that this video is of a different oeuvre to "normal".[8] Indeed, as is customary for the anxiety video, there is the promise of a reveal of a "truer" identity than the viewer has been privy to, drawing viewers in but withholding the *truth* for the big reveal. Zoella states:

> As you are watching this now, you know me as Zoe, I write my blog, I go on my Twitter a lot, and I like all things materialistic. But what you don't often see is a different side of me, which I will begin to describe in this video.[9]

Following the revelation of her true identity as someone struggling with generalized anxiety disorder, Zoella continues to assert that anxiety disorder continues to limit her life significantly. The theme of consumerism as a panacea from anxiety is present within Zoella's series of anxiety videos, often explicitly. For example, speaking on negotiating social anxiety, she advises 'really pamper yourself, take a bit longer picking out your outfit, I always say, like, make up is amazing because it gives that little bit more confidence that they might not have had before . . .'.[10] Anxiety themes also naturally recur in videos otherwise concerned with shopping hauls and grooming practices, as Zoella cites particular brands of smoothies, bath products and candles as having helped her manage stress, anxiety and panic. Zoella has also introduced a range of anxiety merchandise. The mantra "Just Say Yes!", which was coined in her original anxiety video, is now central to Zoella's branding. It is splashed across phone cases, poster prints and make up bags, sold through her company, and independently replicated on sites such as Etsy. In addition, GIFs and memes circulate the internet, featuring Zoella's smiling image positioned next to the slogan. The amplified colours, repetition and stickiness of the GIF lend a sharply magnified affective response, a call to action.[11] However, ultimately, the call to say "yes" to action remains unheeded. In YouTube videos we rarely see Zoella "saying yes"; she does not film herself leaving the house alone, and she regularly discusses how she turns down opportunities due to her anxiety. Moreover, the mantra "Just Say Yes" is symptomatic of a turn towards empowerment and choice in brand culture that utilizes and neutralizes feminist terminology. Ros Gill describes this sensibility as "post-postfeminism"; she argues 'choice in turn is a watchword repeatedly used to underscore the neoliberal fantasy that anything can be achieved if the right choices and correct disposition has been adopted'.[12] Indeed, Zoella's "Just Say Yes" slogan is evocative of empowerment discourses, empty of a criticism of culture or the invocation of feminism directly. This slogan invites a highly individual response that assumes a menagerie of options that young women are denying themselves. It implies that Zoella has numerous options to say yes to, and indeed that these options will be appropriate and fruitful, that Zoella and her fans know what to say yes to and indeed they know to stay away from spaces in which inappropriate questions may be posed.

Algorithm Panic

News media and internet scholars alike have described the online video sharing platform YouTube as "participatory".[13] By definition, participatory media allows any user to design, create and publish their diverse content. For such a vision to be realized, online sharing platforms must be equally accessible; however, on YouTube, a small number of A List participants are promoted by a platform's algorithms, with the majority of users relegated to the long tail of backwater search results.[14] Thus, vloggers hoping to become visible on the platform must produce content that is complicit with YouTube's algorithmic signals. Ultimately, algorithmically privileged content is complicit with advertisers' desires, as the platform attempts to sooth hesitant brand's fears that YouTube content is comprised of skateboarding dogs and surfing videos.[15] Therefore, the YouTube algorithm promotes vlogs that are filmed in HD quality, not aggressive or sexually explicit, and in keeping with commercially desired themes and demographics. To fit within desirable engendered markets, young women are rewarded for producing media that sits within hegemonic traditionally female genres; namely beauty, fashion and shopping. I argue this content is supported and extended by YouTube's myriad algorithmic signals; algorithmic signals function as wire does around a bonsai tree. The signals determine popularity ranking and visibility. Vloggers are well aware that producing "advertiser friendly" content that is synonymous with advertisers' often highly stereotyped and gendered themes and demographics is lucrative.[16] Thus, if femininity is 'a form of symbolic violence in the cultural field that produces transmogrifications', the algorithmic shaping of YouTube vlogging genres is symbolic violence.[17] YouTube's algorithmic signals punish deviant content, straying from their commercial genre, and this too is a form of symbolic violence.

For beauty vloggers, algorithmic signals can be highly affective regulatory powers, increasing feelings of frustration and anxiety for social actors. Crystal Abidin offers the term "visibility labor" to describe the negotiation of such instability by social media influencers.[18] Visibility labor is undertaken to negotiate the anxiety of invisibility, underpinning entrepreneurial participation in online platforms such as YouTube. The task of ensuring they are findable within the noise of online platforms is labour intensive and urgent for entrepreneurial beauty vloggers. For beauty vloggers this algorithmic panic manifests as highly affective and corporal, dictating vloggers' speech patterns, video themes, self-presentation, and grooming decisions. Those who make their living on YouTube are aware of this platform instability, aware that their position can change at the tweak of an algorithm and that even successful and high profile vloggers are at risk of being relegated to anonymity.

The anxiety video genre can be seen as an extension of the manifestation of this algorithm panic, indeed, the video itself is a form of visibility labor or a deliberate participation in a popular online genre with entrepreneurial intent. The anxiety video genre is a popular video genre, and one likely to generate visibility for vloggers who produce content within it. Zoella's hugely visible video "Dealing with Panic Attacks and Anxiety" has been viewed almost four million times, and has been tagged with meta-tags including key words such as "panic attack", "panic attack symptom" and "anxiety".[19] For entrepreneurial beauty vloggers, a widely used strategy to aid discoverability and optimize their content is to tag their content with the same popular tags as those who are successful on the platform.[20] Tagging and labelling a video as part of an existing genre will increase the likelihood of the videos being returned in search, promoted by the platform, included in an "anxiety" play-list, or shared by popular vloggers. In this vein, beauty vloggers' performance of anxiety can be read as a strategy; as Imogen Tyler notes, the intentional performance of affect 'is channeled within and across media with political consequences and we need to theorize these affects as not only unpredictable (which it can be) but also as strategic, and performed'.[21] For many vloggers, creating and tagging videos to fit within an existing genre is an optimization tactic, used to increase search traffic to a vlogging channel, and increase the chances they will be made visible the YouTube algorithm.[22] Therefore, rather than considering each anxiety video as a standalone text, analysis of the generic themes and tropes can be a starting point to unpack the emotional labor involved in creating such a video, and the strategic and entrepreneurial intent that underpins participation within this online genre.

Authenticity and Emotional Labour

The affective excess performed within the anxiety video can be read as an entrepreneurial attempt at signposting authenticity. I have termed this "authenticity labour". To achieve this amateur and "real" aesthetic, vloggers work to composite deliberately clunky editing, minimal cosmetic use, natural lighting and background hum through filming in front of an open window. The authenticity labour and aesthetic choices in the anxiety video genre play homage to an older YouTube genre: the "coming out" video. The coming out video features the protagonist addressing their fans directly, also from within domestic space. The vlogger signals an abject collapse of their per-formed identity, their reveal a true inner self is revealed and they come out. Writing on YouTube coming out videos, Alexander and Losh note:

> An emphasis on revealing a long-hidden, essential truth of unchanging and fixed identity, as opposed to an emphasis on sexual agency and play, may be a reaction to perceptions of flux, instability, and constant change associated with a postmodern, multicultural era.[23]

Indeed, coming out performances are read as oppositional to the evolving, fake, and often contradictory brands of traditional celebrities and therefore neatly fit within YouTube's community values and culture. Coming out videos have historically been very popular on YouTube, some videos gain millions of views, and often work to significantly grow a YouTube channel's visibility. Perhaps in the hope of achieving a designation of popular authenticity, beauty vloggers borrow from the aesthetic of the coming out video in the anxiety video. Anxiety videos work as a humanizing alternative to a perceived commerciality and fakeness; as Sarah Banet Weiser notes 'the creation of the authentic self continues to be understood as a kind of moral achievement'.[24] Indeed, anxiety videos can be read as an attempt at this desirable morality, an attempt at neutralizing the quantities of murky advertising and corporate influence that is often undisclosed by beauty vloggers on YouTube.

Beauty vloggers practice in the dually male dominated spheres of technology and entrepreneurship; women continue to be a minority in this space in the UK, one that is often openly hostile to female participants. In "Womanliness as Masquerade", Joan Riviere turned her attention to successful women in overwhelmingly male spaces. She argues these women's enduring anxiety surrounding their stereotypical performances of hyper-femininity. She states, 'womanliness could be assumed and worn as a mask, both to hide the possession of masculinity and to avert the reprisals expected if she was found to possess it'.[25] In one example of spectacular femininity invoked as a mask in masculine culture, Zoella performs a hyper-feminized teenage girlishness that reads much younger than her 27 years. Subsequently, she is often represented as a teenage girl in news media. In one example, a recent cover feature in *Cosmopolitan* magazine positions her as an acquaintance from school; they state 'is she beautiful? Yes. But no more so than the prettiest girl in your English class'.[26] In addition to a performance of girlishness, the masquerade is manifest through her performances of traditional feminine hysteria and anxiety on the YouTube platform. Indeed, beauty vloggers underwrite their content through documenting their restricting experiences of anxiety. They describe inability to move or to speak, and recall their experiences of (now under control) abject hysteria. The accepted universality of generalized anxiety disorder for young women becomes a point of refrain, even a touchstone within these texts. Then, this normalized description of panic and anxiety of beauty videos means their participation in domestic space is a sense-making strategy. Indeed, in a stark contrast to popular male vloggers—who often document their travels, pranks and music—beauty vloggers limit their participation to this bedroom culture and seldom film videos in public. Ultimately, beauty vloggers rarely undertake their extensive cosmetic labour to *go anywhere*, the make-up is removed at the end of the video.

Performance of anxiety can also be seen as a reassurance of vulnerability and fragility, to offset the fear of retribution in a sphere that young women know is not truly theirs. Eileen Hochschild argues that feminized service work often requires a total emotional submersion into deep acting of happiness, congeniality and pleasantness, as opposed to easily identifiable or fake surface acting.[27] Hochschild argues anger management is encouraged using complex techniques, described as anger desensitization or displacement rather than addressing the source of the anger directly.[28] An expectation of placid goodness is shouldered by beauty vloggers, who are first and foremost invested in being seen as dually feminine and "likeable" good girls, their brands wrapped up in parental approved appropriateness, as role models. Zoella, for example, is very often described in the press as the "anti-Miley Cyrus".[29] Furthermore, beauty vloggers, like many customer facing workers, are required to be perceived as enjoying their jobs. In fact any notion that vlogging is a job runs contrary to the requirement for authenticity on YouTube. Being seen as too commercial is an unforgivable trespass on the platform that can risk vloggers huge quantities of followers and indeed their careers. This is also akin to what Angela McRobbie describes as the authenticity of "passionate work", as hopeful creative workers are required to display unbridled enthusiasm and energy to be hired, paid or (most likely) not.[30] Due to their requirement to appear pleasant, female vloggers do not have the freedom to address their critics directly. As female vloggers do not have the freedom to become directly engaged with the levels of abuse they receive daily online, anxiety videos could be considered to be spaces to perform appropriate, albeit "pathologised" female emotional responses. The appeal of announcing anxiety disorder on camera, and its popularity with female vloggers, is arguably the genuine chance to feel or to perform an authentic emotion. In this vein, anxiety disorder provides the safety umbrella of a diagnosis, whilst assuring viewers this depression and anxiety is an abstraction, aside from the beauty vlogger's *genuine* happy, appropriate, true self.

Notes

1. Angela McRobbie, *Feminism and Youth Culture*, 2nd edition (London: Palgrave Macmillan, 2000).

2. Angela McRobbie, *The Aftermath of Feminism: Gender, Culture and Social Change* (London: Sage, 2009).

3. Elizabeth Nathanson, 'Dressed for Economic Distress: Blogging and the "New" Pleasures of Fashion', inDiane Negra and Yvonne Tasker, eds., *Gendering the Recession: Media and Culture in an Age of Austerity*, (Durham, NC: Duke University Press, 2014), 136–60.

4. Zoella, *Dealing with Panic Attacks & Anxiety | Zoella*, 2012, https://www.youtube.com/watch?v = 7-iNOFD27G4.

5. Tanya Burr, *Anxiety Chat! | Vlogmas Days 5 & 6*, 2015, https://www.youtube.com/watch?v=JVft4hBoEvQ.

6. Estée Lalonde, *STUFF YOU DON'T KNOW ABOUT ME | Estée Lalonde*, 2016, https://www.youtube.com/watch?v=9EOU5qLrBSU.

7. Sprinkleofglitter, *The Big Chat | Sprinkle of Glitter*, 2014, https://www.youtube.com/watch?v=zHsLV8SqT2M.

8. Zoella, *Dealing with Panic Attacks & Anxiety | Zoella*.

9. Ibid.

10. Zoella, *Social Anxiety & Prank Call | #AskZoella*, 2016, https://www.youtube.com/watch?v=h1FY1RXWSlw&t=215s.

11. James Ash, 'Sensation, Networks, and the GIF: Toward an Allotropic Account of Affect', *Networked Affect*, 2015: 119–33.

12. Rosalind Gill, 'Post-Postfeminism?: New Feminist Visibilities in Postfeminist Times', *Feminist Media Studies* 16(4) (July 3, 2016): 610–30, doi:10.1080/14680 777.2016.1193293.

13. Henry Jenkins, Sam Ford and Joshua Green, *Spreadable Media: Creating Value and Meaning in a Networked Culture*, Postmillennial Pop (New York: New York University Press, 2013).

14. Lada A. Adamic and Bernardo A. Huberman, ;The Web's Hidden Order', *Communications of the ACM* 44(9) (2001): 55–60.

15. Mark Andrejevic, 'Exploiting YouTube: Contradictions of User-Generated Labor', *The YouTube Reader* 413 (2009), http://forskning.blogg.kb.se/files/2012/09/YouTube_Reader.pdf#page=204.

16. John Cheney-Lippold, 'A New Algorithmic Identity: Soft Biopolitics and the Modulation of Control', *Theory, Culture & Society* 28(6) (November 2011): 164–81, doi:10.1177/0263276411424420.

17. Beverley Skeggs, 'Context and Background: Pierre Bourdieu's Analysis of Class, Gender and Sexuality', *The Sociological Review* 52(s2) (2004): 19–33.

18. Crystal Abidin, 'Visibility Labour: Engaging with Influencers and Fashion Brands And# OOTD Advertorial Campaigns on Instagram', *Media International Australia* 161(1) (2016): 86–100.

19. Zoella, *Dealing with Panic Attacks & Anxiety | Zoella*.

20. 'Reverse Engineering The YouTube Algorithm', *Tubefilter*, June 23, 2016, http://www.tubefilter.com/2016/06/23/reverse-engineering-youtube-algorithm/.

21. Imogen Tyler, Rebecca Coleman and Debra Ferreday, 'Commentary And Criticism', *Feminist Media Studies* 8(1) (March 2008): 85–99, doi:10.1080/14680 770801899226.

22. Hector Postigo, 'The Socio-Technical Architecture of Digital Labor: Converting Play into YouTube Money, *New Media & Society*, 2014, 1461444814541527.

23. Jonathan Alexander and Elizabeth Losh, 'A YouTube of One's Own? Coming out Videos as Rhetorical Action', *LGBT Identity and Online New Media*, 2010, 37–50.

24. Sarah Banet-Weiser, *Authentic TM: Politics and Ambivalence in a Brand Culture*, Critical Cultural Communication (New York: New York University Press, 2012).

25. Joan Riviere, 'Womanliness as a Masquerade', *Female Experience: Three Generations of British Women Psychoanalysts on Work with Women* (London: Routledge, 1997), 1929, 228–36.

26. Lottie Lumsden, 'The Secret Life of Zoella', *Cosmopolitan*, November 2016.

27. Arlie Russell Hochschild, *The Managed Heart: Commercialization of Human Feeling*, updated edition (Berkeley: University of California Press, 2012).

28. Ibid.

29. Daisy Buchanan, 'Zoella Isn't the Perfect Role Model Girls Think She Is', November 28, 2014, sec. Women, http://www.telegraph.co.uk/women/womens-life/11259853/Zoella-isnt-the-perfect-role-model-teen-girls-think-she-is.html.

30. Angela McRobbie, *Be Creative: Making a Living in the New Culture Industries* (Cambridge, UK: Polity Press, 2015).

12

Chemsex

Anatomy of a Sex Panic

Jamie Hakim

O N 3 NOVEMBER 2015, *The British Medical Journal* published an editorial entitled 'What is Chemsex and why does it matter?' It defined chemsex in the following way:

"Chemsex" is used in the United Kingdom to describe intentional sex under the influence of psychoactive drugs, mostly among men who have sex with men. It refers particularly to the use of mephedrone, γ-hydroxybutyrate (GHB), γ-butyrolactone (GBL), and crystallised methamphetamine. These drugs are often used in combination to facilitate sexual sessions lasting several hours or days with multiple sexual partners.[1]

The editorial reported that chemsex was on the rise and concluded by arguing, 'addressing chemsex related morbidities should be a public health priority'.[2]

This editorial constitutes the height of what can arguably be seen as a moral panic on chemsex within the British media. This panic discourse appeared across a variety of media outlets including news features in *The Guardian*, *The Evening Standard*, *Attitude* magazine, Vice.com, a radio and a TV feature on the BBC, and a feature length film "Chemsex", produced by Vice. Within this discourse, chemsex is represented as a self-destructive sexual practice that "significant" numbers of UK based gay men, are engaging in.[3] Chemsex sessions are organised through geo-locational hook up applications (apps) like Grindr and Scruff, themselves technologies that destroy gay men's capacities to form enduring and meaningful relationships.[4] It is also linked to a recent rise in HIV transmission in the UK, such that its emergence is "ravaging"[5] the gay scene and presents a 'public health time bomb', in the words of Dr. Richard Ma of the Royal College for GPs.[6]

There are a number of issues with this media panic. However, because hook-up apps have been afforded such a pivotal position within it, this chapter seeks to problematise their representation in particular. This problematisation will unfold through discussing this representation in the light of accounts of hook up app use given in interviews with fifteen men who have practiced chemsex. Using a Spinozist framework, this chapter finds that far from destroying gay and bisexual men's capacities for experiencing intimacy, geo-locational hook-up apps have facilitated the production of a new type of collective intimacy in the form of the chemsex "encounter". Often intensely felt, sometimes these encounters are experienced joyfully, other times they are not. Mostly they are a specific mixture of joy and sadness, whose specificity can be understood as a response to a range of material changes that gay and bisexual men living in London have faced during the moment of neoliberal austerity.[7]

Note on Method

In making this argument this chapter contributes to a growing academic literature on gay and bisexual men's use of hook-up apps.[8] In order to problematise the recent moral panic on chemsex in Britain's media it has also had to move beyond this literature in significant ways. It does this through interviewing 15 men who live in London and have had chemsex at least once. In order to understand the affective dimensions of hook up app use in relation to chemsex a Spinozist framework was deployed throughout the interviews. "Chemsex sessions", as they are termed in the sexual health literature, are approached here as chemsex encounters. For Baruch Spinoza an encounter occurs when two or more "bodies" mix. A Spinozist body is an abstract term that can refer to any entity, human or non-human, individual or collective. These bodies are defined by their capacities to affect and be affected by other bodies when they enter into an encounter. A joyful encounter results from a body's capacity to act, or its force of existence being augmented; a sad encounter results from it being diminished. For Spinoza, an ethical life is one in which we are able to consciously create conditions that maximize the potential for joyful encounters for all the bodies that mix in them.[9] This chapter uses this ethical framework to assess chemsex in contrast to the "morality" of the media's moral panic.[10]

In the analysis that follows three major claims made about the role of hook up apps and chemsex within the panic discourse are problematised using material from the interviews. These claims are (1) hook up apps are a primary causal factor in the emergence of chemsex, (2) hook up apps erode gay and bisexual men's capacities to establish intimate relationships, and (3) the most significant affects produced by hook up apps in relation to chemsex are sad. Prior to that, it will be useful to have a working understanding of what constitutes a typical chemsex encounter in order for the analysis to make sense.

Chemsex Encounters

As one of my interviewees said, 'each session is different' and indeed there were a wide variety of types of encounter described in the interviews. Nevertheless there were certain features that were common to many and it is these that will be recounted here. The most common sort of chemsex encounter took place in a private residence somewhere in London and included on average between 5 and 15 men. The majority of these were primarily organised through hook-up apps, Grindr being mentioned most frequently. The encounters described in the interviews typically lasted from a single night to four days. As men arrive at these encounters they undress. They then consume one or a mixture of chemsex drugs; GHB and mephedrone being consumed far more frequently than crystal methamphetamine. All the interviewees described the primary effect of the drugs as being the loss of inhibitions, which led to a range of both sexual and non-sexual activities taking place. As much as these men had often very intense sex, they are also engaged in "stupidly deep" conversations (Dennis). Another common activity was collectively or individually browsing Grindr. This meant as some men left the encounter others would join. Some would go from encounter to encounter. These are the bare bones of what might be described as a typical chemsex encounter. More details of individual encounters are included throughout the analysis below.

Media Claims

Claim 1. Hook up apps are a primary causal factor in the emergence of chemsex

The first claim within the media panic discourse is that hook up apps are a primary causal factor in the emergence of chemsex as a cultural phenomenon. For example, on Vice.com's music platform *Thump* is the claim:

It seems like more and more people in London are swapping chemsex parties for "actual" parties. These events have become popular because they're easily accessible and technological advances have made it incredibly simple to either host or attend a party. Getting hold of drugs is easier, too.[11]

It is common for popular media coverage of new technologies to presume a simple cause and effect relationship between a technology's affordances and their perceived, frequently negative, social and cultural effects.[12] This has been exactly the case in the media's representation of hook-up apps and chemsex. Cultural studies has long argued against this sort of technological determinism.[13] Although, it was clear from the interviews that hook-up apps played a central role in London's chemsex culture, this is not equivalent to their being a primary reason why chemsex has emerged as a distinct sexual practice in London in recent years. In order to understand why any cultural practice (sexual or otherwise, digital or not) increases in popularity in a given place and time, the analytical net must be cast much wider than simply the contributing technological factors.

Chemsex was first reported to UK sexual health clinics in sufficient numbers to warrant a coordinated response in 2011,[14] putting the emergence of this digitally mediated sexual practice squarely within the historical period dominated by neoliberal austerity. Geographically, it almost exclusively takes place within London, specifically in the boroughs of Lambeth, Southwark, and Lewisham. A variety of shifts have occurred within these boroughs during this period that have affected the lives of the gay and bisexual men living there. It is in the context of these shifts that the emergence of chemsex can most productively be understood.

The UK-wide conditions include stagnating wages, cuts to public services, increasingly precarious employment arrangements, decreases in disposable income, and widening inequality across a range of axes of power. The rise of both homonormativity[15] and homonationalism,[16] as organizing principles of contemporary gay culture, must be understood within the framework of the continued privileging of individualism over collectivity as the advantaged mode of being in the world.[17] The ways these general conditions are affecting gay and bisexual men—living in Lambeth, Southwark and Lewisham, specifically—is primarily through the gentrification of Vauxhall, an area historically associated with a large gay nightlife scene.[18] During this period, Lambeth council has been successful in attracting global property developers to the area, in a way that has increased property prices across the area. One of the deleterious effects of this on Vauxhall has been either the closing down of its gay nightlife venues or their becoming too expensive for large numbers of people to enjoy.[19]

This means a largely migrant gay and bisexual community (from both within and outside the UK) had to invent new forms of collectivity in private accommodation, because the more public spaces where the older forms took place are diminishing. Coupled with recent developments—post-exposure prophylaxis(PEP), pre-exposure prophylaxis (PrEP) and "treatment as prevention"—that have made HIV prevention strategies more successful and sex between men less risky, I suggest that chemsex emerged as a distinct cultural practice in response to these material changes. Vauxhall's dance floors and darkrooms have diminished and it would seem they have been, in part, replaced by chemsex encounters where there is no prohibitive entry fee, no expensive drinks and no kicking out time. Hook-up apps might help mediate these new forms of collectivity but they are not a primary reason for their emergence.

Claim 2: Hook-up apps erode intimacy. The rise of chemsex is evidence for this

Understanding chemsex as a digitally mediated form of collective intimacy is quite different to how this sexual practice has been represented within the panic discourse. There, hook-up apps are straightforwardly held responsible for eroding gay men's capacities to form enduring and meaningful relationships. For example, David Stuart, substance abuse lead at the sexual health clinic on 56 Dean St is quoting as saying:

> the overnight switch from real life socializing to online hook ups robbed us of a very important skill set, that involved forming bonds and intimacy before the sexy stuff happens.[20]

As previously discussed, the majority of chemsex encounters described by the interviewees were organised through online hook up apps. However unlike the panic discourse, there were also multiple descriptions of intensely felt intimacy experienced during these digitally mediated offline encounters:

> chemsex lubricates it so we feel connected to somebody and that's what we want don't we? We all want a bit of connection. That's why we're here as human beings. Sex is in some way the ultimate connection and chems make it much more intense. (Daniel)

One of the interviewees talked specifically about how collectively browsing Grindr during a chemsex encounter not only further bonded the men who were there but also created the potential for further joyful encounters:

The idea of chemsex is not just to meet people where you are but also going online with other people. That's your opportunity to chat to as many people as you want to . . . being in a situation and everyone thinking exactly the same as you're thinking. (Antonio)

The idea, advanced in the panic discourse, that these actual or virtual connections were somehow illusory[21] or necessarily ended once the encounter finished was contradicted by five of the interviewees. Below are three examples:

Have you made friends there?

Absolutely. Yeah. This one guy has become a real friend. I keep in touch with him a lot. (Andrew)
    Most of my friends now are guys that I met at those parties. (Tomas)

**Did you form any relationship with those people out of
chill outs.**

Somebody I lived with for 4 months. Another one I used to hang out with. Some yeah. (Michael)

It is important to note that the above quotes do not represent the entirety of the sorts of chemsex intimacies described in the interviews. For instance, one interviewee explained that he attended chemsex sessions for a year because he felt depressed. The effect of his drug consumption was that he spent considerable time in the corner of the room scrolling through Grindr; however, it might be considered significant that he repeatedly did this surrounded by a group of people. Either way, the overwhelming picture painted by the interviews was not as straightforwardly anti-relational as the panic discourse would suggest. As might be expected, a multiplicity of intimacies was potentiated within the different chemsex encounters, many of which were joyfully experienced during the encounter and endured beyond it.

Claim 3. The most significant affects produced within chemsex encounters were sad

Within the media panic narrative was the claim that hook-up apps have the capacity to erode intimacy via the faciliatation of chemsex encounters in which the most significant affects produced were sad. These claims include:

exhaustion, feeling emotional, paranoia, trauma,[22] anxiety, depression, panic attacks, fatigue,[23] HIV and other sexually transmitted infections (STIs),[24] psychosis, suicide and death.[25] Descriptions of sad affects did, in fact, appear throughout the interviews. Four of the interviewees talked about the negative influence that chemsex had on their lives. One said it increased feelings of depression. Another said he had a psychotic episode after a long stint of chemsex. Another regularly attends Narcotics Anonymous meetings for his "chemsex addiction". However descriptions of joyful chemsex encounters also appeared in the interviews:

> the sex would be absolutely . . . elemental somehow. It's basic and raw and intense. It's that sort of intensity. . . . That's the point—it makes everything feel amazing. The drugs give you that feeling—this is the best encounter ever. (Patrick)

Some related to less intense affective states of feeling comfortable within a group:

> The drugs make you lose all inhibitions. There are bad things of course, but at the moment, you don't have to worry about anything because you're going to be in an environment where you feel safe, and whatever you do, whatever you think, whatever you say you'll be very much accepted. (Antonio)

In the media discourse these joyful affects did appear but did not significantly inform the conclusions drawn on what chemsex meant for the men who engaged in it. Bearing this in mind, we might usefully theorise the sum of chemsex encounters as a Deleuzo-Guattarian assemblage that is held together by a set of intense, affectively contradictory forces. Following one of cultural studies foundational insights, that cultural practices reveal something about their historical period emergence, it then becomes possible to read these affective contradictions as indicative of broader structures of feeling generated within the conditions of neoliberal austerity outlined above. Interviewee Michael, a 24 year old, white, middle class, politics and psychology graduate, began exactly this sort of analysis in his interview:

> I think in the wider population there's more a focus on the individual. . . . I'd probably draw comparisons with what's happening with the far right at the moment and Donald Trump, populist campaigns. . . . Brexit. I think people are looking for places where they fit in. And there's less of a gay culture now. There's more equality so there's less of a reason to go to a gay bar. They can go to a straight bar and not hide who they are in public. So they don't go to the gay villages.

How do the chill-outs fit into that?

> They give you a sense of belonging. You find yourself in a situation where you suddenly love everyone and everyone loves you and you tell each other everything. You tell each other your secrets. You have this enormous rush of drugs and the rush of sex and everything. . . . It's intoxicating.

Here, Michael makes sense of the collectively experienced, affective intensities of chemsex within a wider cultural terrain that has been shaped by two of neoliberalism's animating principles: (1) the re-privileging of the individual over other forms of being in the world and (2) the concomitant liberalization of attitudes to sexual minorities—cis-gendered, white, middle class, consuming gay men in particular. As Michael points out, this is a cultural terrain that has produced what might be seen as other, darker, desires for collectivity—those that animate Trumpism and the desire for Brexit. In this quote, Michael describes the joy of chemsex—its intoxicating sense of belonging to a group—as a response to living in material conditions shaped by neoliberalism.

Conclusion

Overall, the accounts of hook up app use in relation to chemsex given by the interviewees complicates the simplistic and mostly negative one portrayed in the British media. It is not that the media panic is "incorrect", as it were, it is that it is too partial in what it reveals—gesturing towards real limitations in the public discourse on austerity and its ability to grasp the profound and unexpected rearrangements of British culture engendered by austerity.

Addressing the first and third claim delineated in this chapter: hook-up apps have played their part in the rise of chemsex, although they are not a primary cause; and while there is evidence of sad affects produced in and by chemsex encounters, much joy was found in them too. As for the second claim, there was little evidence that hook-up apps eroded gay and bisexual men's capacities for forming enduring intimate relationships. In fact, in the context of chemsex, hook-up apps appeared to have enabled a digitally mediated form of affectively intense, collective intimacy. The contradictions of this affectivity can arguably be seen as a response to a set of shifting material conditions in which neoliberalism has made collectivity itself so difficult to achieve.[26] It is precisely because the desire for collectivity becomes so strong within these material conditions that this desire burns so intensely within chemsex encounters. Conversely it is precisely because neoliberalism has been so successful at diminishing the material spaces where collectivities can endure, that the "lines of flight"—its intoxicating sense of belonging—generated within the chemsex encounter can so easily mutate into "lines of death"—depression, psychosis or death itself—the morbidities of *The British Medical Journal* editorial.

Notes

1. Hannah McCall, Naomi Adams, David Mason and Jamie Willis, 'What is chemsex and why does it matter? It needs to become a public health priority', *The British Medical Journal* 351 (2015): 1–2.

2. Ibid., 2.

3. Paul Flynn, 'Chemsex Film Review', *Attitude* (December 2015): 78; Matthew Todd, 'When do drugs become a problem?' *Attitude* (December 2015): 10.

4. Patrick Cash, 'What's Behind the Rise of Chemsex?' *Vice.com*, November 30, 2015, accessed February 8, 2016. https://www.vice.com/en_uk/read/whats-behind -the-rise-of-chemsex-902; Patrick Cash, 'Patrick Cash on Gay Sex and Drugs'. *Attitude* (December 2015): 77.

5. Rebecca Nicholson, 'Welcome to Chemsex Week'. *Vice.com,* November 30, 2015, accessed February 9, 2016. https://www.vice.com/en_uk/read/welcome-to -chemsex-week-992.

6. Zoe Cormier, 'Chemsex: How Dangerous Is It?' *The Guardian*, November 9, 2015, accessed February 8, 2016, http://www.theguardian.com/lifeandstyle/shortcuts/ 2015/nov/05/chemsex-how-dangerous-is-it.

7. This refers to the period beginning in 2010 when Britain's coalition government introduced a full-blown "austerity" programme as a response to the 2008 global financial crisis, and ends in 2016, when the interviews for this project were completed.

8. For example, Kath Albury and Paul Byron, 'Queering Sexting and Sexualisation.' *Media International Australia Incorporating Culture and Policy* 153 (2014): 138–47; Kath Albury and Paul Byron, 'Safe on My Phone? Same-Sex Attracted Young People's Negotiations of Intimacy, Visibility, and Risk on Digital Hook-Up Apps', *Social Media + Society* 2(4) (2016): 1–10, accessed January 27, 2017. DOI: 10.1177/ 2056305116672887; Carl Bonner-Thompson, 'The "Meat Market": Production and Regulation of Masculinities on the Grindr grid in Newcastle-upon-Tyne, UK'. *Gender, Place & Culture* (2017), accessed August 7, 2017. DOI: 10.1080/0966369X. 2017.1356270; Mark Davis et al., 'Location, Safety and (non) Strangers in Gay Men's Narratives on 'Hook-up' Apps', *Sexualities* 19(7) (2016): 836–52; Shaka McGlotten, *Virtual Intimacy: Media, Affect and Queer Sociality* (Albany, NY: State of University Press, 2013); Kane Race, 'Speculative Pragmatism and Intimate Arrangements: Online Hook-up Devices in Gay Life', *Culture, Health & Sexuality* 17(4) (2014): 469–511; Kane Race "Party and Play": Online Hook-up Devices and the Emergence of PNP Practices among Gay Men', *Sexualities* 18(3) (2015): 253–75.

9. Baruch Spinoza, *A Spinoza Reader: The Ethics and Other Works,* translated by Edwin Curley (Princeton, NJ: Princeton University Press, 1994 [1677]).

10. Gilles Deleuze elaborates on Spinoza's distinction between ethics and morality.

Whereas an ethical life is one in which joyful encounters are consciously cultivated between different bodies, morality refers to laws—imposed from above and blindly followed——separate bodies from pursuing a joyful life. See Gilles Deleuze, *Spinoza: Practical Philosophy,* translated by Robert Hurley (San Francisco: City Light Books, 1988 [1981]), 22–29.

11. Thomas Hibbitts, 'Is Chemsex Killing Gay Clubbing?', *Thump,* November 30, 2015, accessed, February 9, 2016. http://thump.vice.com/en_uk/article/is-chemsex -killing-gay-clubbing.

12. Kristen Drotner, 'Dangerous Media? Panic Discourses and Dilemmas of Modernity', *Paedagogica Historica* 35(3) (1999): 593–619.

13. Raymond Williams, *Television: Technology and Cultural Form* (London: Routledge, 1990 [1974]).

14. Adam Bourne et al., *The Chemsex Study: Drug Use in Sexual Settings among Gay & Bisexual Men in Lambeth, Southwark & Lewisham* (London: Sigma Research, London School of Hygiene & Tropical Medicine, 2014), accessed October 23, 2015. www.sigmaresearch.org.uk/chemsex.

15. Lisa Duggan, *The Twilight of Equality? Neoliberalism, Cultural Politics and the Attack on Democracy* (Boston: Beacon Press, 2003).

16. Jasbir Puar, *Terrorist Assemblages: Homonationalism in Queer Times* (Durham, NC: Duke University Press, 2007).

17. Jeremy Gilbert, *Common Ground: Democracy and Collectivity in an Age of Individualism* (London: Pluto Press, 2013).

18. Johan Andersson, 'Vauxhall's Post-industrial Pleasure Gardens: 'Death Wish' and Hedonism in 21st-century London', *Urban Studies* 48(1) (2017): 85–100.

19. Robert Booth and Helena Bengtsson, 'The London Skyscraper That is a Stark Symbol of the Housing Crisis', *theguardian.com,* May 24, 2016, accessed June 21, 2016, https://www.theguardian.com/society/2016/may/24/revealed-foreign-buyers -own-two-thirds-of-tower-st-george-wharf-london?CMP = Share_iOSApp_Other; Ben Walters, 'Closing Time for Gay Pubs—A New Victim of London's Soaring Property Prices', *theguardian.com,* February 4, 2015, accessed February 5, 2015, https://www.theguardian.com/society/2015/feb/04/closing-time-gay-pubs-lgbt-venues -property-prices.

20. Patrick Cash, 'Patrick Cash on Gay Sex and Drugs', *Attitude* (December 2015): 77.

21. Ibid., 77.

22. Ibid., 74.

23. Zoe Cormier, 'Chemsex: How Dangerous Is It?', *The Guardian,* November 9, 2015, accessed February 8, 2016. http://www.theguardian.com/lifeandstyle/shortcuts/ 2015/nov/05/chemsex-how-dangerous-is-it.

24. Anonymous, 'I Woke Up Naked on the Sofa—I Had No Idea Where I Was', *Evening Standard,* November 12, 2015, 20–21; David Stuart quoted in Patrick Cash, 'Patrick Cash on Gay Sex and Drugs', *Attitude* (December 2015): 74; Matthew Todd 'Attitude, Editor's Letter', *Attitude* (December 2015).

25. Anonymous, 'I woke up naked on the sofa; Cash, 'Patrick Cash on Gay Sex and Drugs'; Todd, 'When Do Drugs Become a Problem?'

26. Jeremy Gilbert, *Common Ground: Democracy and Collectivity in an Age of Individualism* (London: Pluto Press, 2013).

13

Designing Life? Affect and Gay Porn

Stephen Maddison

H OW DO SO-CALLED "lifestyle" values become installed culturally? What are the drives, emotions and skills through which we negotiate those values? This chapter will attempt to consider ways in which gay men negotiate lifestyle in their consumption of porn cultures. Thirty years of scholarship on gay porn has produced one striking consensus—that gay cultures are especially "pornified".[1] Mindful of John D'Emilio's assertion that lesbians and gay men 'are a product of history . . . their emergence is associated with the relations of capitalism',[2] my aim here is to consider the relationship between gay citizenship, and the skills and emotions required to produce it at the current conjuncture. If consuming porn has always entailed an arguably over-determined relation to subject formation for gay men, this is partly because consuming porn has historically carried politically significant affects of urgency and liberation. But gay men are no longer marginalized and castigated by popular media, and by the state governments of the "advanced" democracies, as we once were.

At the same time, neoliberal cultures have transformed the operation and meaning of sexuality, installing new standards of performativity and display, and new responsibilities attached to a "democratisation" that offers women and men apparently expanded terms for articulating both their gender and their sexuality. High levels of production and consumption, across a range of commercial and social media platforms, would suggest substantial affective intensity continues to be attached to gay porn. If being a happy gay man attuned to the erotic and cultural implications of his disposition necessarily means having a relationship with porn—as Waugh, Dyer, Burger and Mowlabocus have suggested (see note 1)—that man's erotic and cultural life is a function of local and corporate commercial arrangements, his ability to access online networks and develop technical skills, his ability to understand and circumvent legal statute and its enforcement, his ability to negotiate social networks on and off the scene and on- and off-line, as well as his tastes, access to privacy, leisure time and money. In short, the pornification of gay men suggests that we are entrepreneurial voyeurs[3] whose individual and subcultural journeys towards "hard imagings"[4] have produced a subjectivity organized around the accumulation and appreciation of our human capital to a degree that implies that we are ideal neoliberals.

If distinctions between work and life, labour and leisure, are collapsing, this has in some ways benefited gay men: our history partly derives from a dissident appropriation of nineteenth century leisure class aestheticism and decadence.[5] As David Alderson suggests, after gay liberation, the decadent and effeminate associations of gay men were preserved and reinforced by 'the purposeful marketization of gay subcultures'.[6] Evangelos Tziallas similarly suggests that the rise of gay male social networking applications (GMSNAs) 'whittle down Gay Liberation's utopic vision . . . but maintains its coded dream of a pure market economy'.[7] Gay men inherit an investment in taste choices, and in articulating their identity through aestheticism, from a history of gender dissent. Richard Dyer has noted that as a young gay man he was positively drawn to culture and the arts because of its associations with sensitivity and femininity: 'being queer was not being a man'.[8] The shift from a consumer society, largely understood as female or adolescent, in the 1960s and 1970s, to a universalization of market relations in late neoliberalism, has reconfigured masculinity and collaterally privileged gay men who have financial resources. Decadence is no longer unmanly, but effeminacy remains troubling, possibly more than ever for so-called "metrosexual" men.[9]

Alongside this shifting trajectory of gender and consumerism, Ros Gill, Laura Harvey and Feona Attwood,[10] amongst others, have noted complex patterns of empowerment and containment associated with processes of sexualisation. Gay male identities have been vulnerable to assimilation through those very cultural modes that can often feel most subcultural, resistant and reinforcing. The proliferation of pornography in the last twenty years, driven by digitization and networked cultures, has offered consumers greater choice, and for a range of sexual minorities—including gay men—this has intensified both our access to "the image of desire"[11] and the penetration of porn 'into the code of gay men's everyday lives'.[12] But these choices and freedoms are available only within an increasingly privatized zone of entitlement, the desirability of which is used to legitimate the radical abandonment of the public sphere by state governments of the so-called advanced democracies.[13]

Michel Feher has suggested that neoliberal policies define us as subjects constantly seeking to appreciate our value.[14] This value is derived from a combination of innate (genetic background), contextual (social environment), and collateral factors (physical and psychological make-up, diet and recreation). Lazzarato and others describe the value to the economy derived not just from our labour, but from our tastes, creativity, social networks and emotions as "immaterial" labour.[15] Neoliberalism incites us to govern ourselves through the management of these assets, which can appreciate or depreciate in value: 'the things that I inherit, the things that happen to me, and the things I do all contribute to the maintenance or the deterioration of my human capital'.[16]

Gay men, like other porn consumers, must act entrepreneurially to exercise discrimination upon a bewildering array of porn choices that not only must deliver private, fleeting experiences of pleasure, but which additionally work to constitute their gay self: porn designs life. And as we have seen, this determining quality of porn to selfhood for gay men isn't simply a function of the intensification of both network cultures and neoliberal effects in the last twenty years. Burger suggests that gay porn serves as "popular memory" in which individual 'porn-induced queer orgasm[s]' are 'a political act, no matter how private'[17] and Waugh notes that "fuck photos" are 'our cultural history and political validation'.[18] I would argue that as porn consumption increasingly occurs on social media platforms we can see how these culturally urgent patterns of desire transact not only erotic and libidinal affects, but become attached to consumerist and aspirational fantasies and images that signify the successful acquisition of a gay lifestyle. Successful consumption of gay porn in an increasingly standardised market, defined by a demand for high volume of content throughput, depends upon managing networks and social media apps where we must demonstrate entrepreneurial skill, choosing appropriate subscriptions, following links and recommendations, screening and filtering feeds and contacts, keeping up with blogs and feeds to ensure we aren't missing out on opportunities not only to realize our desires but to become properly gay.

Given this, to what extent is gay identity foreclosed in its entrepreneurial voyeurism? We can assert on the one hand the particular force porn has had in determining contemporary gay male identities in the metropolitan cultures of the US and UK, and on the other hand, the conditions in which the enterprise society seeks to limit social relations that don't manifest opportunities to maximize our human capital. But is this necessarily so? The appropriation by queers of nineteenth century decadence may have subsequently lubricated the marketization of gay subcultures, as David Alderson has argued, but effeminate aestheticism and performed decadence also gave rise to formations that dissented against the 'manly purposefulness of industry and empire' as Alan Sinfield asserts.[19] More recently, David Halperin has suggested that whilst "gay identity" may imply assimilation, "gay subjectivity" may offer a 'dissident way of feeling and relating to the world'.[20] The pornification of gay culture, implying intense modes of commodification and sexualisation, may produce entrepreneurial voyeurs willingly speculating on their human capital,[21] but it may also, at the same time, continue to articulate the kind of dissidence Halperin envisages, and which Waugh and Burger identify as distinguishing the meaning of porn in late twentieth century gay cultures.

As one would expect in a context where consumer choices proliferate and taste decisions articulate significant cultural meanings, there are a number of gay porn blogs that profile the weekly releases by the major studios and artisanal producers and which purport to help consumers make the right choices in terms of purchasing individual clips and rolling subscriptions. Many of these, such as gaypornblog.com and waybig.com, are effectively shop fronts that offer a minimal review function, and are economically tied to producers' sites by aggregating pay wall access. As interesting as these sites are, here I want to focus on a blog that has a less integrated relationship with commercial producers, so as to gain some perspective on the culture of gay porn consumption. "craigdesigninglife" is a Tumblr feed, maintained by an anonymous poster who describes himself/themselves as 'Gay architect Miami Loving Life—Here's a combination of my work, the work of others I admire, things I love, a few personal pics thrown in here and there! Oh + Hot Men!' The profile picture appears to show a muscled dark haired young man with his shirt off, and the micro-blog's wallpaper shows a sunny image of a Miami beach front, with palm trees, blue sea and tower blocks. The blog title reads: "Luxury Lifestyle Gay Houses Food Travel and Men!", and each post, invariably an image, includes the standard text: 'THE ULTIMATE LUXURY LIFESTYLE BLOG FOR THE GAY MAN.'

Tumblr is a microblogging platform that hosts over 243 million blogs[22] and is well known for its pornographic content; the format allows easy posting of text and images via web-based or app-based platforms, as well as enabling comments and reblogging, as you would expect from a social media service. Users subscribe to blogs, which then appear in their news feed. On March 5–6, 2017, sixty-six posts were made to the craigdesigninglife blog, all of them comprising images. Of these, ten were soft-core pornographic images of naked or semi naked men, including selfies; fifteen were hard-core images (all apparently taken from commercial gay videos), comprised of multiple images showing sequences of genital acts; twenty-one were images of exotic and luxurious travel locations; eleven showed luxurious houses or interiors; six were images of expensive cars (Lamborghini, Bentley,

Ferrari, etc); three contained images of "super-yachts"; and one was a motivational slogan (a pendant attached to a wall with the slogan "fuck it"). This distribution of topics in posts is representative of the content on craigdesigninglife.

Almost all of the non-porn posts focus on aspirational images of luxury goods and locations; these posts rarely include titles or descriptions, and rely on the follower to know what or where it is. We might suggest that in such cases the specific detail of the post is less meaningful than the overall effect of luxury that is connoted. This is especially notable in relation to the travel images, which foreground a mode of travel and a type of destination, rather than offering a general celebration of diverse geographical locations: one high-end beach resort is much like any other, and this culture of tourist travel seems to exist at a trans-national, trans-cultural, neo-imperialist level. The mode of travel is always luxurious, and the blog frequently features images of hotel rooms, resort beach huts and so on; similarly, destinations are either white sandy beaches or metropolitan urban cityscapes, or both (as in the case of the image of Miami Beach used in the profile wallpaper). The porn images are similarly predictable in style and content: they feature commercial and selfie photos, with muscled, tanned, sometimes hairy men, often engaged in oral or, more frequently, anal sex. The blog is striking for the way in which it combines these two sets of porn and non-porn content in a seamless way, almost as though one stands in for the other: muscled attractive men and energetic sex acts comprising a menu of potential acquisitions, alongside expensive cars, resort destinations and up-scale interiors, all denoting 'THE ULTIMATE LUXURY LIFESTYLE . . . FOR THE GAY MAN.'

If making appropriate shopping choices, and assimilating neoliberal, trans-cultural values, are part and parcel of successful selfhood in late neoliberalism, then one way of reading craigdesigninglife is that it serves its followers by helping them to exercise informed discrimination in their taste choices in both a literal, didactic sense, and by associating those choices with libidinal intensity and culturally urgent affects associated with gay porn. In this reading, craigdesigninglife provides gay men with the means to maintain and enhance the value of their human capital by empowering consumer choices that will align their tastes with those of super-rich neoliberal elites: the "portfolio" that comprises this human capital reconciles gay desire and lifestyle with that of the elite. The combination of pornographic images and gifs, and images of conventional, albeit luxury, consumer goods and services, intensifies "affective resonance",[23] fostering libidinal as well as aspirational desire. Thus, the codification of porn in gay men's everyday lives here would seem to reinforce homonormative assimilation.

Yet, this seems too simplistic an account of the meanings generated by this microblog. Sometimes the juxtaposition of porn and non-porn posts creates dissonant effects, rather than mutually reinforcing ones. This often occurs when posts of commodities associated with mainstream heterosexual masculinity (watches, motorbikes, sports cars) appear adjacent to images from gay hardcore. Here, it is the aesthetic mode, as well as the content, which generates the dissonance. The images of cars and boutique interiors reposted on the blog deploy the visual codes of a glossy magazine, with lighting and photography derived from labour-intensive and expensive staging and post-production. The porn images reblogged are brightly lit to reduce shadow and highlight the "meat"[24] performance. Generically, one evokes a public world of celebrity and lifestyle culture, men's lifestyle magazines, wealth and luxury, and the other evokes a private world of personal pleasures reinforced by subcultural histories and practices. Thus, we might suggest that rather than the images of luxury goods and services having the effect of de-gaying or de-ghettoizing the porn images—assimilating the gay follower of craigdesigninglife to an aspirational, homonormative disposition where the porn simply serves to intensify the excitement attached to such assimilation—we could say that the porn imagery "queers" the unattainable, implicitly heterosexual, masculinized world of supercars and resort destinations,[25] reinscribing the "everyday reality" of aspirational consumerism in a homoerotic fantasy that 'actively violate[s] masculinist norms' and deconstructs 'oppressive social standards'.[26]

Given the meta-evidence, 'luxury lifestyle . . . things I love, places I love', I would suggest that in intent the craigdesigninglife microblog is nearer to the first, assimilationist approach, than to the second, dissident one. But clearly the two are not mutually exclusive. Messages and posts from followers indicate a high degree of investment in a mode of consuming the microblog that flattens distinctions between the porn and non-porn content, seeing both sets of material as mutually reinforcing. For example, the following exchange between a follower and the blogger appeared on July 7, 2015:

Follower: I saw the photo of you and your husband in the paper here in Miami. You are such a hot couple & a great example of a gay couple living life like any other really successful married couple. I hope I have that too one day. I think you guys are amazing.

craigdesigninglife: Geeez thank you! I want to just say we aren't living our life "LIKE" a regular couple, WE ARE just another couple! We don't think of ourselves as a "gay" couple. We honestly don't put any real time or thought into it! We're both to [sic] busy and we're simply a married couple.

I'm sure you'll find what you're looking for and again, thanks man!

And the following exchange appeared on July 6, 2015:

Follower: Dude, you posted a gif of a guy rubbing a guy's boner wearing andrew Christians. . . . Do you happen to know who they are? It's for educational purposes.

craigdesigninglife: No I don't but I wish I did! I'd just love to help you advance your education! Goals are good, keep it up bud! ;-)

Here meaning lies not only in the content of specific exchanges, but in their form, and in the affective intensity: values articulated in the conversations straightforwardly animate an assimilationist agenda in which gay men follow craigdesigninglife precisely to learn about how to be gay in the contemporary moment by exercising appropriate choices in both erotic/libidinal and luxury/fashion commodities, and in which such pursuits underwrite a denial of the very distinctiveness of "gay" due to both the pressures of work in a neoliberal context and the desire for normality. Dissatisfaction or critique is ostensibly limited to frustration at not knowing the origin of a particular image, or the label associated with a particular commodity, and yet the transactions seem haunted by anxiety associated with not being able to achieve appropriate skills, knowledge, emotions, and of course, wealth.

If the "affective resonance" produced by the association of pornographic and erotic images with images of luxury goods and services on craigdesigninglife has the effect of either eroticizing gay assimilation to late neoliberal consumerism, or effects a homoerotic appropriation of familiar symbols of unattainable economic prestige, then in both cases the blog forecloses the pleasurable affects associated with consuming pornographic images to a field of entrepreneurial voyeurism. In other words, whether conforming or dissenting, the preoccupation is with the relationship between gay porn and consumer culture. Craigdesigninglife schools its followers in both the kinds of taste choices through which they can display their accumulation of human capital, and patterns modes of social engagement that enable followers to speculate on that human capital—competitive, masculine, commensurating.

Notes

1. See Richard Dyer, 'Coming to Terms: Gay Pornography', reprinted in Dyer, *Only Entertainment* (London: Routledge, 1985/1992); Richard Dyer , 'A conversation about pornography', in Simon Shepherd and Mick Wallis, eds., *Coming on Strong: Gay Politics and Culture* (London: Unwin Hyman, 1989); Thomas Waugh, 'Men's

Pornography Gay vs. Straight', *Jump Cut*, March 30, 1985, 30–35; Thomas Waugh, *Hard to Imagine: Gay Male Eroticism in Photography and Film from Their Beginnings to Stonewall* (New York: Columbia University Press, 1996); John R. Burger, *One-Handed Histories: The Eroto-Politics of Gay Male Video Pornography* (London: Routledge, 1995); Sharif Mowlabocus, 'Gay Men and the Pornification of Everyday Life', in Susanna Paasonen, Kaarina Nikunen and Laura Saarenmaa, eds., *Pornification: Sex and Sexuality in Media Culture* (Oxford, UK: Berg, 2007).

2. John D'Emilio, 'Capitalism and Gay Identity', reprinted in *The Lesbian and Gay Studies Reader,* Henry Abelove et al., eds. (London: Routledge, 1983/1993), 468.

3. Stephen Maddison, 'Beyond the Entreprenial Voyeur? Sex, Pain and Cultural Politics, *New Foundations* 80–81, 2013.

4. Thomas Waugh, *Hard to Imagine: Gay Male Eroticism in Photography and Film from Their Beginnings to Stonewall.* New York: Columbia University Press, 1996, 5.

5. Alan Sinfield, *The Wilde Century: Effeminacy, Oscar Wilde and the Queer Moment* (London: Cassell, 1994), 93–97.

6. David Alderson, *Sex, Needs and Queer Culture: From Liberation to the Postgay* (London: Zed Books, 2016).

7. Evangelos Tziallas, 'Gamified Eroticism: Gay Male "Social Networking" Applications and Self-Pornography', *Sexuality & Culture*, 19: 759–75.

8. Derek Cohen and Richard Dyer, 'The Politics of Gay Culture', in Gay Left Collective, eds., *Homosexuality: Power and Politics* (London: Allison & Busby, 1980), 178–79.

9. Stephen Maddison, 'Is the Queen Dead? Effeminacy, Homosociality and the Post-Homophobic Queer', *Keywords* 13, 2015.

10. Rosalind Gill, 'From Sexual Objectification to Sexual Subjectification: The Resexualisation of Women's Bodies in the Media', *Feminist Media Studies*, 3(1) (2003); Laura Harvey and Ros Gill, 'Spicing It Up: Sexual Entrepreneurs and the Sex Inspectors', in Ros Gill and Christina Scharff , eds., *New Femininities: Postfeminism, Neoliberalism and Subjectivity* (London: Palgrave, 2011); Feona Attwood, 'Sexed Up: Theorising the Sexualisation of Culture', *Sexualities*, 9 (2006); Feona Attwood, 'Sexualisation, Sex and Manners', *Sexualities* 13 (2010).

11. Waugh, 'Hard to Imagine', 4.

12. Mowlabocus, 'Gay Men and the Pornification of Everyday Life', 61.

13. Finn Bowring, 'Repressive Desublimation and Consumer Culture: Re-Evaluating Herbert Marcuse', *New Formations* 75 (2012): 8–24.

14. Michel Feher, 'Self-Appreciation; or, The Aspirations of Human Capital', *Public Culture* 21(1) (2009).

15. Maurizio Lazzarato, 'Immaterial Labor', http://www.generation-online.org/c/fcimmateriallabour3.htm, 1999.

16. Feher, 'Self-Appreciation', 26.

17. Burger, '*One-Handed Histories*', 105.

18. Waugh, 'Hard to Imagine', 5.

19. Sinfield, 'The Wilde Century', 97.

20. David Halperin, *How to be Gay*, Cambridge, MA: Harvard University Press, 2014, p. 12–13.

21. Feher, 'Self-Appreciation', 34.

22. https://www.tumblr.com/about

23. Susanna Paasonen, *Carnal Resonance: Affect and Online Pornography* (Cambridge, MA: MIT Press, 2011).

24. Paul Willeman, 'For a Pornoscape', P. Gibson, ed., *More Dirty Looks: Gender, Pornography and Power* (London: BFI, 2011), 21.

25. Many of which, like Sandals, have a well-known history of refusing bookings from gay couples. See http://www.theguardian.com/uk/2004/oct/12/gayrights.immigrationpolicy, accessed 10/3/17.

26. Burger, *'One-Handed Histories'*, 41.

Part IV

Contagion: Image, Work, Politics and Control

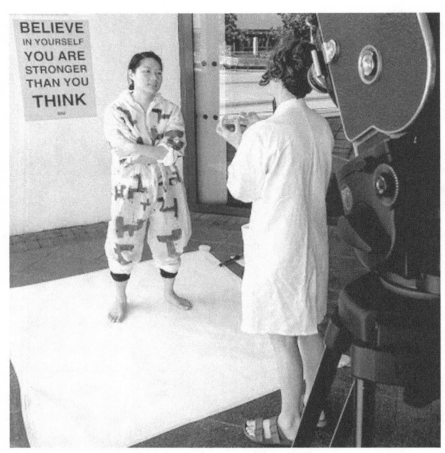

Artists Bettina Fung and Bea Haute at the Third Sensorium. Photo by Mikey Georgeson.

Introduction to Part IV

Affective Contagion: I Heard a Rumour

Tony D. Sampson

L ET'S BEGIN THIS FINAL PART with a series of questions to mull over concerning the generalities of the contagion metaphor and the concept of affective contagion more specifically. To start with, I ask the reader to consider if social and cultural events spread in non-biological contexts in a similar way as viruses do in biological contexts? This is important since, on the one hand, the biological metaphor adds a lot of discursive weight to the notion of spreading phenomena, and on the other, it suggests a particular kind of mechanism is at work across both contexts. For example, can we say that a contagious rumour is *virus-like,* or, as the "science" of memetics would argue, is culture itself coded like a neo-Darwinian gene? Similarly, can we say that the spreading of such a rumour, enmeshed in the vectors of social media, becomes accelerated in ways comparable to the spreading of biological viruses in social networks? It is indeed these and other comparisons that have inspired network scientists, science fiction writers and marketers alike to draw on the biological metaphor of contagion in order to conceptualise the spreading of social and cultural phenomena in numerous non-biological contexts. Some claim that rumours are subject to universal viral network models, and analogous to epidemiological thresholds and genetic coding.

These questions concerning the validity of the viral metaphor have been widely debated in recent years. But what if the questions posed by the metaphor are the outcome of a badly formulated problem? What if a far more radical and profoundly stated series of questions shift the problem of contagion to a completely different place to that defined by linguistic concerns about metaphors? That is to say, what happens if we bypass the assumption that biological and non-biological contexts are somehow different to each other at all? To put it another way, why do we assume that culture is nothing more than analogous to nature. Why not simply remove a divide that can only be reconciled, it seems, by constructing an analogical or metaphorical artifice? Let's instead reimagine the contagious rumour as part of a nature-culture continuum.

In many ways, this radical reimagining is where we begin to conceive of the specificities of affective contagion. This is not an exclusively mindful contagion, as in a rumour that goes on to simply act *like* a language virus, while, at the same time, seemingly bifurcating itself from the natural forces we compare it to. It is instead an intensity of an affect that spills over into a nature-culture continuum that includes the emotions and personal felt experiences of those contaminated, but is always in mixture with bodily and environmental affect. Arguably, affective contagion reminds us that humans can often falsely sense themselves as the command post of a consciousness that somehow hovers above these natural forces. Indeed, by thinking that our relation to the contagions of the natural world are merely metaphorical, do we not simply reveal the mere "foothold" human consciousness has in nature?[1]

Affective contagion is evidently a contested term, but despite not being able to agree on stable definitions, it has become a significant way of understanding the nature-culture continuum, and alongside affective atmospheres has allowed media theorists, philosophers, psychologists and even designers to grasp social media in novel ways. For example, in his chapter, Yiğit Soncul innovatively explores the contagion of images that work in-between non-biological and biological contexts. The image of the Ebola mask that seemingly defends the orifices of the head from infection therefore does more than protect us from deadly biological threats. This image can be scaled up to an anxiety contagion that threatens national borders. Although Stephen Juke's rendering of affective contagion is not theoretically couched, it nevertheless enables the reader to feel the full force of affect in the practices of the young journalist's workplace. Juke's chapter is indeed a quite shocking depiction of the vulnerability of young journalists, at the bottom of the media career ladder, exposed to the affects of violent social media war porn. As an affect theorist it is quite refreshing to get away from the theory and bump one's nose up against the raw realities of felt experiences in the real world.

Kimmich takes a very different turn with contagion, more specifically referring to a generic concept of emotional chains rather than affect. Although understood in the grounded approach to theory we expect from such data driven research projects, the chapter comes up with very interesting and highly pertinent thoughts concerning the politics of emotional contagion. The emotional chains of political affect are not, accordingly, a simple refrain of passive affect, but contain within each link large doses of scepticism, frustration and humour in the face of attempts by politicians to emotionally manipulate their social media audiences.

In stark contrast, Wright's concluding piece locates the social media epidemics of the "like" economy hiding in a dystopian behavioural panoptic system. This is a very different notion of affective capitalism, in which we find a dreadful mixture of Foucault, Skinner and Charlie Brooker. In the invisible tower of the social media panopticon Wright argues that two occulted and disavowed levels of user manipulation are in operation. Perhaps it is because of the aforementioned mere foothold of consciousness that we fail to see that the most successful dystopias are often dressed up as utopias!

Note

1. Here I borrow the terminology used by Isabelle Stengers to describe A. N. Whitehead's concept of nature in which human consciousness exists in a nonbifurcated relation to the natural world. See I. Stengers, *Thinking with Whitehead: A Free and Wild Creation of Concepts*. Michael Chase, trans. (Cambridge, MA: Harvard University Press, 2014); originally published in French in 2002.

EEG art in the EmotionUX Lab at Sensorium Two. Photo by Dean Todd.

14

The Mask of Ebola
Fear, Contagion and Immunity

Yiğit Soncul

THERE HAD BEEN a considerable number of outbreaks since the identification of Ebola virus disease (EVD) in 1976, yet none came close to the scale of the twenty-first-century regional epidemic in West Africa. Officially declared in Guinea on 22 March 2014, the epidemic progressed to affect neighbouring West African countries Liberia and Sierra Leone, and claimed more than 11,000 lives until being declared over, two years later, on 14 January 2016.[1]

This particular outbreak instantiates some contemporary cultural anxieties about global pandemics, where the connectivity of our species is imagined as a condition that poses an existential threat to itself.[2] These anxieties were acknowledged in a 2016 report by the Global Challenges Foundation that lists the risk of a fatal pandemic amongst the potential catastrophes we are facing which could 'lead to the deaths of approximately a tenth of the world's population'.[3] The risk is connected to the factor of increased 'transmission of pathogens through society . . . by global travel and dense populations.[4] Happening in an era in which not only commodities and organisms move beyond specific localities but also images, via social media, in an escalating speed, the Ebola epidemic makes discernible some of the technological, cultural and political dynamics that underpin the present.

General Director of Médecins Sans Frontières (MSF), Bruno Jochum—in the foreword of a report, entitled, "Epidemics: Neglected Emergencies?"—puts the significance of the epidemic in context as follows: 'The Ebola outbreak that hit West Africa in 2014 dominated the headlines for months, eclipsing coverage of other medical emergencies. But if we focus too intently on any single disease, we risk overlooking less spectacular but far more common outbreaks'.[5] Although Ebola is amongst the viral diseases with the highest fatality rates, the affected number of people is dwarfed in comparison to more common epidemics such as malaria or the common flu.[6] For example in the year 2015 alone malaria claimed about 438,000 lives.[7] Yet still, as Jochum emphasises, Ebola 'dominated the headlines for months', if not years. The significance of the Ebola Virus Disease (EVD), then, cannot be exhausted through its high mortality risk and pathophysiological consequences alone but pertains to effects that are not immediately biological.

Viral outbreaks are not merely biological events. They unfold as assemblages through polyscalar networks. The immediate biological effects of a disease constitute only a part of the outbreak assemblage.[8] Discussing Ebola in these terms allows for a broad framework where the fatality of the infection is not separated from the discourses, visual and beyond, and techniques that surround it, as well as the technological relationalities at stake. This reading acknowledges the radical interrelations between these disparate elements. Media scholar Joost Van Loon posits that it may be analytically infeasible to divide real and imaginary risks associated with outbreaks within network ecologies.[9] Imaginaries articulate the real and the reality feeds into the repertoire of the imaginable.

To read the Ebola outbreak of 2014 as an epidemic of images I look here at the image of the mask that appears both in affected localities on human bodies and on the screens of global media. In retrospect, it is clear that the tools of containing biological entities within the geographical regions worked fairly well despite national and regional borders being rendered porous by logistic and transportation networks. However, containment does not work to that degree when it comes to the images of such biological epidemics— when it comes to the distribution or flow of images over geographical regions through networks of information.

In other words, although the Ebola virus contaminated biological matter and human bodies within a restricted geographic range, its images, whether we are talking about the microphotography of the virus, or the personal protective equipment (PPE), including the significant mask, appeared on the materiality of our networked screens globally. Hence, the phenomenon's geographical containment was only partial. Or to put it another way, its biological containment was only possible with an image epidemic on a global level, a point to which I will return to later.

The contagion theme in this chapter is discussed in relation to the emergence of images on a wide scale across varied materialities and how these materialisations relate to certain kinds of affective embodiments. Furthermore, I discuss the notion of contagion in relation to the "paradigm of immunization" as proposed by contemporary political philosopher Roberto Esposito.[10] My emphasis in this regard is on the stigmatisation and medicalisation of human bodies and how the circulation of images reproduces the established asymmetries of power: at once penetrating and reinforcing the borders of the individual bodies and the body politic. The former concerns the situatedness of bodies in milieux whereas the latter articulates a biopolitics of immigration.

The Body

Analogous to epidemics of viruses which may communicate through the orifices of the head, facial masks emerged and proliferated in the affected localities. EVD can be transmitted from human to human via bodily fluids, hence openings throughout the body may constitute portals of entry.[11] Accordingly, the protection suit involves not just a mask that covers the mouth and the nose, but a full covering of the body.[12] When news of the outbreak started hitting outlets around the world, images of the medical staff and patients in PPE—photographed in the affected-localities like Sierra Leone and Guinea—appeared in articles and social media posts alike.

This may have reached its apex of visibility when *Time* Magazine chose "The Ebola Fighters" as their "person of the year" in 2014. Significantly, the magazine offered five different covers for this one issue. The most distinct among the group features a doctor in apparent full hazardous material (hazmat) suit, with his surgical mask and goggles. Its distinctiveness is emphasised by the arrangement of the covers in the microsite dedicated to the issue, where the image in question has been located in the very middle, covering as much space as the other four combined.[13] Here we see how the PPE's mask quality is emphasised by the prevalent genre of portraiture, and also how it becomes one of the "faces" of the phenomenon, in the sense of being representative of it. Even though the virus was contained successfully—in contrast to initial projections and anxieties—within a circumscribed geographic region, these images permeated the screens of networked devices globally.[14] In other words, the images took on a life of their own by becoming vectors of repetitive embodiments and exceeding not just their localities, but also specific materialities—that is, a viral vector that gives its form to virtually any materiality with which it comes into contact.

The appearance of Ebola-associated versions of PPE was not only restricted to journalistic contexts. Sexualised versions of the hazmat suit were commercially sold as Halloween costumes, including the "Sexy Ebola Costume" (see figure 14.2). This point may be pertaining more to the contemporary culture of image dissemination and production than this particular

FIGURE 14.1.
ST1 Ebola treatment unit (ETU) run by the Ministry of Health and the Armed Forces of
Sierra Leone. Freetown, Sierra Leone, on December 12, 2014. Photo credit: UNMEER/
Martine Perret; https://www.flickr.com/photos/unmeer/15623976644/in/album-72
157650226766535/

phenomenon. The commodification of cultural images and objects that gain wide visibility is not a novel phenomenon in and of itself. Nevertheless, it is striking that images of such crises are propagated in this way. They lose their immediate association with anxieties that surround the contagion of fatal diseases and become a repetitive series of images fuelled by anxiety. The image itself becomes contagious—it contaminates organic and inorganic materialities alike, across geographies and contexts. The images that originally articulate biological viruses begin to transgress into non-biomedical contexts.

How are we to analyse this phenomenon, with all its complexity, through its images? One way might be to follow the approach of the German art

FIGURE 14.2.
redit: Johnathon Weeks, Brands On Sale, Inc (www.costumeish.com) http://ep.yimg
.com/ay/brandsonsale-store/sexy-ebola-costume-7.jpg

historian, Hans Belting, whose 2011 book, *An Anthropology of Images* is concerned with images that appear on a variety of materials. As Belting puts it:

> What in the realm of bodies and objects is their matter, in the world of pictures is their medium. As images by definition have no body, they need a medium in which they become embodied.[15]

The relationship between bodies and media, manifested through their materiality, is key here. What we call pictures, from this angle, are embodiments of images by objects. These objects can be technological media, like paper or screen, or biological media, the human body. This angle allows us to map the proliferation of the image of Ebola on an array of media whilst still talking about a single phenomenon.

The question of what the embodiment of this image on different media indicates should also be addressed in relation to the paradigm of immunisation as proposed by Esposito (see note 10). For example, what kind of immunitary capacities does this case denote? The hazmat suit performs exclusions and enables inclusions on the immediate level when embodied by medical staff and patients on the ground. It physically separates the wearer from the (dangerous) environment, but also it renders this cohabitation possible. When this image is embodied by human bodies, it marks a spatial separation from the hostile environment. It operates as a border between self and nonself. An immunisation is realised by exclusion from a contaminated sphere.

The Body Politic

I am, however, also interested in the global circulation of the photographs of hazmat suited bodies taken in their localities which may be read as a sign of threat—an image that produces danger through fear as an *affective fact*.[16] To be sure, exposure to images of Ebola does not constitute an immediate danger to the person who is holding a magazine or in front of their screen in a part of the globe where the photo was not taken. Nevertheless, its effects operate on an affective level at which the non-biological elements gain "(f)actuality".[17] This indicates a further immunitary capacity that manifests itself through perception, as it creates fear and anxiety about the physiological dangers of contagion. Although the threat is neither immediate nor existent for the person in front of the screen, it still emerges as an affective reality. Here, if there is an affective contagion, it is perhaps an anticipated fear of contamination through images that are propagated. To use Richard

Grusin's term, this fear of propagation might be considered an immunization by way of premediation: if we understand it as pre-mediating possible future events as a way of pre-emptive and anticipatory governance of both the present and potentialities of the future.[18] Contagion of the image itself functions as an immune response to contain the virus in a limited geography.

If we use the definition of immunity as becoming exempt from physiological danger, such images are a means through which anxiety becomes distributed and the immunisation of the collective possible. This is what media theorist Tony D. Sampson calls "immunologic" as it 'involves the spreading of fear relating to encounters between a knowable self and an unknown nonself'.[19] On one hand, by depicting the bodies around the infected as requiring spatial differentiation, the hazmat suit becomes an image of separation. On the other hand, it renders bodies without masks as susceptible to infection.[20] The need for protection that the body in PPE offers while situated in an environment communicates a dangerous milieu. When circulated in the photographic form, this codifies the affected-localities (along with the people who inhabit those spaces) as dangerous.

In the arrangement of the covers for the microsite, *Time* magazine chose to photograph the bodies with darker skin tones in explicitly medical garments.[21] The fully hazmat suited doctor is at the very centre. Such arrangement by one of the most central image disseminators of our age gives a strong lead: a clear visual intervention was apparently seen essential to transform the bodies with darker skin tones from possible Ebola patients into Ebola fighters, from members of a contaminated community in West Africa, into provisioners of immunity. Evidently, not many signs that are overtly medical were needed in the other two photographs, where white medical specialists pose in attire that do not strictly signify their profession, as "the Ebola fighter" quality of the bodies within them was less questionable in relation to racial dynamics of the geography. The relation between bodies in these depictions is not unique but articulates a colonial imaginary rooted in the Western visual cultures.

Donna Haraway, writing after the AIDS epidemic, posited that the '[e]xpansionist Western medical discourse in colonising contexts has been obsessed with the notion of contagion and hostile penetration of the healthy body'.[22] The image of the healthy body (of the nation) juxtaposed with that of the infected migrant is at the core of the immunologic operative in international responses. The colonial history of the region deserves a moment of reflection here. The germ theory which we are more familiar with now in medicinal sciences only became dominant around the nineteenth century.[23] The miasma theory was the general model before this time for the communication of infectious diseases and it was influential in the discourses of hygiene during industrialisation and colonisation processes where 'the poor and the uncivilised' were seen as in need of 'moral and hygienic regulation and education'.[24] It is against this colonial backdrop that the present emergency becomes more meaningful.

Crossing Bodies

As stated in an MSF report, 'part of the problem [with Ebola] is [that of] a "defensive" posture whereby international action is taken only when a potential threat crosses a border'.[25] The crossing of the border by the infected body becomes an immunogenic phenomenon as it actualises the movement of the virus beyond its initial locality and catalyses (inter)national action. The image gets into the wider collective imaginaries outside the locality once the virus crosses the border, or when it poses a threat to transcend the continent. In other words, a material crossing of the border needed to happen first for these images to claim a life of their own.

Governments and other institutions capitalise on these images of threat and fear. As written in the introduction to a *Theory, Culture & Society* issue on emergencies, 'in some circumstances [such crises] become politically expedient because it leads beyond its immediate condition, justifying policies and responses that are disproportionate'.[26] For example, Reuters reported that students of West African citizenships were denied admission by some universities in the United States after the breakout, while the Australian Department of Immigration and Border Protection suspended issuing visas to individuals from these countries on November 2014.[27] Evident in these reports is the way in which immunisation of the body articulates a biopolitics of immigration. In other words, the exclusion not only works at the level of the body of the individual through fabric and skin, but also the "body" of the nation through legislation, fences and biometrics.

We can locate a similar assessment in Esposito's project as well. He asserts that 'in addition to constituting a threat to the public order, immigration is commonly presented by the media as a potential risk to the host country, according to a model that pathologises the foreigner'.[28] The dangerous milieux that images communicate, articulate the regulation of movement of the bodies across borders, based on nationality and citizenship. In the case of epidemics, national borders, analogous to the Hobbesian body politic, are imagined as the borders of the body. The discourses about the masking of the latter translate into the policing of the former.

Brian Massumi problematises this preemptive operative logic which legitimises itself through the unknowability of these potential threats.[29] It is not important whether or not these epidemics or attacks are *actual* threats, they always *could be* or could have been.[30] As Massumi argues:

> Preemption is when the futurity of unspecified threat is affectively held in the present in a perpetual state of potential emergence(y) . . . so that a movement of actualization may be triggered that is not only self-propelling but also effectively, indefinitely, ontologically productive, because it works from a virtual cause whose potential no single actualization exhausts.[31]

This logic becomes an operative part of the ecology of stigmatisation whereby "the other" is imbued with all kind of dangers.

A comparable logic may be located in a widely circulated documentary, produced during the outbreak. *Vice News*, which was amongst the first news organisations to disseminate images from ground-zero, posted a short piece on June 26, 2014 on YouTube, preceding the peak of the outbreak, entitled "Monkey Meat and the Ebola Outbreak in Liberia".[32] After speculating causes to the current outbreak, the video ends with a note by the narrator, Kaj Larsen: 'the next global pandemic exists somewhere, the virus just has to jump that gap the way HIV did decades ago and the Ebola did today'. It is not necessary that this particular epidemic is a potential catastrophe in the making, so the reasoning of the narrator goes, but a pandemic will emerge from this already stigmatised locality. This, as evidenced from the legislative gestures in the present, is politically operationalised as an affective fact.

The screen theorist Pasi Valiaho argues that '(a)rrangements of power do not become operative without the desires, fears, beliefs, thoughts and actions that images animate'.[33] Similarly, as the images of Ebola contaminate various bodies and media, they reinforce fears, thoughts and beliefs. Images that immunise and stigmatise essentially, in our case, mainly work for maintaining the exclusion of the already excluded. The dynamics of immunity and contagion at play, in the case of EVD, are symptomatic of the contemporary politics of images, which does not pertain only to what is imaginable and imagined, but also to the ways in which we relate to one another, be it in each other's physical or mediated presences.

Notes

1. MSF, 'Ebola Crisis Update, 14 January 2016', *Médecins Sans Frontières*, http://www.msf.org/en/article/ebola-crisis-update-14-january-2016.

2. Priscilla Wald, *Contagious Cultures, Carriers, and the Outbreak Narrative* (Durham, NC: Duke University Press, 2008), 7.

3. Owen Cotton-Barratt et al., 'Global Catastrophic Risk Annual Report 2016',

Global Challenges Foundation, http://globalprioritiesproject.org/wp-content/uploads/2016/04/Global-Catastrophic-Risk-Annual-Report-2016-FINAL.pdf.

4. Ibid.

5. MSF, 'Epidemics: Neglected Emergencies?', *Médecins Sans Frontières*, http://www.msf.org.uk/sites/uk/files/final_rapport_epidemies_eng.pdf.

6. Ibid.

7. WHO, 'Fact Sheet: World Malaria Report 2015', *World Health Organization*, http://www.who.int/malaria/media/world-malaria-report-2015/en/.

8. I use assemblage here as introduced by Gilles Deleuze in Gilles Deleuze and Claire Parnet, *Dialogues II* (New York: Columbia University Press, 2002), 69.

9. Joost van Loon, 'Virtual Risks in an Age of Cybernetic Reproduction', *The Risk Society and Beyond: Critical Issues for Social Theory*, Barbara Adam, Ulrich Beck and Joost van Loon, eds. (London: Sage, 2000), 165–82.

10. In the book *Immunitas,* Esposito maps the immunitary capacities operative in contemporary politics, on the level of individual and collective alike. Roberto Esposito, *Immunitas: The Protection and Negation of Life,* Zakiya Hanafi, trans. (Cambridge, UK: Polity, 2011).

11. CDC 'Transmission', Centres for Disease Control and Prevention, http://www.cdc.gov/vhf/ebola/transmission/index.html.

12. The hazardous material (hazmat) suit is a version of PPE that is worn in places and situations that pose danger to human life. PPE is an umbrella term for a variety of protective garments and kits against a list of conditions, ranging from radioactive contamination to excessive-heat.

13. Nancy Gibbs, 'Person of the Year, The Choice', *TIME*, http://time.com/time-person-of-the-year-ebola-fighters-choice/.

14. WHO Ebola Response Team, 'Ebola Virus Disease in West Africa: The First 9 Months of the Epidemic and Forward Projections', World Health Organization, http://www.nejm.org/doi/full/10.1056/NEJMoa1411100#t = article; Sherry Towers et al., 'Mass Media and the Contagion of Fear: The Case of Ebola in America', *PLoS ONE* 10(6): e0129179. https://doi.org/10.1371/journal.pone.0129179,2015.

15. Hans Belting, *An Anthropology of Images*, Thomas Dunlap, trans. (Princeton, NJ: Princeton University Press, 2011),13.

16. Brian Massumi, *Ontopower: War, Power and the State of Perception* (Durham, NC: Duke University Press, 2015), 189–206.

17. Ibid, 199.

18. Richard Grusin, *Premediation: Affect and Mediality After 9/11* (New York: Palgrave Macmillan, 2010).

19. Tony D. Sampson, *Virality: Contagion Theory in the Age of Networks* (Minneapolis: University of Minnesota Press, 2012), 127.

20. Grusin, *Premediation*.

21. Nancy Gibbs, 'Person of the Year, The Choice', *TIME*, http://time.com/time-person-of-the-year-ebola-fighters-choice/.

22. Donna Haraway, *Simians, Cyborgs and Women: The Reinvention of Nature* (New York: Routledge, 1991), 223.

23. Joseph P. Byrne, *Encyclopaedia of the Black Death* (Santa Barbara, CA: ABC-CLIO, 2012), 235.

24. Eric D. Nelson, 'Air and Epidemic Diseases', *Encyclopedia of Pestilence, Pandemics, and Plagues*, Joseph P. Byrne, ed. (Westport, CT: Greenwood Press, 2008), 19.

25. MSF, 'Epidemics: Neglected Emergencies?'

26. Peter Adey et al., 'Governing Emergencies: Beyond Exceptionality'. *Theory, Culture & Society* 32(2015): 3–17.

27. 'With U.S. Ebola Fear Running High, African Immigrants Face Ostracism', Reuters, http://uk.reuters.com/article/us-health-ebola-usa-xenophobia-idUSKCN0I D1J420141024; 'Australia Suspends Visas for People Travelling from Ebola-hit Countries', BBC, http://www.bbc.co.uk/news/world-australia-29783106.

28. Esposito, *Immunitas*, 4.

29. Massumi, *Ontopower*.

30. Ibid., 194–99.

31. Ibid., 15.

32. Vice News, 'Monkey Meat and the Ebola Outbreak in Liberia', *Youtube*, https://www.youtube.com/watch?v=XasTcDsDfMg.

33. Pasi Väliaho, *Biopolitical Screens: Image, Power, and the Neoliberal Brain* (Cambridge, MA: MIT Press, 2014), 25.

15

The Newsroom is No Longer a Safe Zone

Assessing the Affective Impact of Graphic User-generated Images on Journalists Working with Social Media

Stephen Jukes

The ubiquity of the image in our lives, and the new ontology of imagery, is the stage on to which Jihadi John[1] and the other Islamic State murderers have made their swaggering entrance . . . ours is the culture of the repeat, the freeze-frame and the slow-motion action sequence.[2]

E VER SINCE THE TERROR ATTACKS of September 11, 2001 (9/11), user-generated images and video have dominated news media. It is hard to think of today's news coverage without focusing on the all-pervasive nature of digital images. They become engraved in our mind as readers and viewers of the news, not least, as the author and journalist Will Self observes in his essay *Click Away Now*, because of the ability to freeze the digital frame or replay scenes on a continual loop.[3] It has become standard practice for passers-by to capture graphic images of violence and terror, from the London street killing of an off-duty soldier in Woolwich to attacks on members of the public walking across Westminster and London bridges; from slaughter in the heart of Paris, Nice and Berlin to the suicide bombing of teenage concert-goers in Manchester. At other times, extremists have used social media to distribute their message using what have become labeled "perpetrator images".[4] Much has been written about the affective impact of images from 9/11 on consumers of news[5] or that of the gruesome "selfies" taken by U.S. soldiers as they tortured prisoners of war at Abu Ghraib jail in Iraq.[6] But the affective impact of these images on the journalists handling them, in what used to be thought of as the safety of the newsroom, has gone largely unnoticed. It is no longer just foreign correspondents covering conflict and disaster who are exposed to trauma. Today, according to Eyewitness Media Hub, the newsroom has become the new "digital frontline":

> Office-bound staff who used to be somewhat shielded from viewing atrocities are now bombarded day in and day out with horrifically graphic material that explodes onto their desktops in volumes and at a frequency that is very often far in excess of the horrors witnessed by staff who are investigating or reporting from the actual frontline.[7]

This chapter begins by exploring the explosion of social media images in today's news landscape. It then examines the studies that are emerging into the traumatic impact of graphic content on the newsroom and—through a series of interviews with those working on social media "hubs"—explores the lived experience of journalists sifting through a torrent of material each day. The chapter also looks at measures being introduced to mitigate the affective impact on journalists and to minimize any affective contagion into other areas of the news production environment.

From the Boxing Day Tsunami to ISIS—The Relentless Rise of Images

News organizations have traditionally relied on images. Indeed, aside from the cliché that a picture is worth 1,000 words,[8] there has been detailed academic investigation of the way in which pictures attract readers and viewers to news,[9] including a series of influential eye tracking studies in the pre-Internet era.[10] More recent research has shown how news organizations are using emotive social media content to drive traffic and promote audience engagement.[11] Until the start of this century such images were typically captured by *professional* news photographers or cameramen and the sheer economics and logistics of managing an editorial operation imposed practical limits on the volume. But in the past 10–15 years, the floodgates have opened. Since the watershed news stories that were 9/11, the Boxing Day tsunami of 2004 and the 7 July London bombings the next year, *amateur* photography has become a powerful—and problematic—new source for established news organizations.[12] Moreover, as Linfield notes, a further dimension has been added by what she calls the "perpetrator image" or "terrorist selfie" through which social media images are used to celebrate acts of violence:

> We live in the age of the fascist image. The cell-phone camera and lightweight video equipment—along with YouTube, Facebook, Instagram, and all the other wonders of social media—have allowed perpetrators of atrocities to document, and celebrate, every kind of violence, no matter how grotesque.[13]

The explosion in the number of images has been accompanied by the speed of their circulation, both through social media and by their inclusion within the various outlets of professional news organizations. The opportunities and threats of the torrent of such images have been well rehearsed in academic literature over the past decade. On the one hand, they provide coverage of events the consumer of news would otherwise never have seen and often in real time[14]; they provide an inexpensive opportunity for news organizations to intensify their links to their customers and generate public trust at a time of economic pressure on the industry[15]; and the fact that they are not edited or digitally enhanced can make the impersonal detachment of mainstream news photography and journalism's preferred framing seem outmoded.[16] In this sense, such material can be considered by the public to be 'more real and less packaged', adding drama and human emotion to an otherwise dry news environment.[17]

Social Media "Hubs" Emerge in Newsrooms

Helen Boaden, who was the BBC's Director of News at the time of the London bombings on 7 July 2005, identified the attacks as a watershed and 'the point at which the BBC knew that newsgathering had changed forever'[18]:

> Within 24 hours, the BBC had received 1,000 stills and videos, 3,000 texts and 20,000 e-mails. What an incredible resource. Twenty-four-hour television was sustained as never before by contributions from the audience; one piece on the Six O'clock News was produced entirely from pieces of user-generated content. At the BBC, we knew then that we had to change.[19]

It was then that the BBC established its social media "hub", setting a trend for the rest of the industry. But it was not until nearly a decade later (2014) that the first investigation into secondary traumatic stress related to journalists handling graphic images in the newsroom was published. In a study of 116 English-speaking journalists in three newsrooms working with user-generated content (UGC), the psychiatrist Anthony Feinstein found that frequent, repetitive viewing of traumatic images raises journalists' vulnerability to a range of psychological injuries, including anxiety, depression and Post Traumatic Stress Disorder (PTSD).[20] He noted that much of the material that such journalists are exposed to is 'deemed too shocking to be shown to audiences',[21] and that many of the journalists on the specialist desks he studied had little experience with such exposures. Of this cohort, 40.9 percent had daily exposure to such images.[22] A subsequent 2015 survey by Eyewitness Media Hub found that 37 percent of the 122 journalists working in newsrooms experienced adverse effects from handling UGC in their job. This ranged from formal diagnosis of PTSD and long-term sick leave to a disruptive and disturbing effect on their personal and home lives.

The Affective Impact on Journalists Handling UGC

The journalists trawling through user-generated content, which is now flooding into newsrooms, are often inexperienced. Many of them are freelancers on casual contracts, sometimes hired for their social media skills and sometimes, given the prevalence of material from the Middle East conflicts, for their Arabic language skills. These are often entry level jobs, with those working on social media hubs keen to progress to more traditional roles. To investigate the impact of handling such material, the author conducted interviews with ten journalists at UK news organizations—both those working "on the digital frontline" and with more senior journalists overseeing operations.[23] The picture that emerged is of a new role that can sometimes isolate social media journalists from their colleagues working in more traditional areas. It is a role in which the desktop screen, and in some cases headphones, serve as an affective site of connection to a diet of disturbing images and sound that can pose serious mental health risks.

Part of the risk lies in the contrast to more traditional roles in journalism and the potential for isolation. As Morrison and Tumber observed in relation to the Falklands conflict, war correspondents in the field may feel part of a collective heroic force, with newspaper journalists particularly prone to living in a "press pack" at a particular hotel and sharing information.[24] That common identity, an affective community of shared practice, is one important way in which journalists shield themselves from the trauma of what they are covering. They are mentally prepared to encounter danger. In contrast, the newsroom was always considered to be a "safe" zone; however, the sudden intrusion of violent images challenges that assumption. Gavin Rees, director of the Dart Center for Journalism and Trauma[25] in Europe, explains it in the following way:

> One of the reasons it foxes us is that we don't take on board the fact that that images, now with very realistic sound and in High Definition, are coming into environments that we assume to be safe. So, if you are a war reporter and you are working in a conflict zone, you would expect to be a bit hyper, you would expect to have certain types of trauma responses. But if you are working in an office block somewhere in London, then it is hard to find the language for that. You may have some people who are immersed in traumatic images and other people at the water cooler talking about how Arsenal did the night before.[26]

One of the young social media producers interviewed described how the vast majority of her work is conducted from her desk as she views repeated video clips from the Middle East. There is little scope to avoid or skip over the most graphic material if she is to do her job. She explained how when the first videos of the chemical weapons attack on the Ghouta suburb of Damascus started being uploaded in August 2013[27] her job was to go through every single piece of footage, every photo and every YouTube clip to help create a narrative for the reporters working on it. The affective impact is amplified across the screen by the ability to reach out to those caught up in the Middle East conflict through contacting them on social media platforms. But a virtual connection established one day can disappear the next, leaving a sense of loss:

> I've lost contact with all of those guys because they no longer appeared online. Some of them I knew had been killed in the shelling. Everything was eaten up in Homs. There wasn't anything left. So, that was the most difficult time for me. But because it was also the busiest time working as a journalist, I didn't really have time to stop and think about it . . . eventually, as the months progressed, the videos got more and more graphic. Situations and scenarios just became more unbearable. Up until the point, I tried to avoid looking at things that I didn't really have to look at, videos and stuff.

The newsroom screen thus becomes an affective site or "point of emergence",[28] facilitating flows of affect between complete strangers thousands of miles away. It is not dissimilar to the relationship foreign exchange dealers are said to forge with their screens.[29] While traders used to talk to each other on the phone, interaction is now mainly through an impersonal screen transaction. In these "post social" relationships, the screen becomes a social entity with which traders become strongly, even excessively, engaged.[30]

This affective dynamic came through in interviews in another newsroom, illustrating the power of images to captivate individuals however far away and however repulsive they might be. A senior producer overseeing a social media hub explained how one incident prompted a re-evaluation of its practice. In the early days, they ran five-day, eight-hour shifts until, in a key moment, the producer became conscious of the impact on one young journalist working there:

> We didn't think deeply enough about how these kids, fresh from college, would respond to these stories. As a result, we kept . . . these two boys on for weeks at a time, weeks and weeks, and then . . . after James Foley[31] was executed and put everything onto a new level, I became aware of one of these boys, on the intake desk near to me, plugged in with cans as I am, I just noticed that he was constantly (she makes a ducking motion) . . . and he did it again and again and again.

He had been watching a video from Syria of two young Shiite boys being tortured by ISIS. And he had been reviewing similar material all day. It had, the producer said, been so far outside his cultural points of reference that he even started investigating such material after work to try to understand what was going on. That one experience led to a thorough review of the operation and a series of guidelines, discussed later in this chapter, designed to protect those handling such material.

Those interviewed recounted a classic mix of trauma-related symptoms, echoing those found by Feinstein in his 2014 study. These included anxiety, depression, and avoidance.[32] Often, the intense pressure of the daily news flow would mean such symptoms were suppressed, with the journalist operating on a form of "autopilot". But there were times when the cumulative impact caught up with them. One social media producer said:

> Some days, it would not affect me at all and I'll just get on and it's fine, doing stuff. And I think usually, surprise, surprise towards the end of the week, I would start feeling more and more down and upset and just really more or less antisocial. I think I became a lot more withdrawn and didn't really want to speak to as many people.

Affective Contagion and Best Practice Guidelines

There was a broad consensus among interviewees that the recent wave of ISIS beheading videos, although drawing on a long history of terror and propaganda, had taken graphic imagery to a new level.

It is difficult to see how this sheer volume of graphic UGC, and its now pivotal role in news production, cannot spill over contagiously into the wider news culture. Even the editing dynamic for video material is different. While, in the past, a field producer may have done a raw edit in a combat zone and sent material through to London, UGC comes with no such filter and can potentially be viewed "raw" by a large number of journalists in the newsroom. Equally, social media can quickly influence other editorial practices. One journalist interviewed told of cases where news desks can become wrapped up in social media content to the extent that sometimes the "tail starts wagging the dog". Journalists then come under pressure to write a story based on breaking social media feeds rather than standing back on the story and checking the facts of what had happened.

Many of the journalists had begun to formulate their own coping strategies. The more senior could afford the luxury of choosing not to view disturbing material, but some of the younger ones felt less able to refuse jobs for fear of being passed over for promotion. One senior journalist summed up the dilemma as follows:

> They are young and ambitious and so, you know, they don't want to say . . . 'I can't deal with this, I really need a day not looking at this stuff', because they don't want to lose their position or be seen as too weak.

Another echoed this risk:

> When you're starting out, you feel like you can't say things about feeling scared, feeling depressed and so on . . . you're not in a position to do that when you're starting out.

Mainstream news organizations have tried to dilute the macho culture by assuring journalists that they *can* freely decline to view such material. Most are now introducing guidelines. These are often based on best practice set out by the Dart Center in 2014,[33] which advocated six guiding principles. These include the need to minimize exposure, avoiding unnecessary and repeat viewing, experimenting with means of distance and detachment,[34] taking regular breaks from the screen, developing a self-care plan and ensuring that a journalist does not cut him or herself off from friends and a social life. One of the key principles is that no journalist should ever attach a file of disturbing images and send it around the newsroom without a clear warning. Turning down the volume on video has also become an important safeguard since sound can be just as disturbing as images.

Conclusion

The technological revolution that is social media has introduced a powerful new affective dimension into the newsroom and is posing a risk to a generation of young and vulnerable journalists. Those working at social media hubs can be exposed to a daily diet of horrific images that in turn are finding a strong resonance with news organizations seeking a cheap source of new material to attract new subscribers and re-engage disaffected audiences. The vulnerability is compounded by the entry-level nature of these jobs, attracting young and inexperienced journalists who may have difficulty admitting that they find the material they are handling disturbing. The affective and contagious impact of these images and their audio tracks is compounded by newsroom technology that allows journalists to form virtual relationships across the screen with those caught up in conflict and disaster thousands of miles away. Slowly but surely, news managers are realizing the early mistakes they made and are starting to adopt measures to protect their journalists.

Notes

1. Jihadi John was the name given by the British media to the masked ISIS militant seen as an executioner in many of its beheading videos. He was subsequently revealed to be Muhammad Emwazi, of Iraqi origin, whose family had settled in North Kensington, London, when he was six years old.

2. Will Self, 'Click Away Now: How Bloodshed in the Desert Lost its Reality', *The Guardian,* December 23, 2014. Available from: http://www.theguardian.com/news/ 2014/dec/23/-sp-passive-consumers-pornography-violence.

3. Ibid.

4. Susie Linfield, 'Perpetrator Images of Atrocity and Suffering: Then and Now', *The Visual Politics of Human Images in Humanitarian and Human Rights Communication* (London: London School of Economics, 2015).

5. Stuart Allan, *Citizen Witnessing: Revisioning Journalism in Times of Crisis* (Cambridge, UK: Polity Press, 2013); Lilie Chouliaraki, *The Spectatorship of Suffering* (London: Sage Publications, 2006); Richard Grusin, *Premediation: Affect and Mediality after 9/11* (Basingstoke, UK: Palgrave MacMillan, 2010); Victor Seidler, *Remembering 9/11: Terror, Trauma and Social Theory* (Basingstoke, UK: Palgrave Macmillan, 2013).

6. Grusin, *Premediation: Affect and Mediality after 9/11;* Andrew Hoskins and Ben O'Loughlin, *War and Media—The Emergence of Diffused War* (Cambridge, UK: Polity Press, 2010); Linfield, *Perpetrator Images of Atrocity and Suffering: Then and Now.*

7. *Eyewitness Media Hub, Making Secondary Trauma a Primary Issue: A Study of Eyewitness Media and Vicarious Trauma on the Digital Frontline,* 2015. Available from: http://eyewitnessmediahub.com/research/vicarious-trauma.

8. The phrase dates back to slogans used in U.S. newspapers in the period before World War I.

9. David Domke, David Perlmutter and Meg Spratt, 'The Primes of Our Times? An Examination of the Power of Visual Images', *Journalism* 3(2) (2002): 131–59.

10. Mario R. Garcia and Pegie M. Stark, *Eyes on the News* (St. Petersburg, FL: Poynter Institute, 1991).

11. Jessica Gall Myrick and Bartosz W. Wojdynski, 'Moody News: The Impact of

Collective Emotion Ratings on Online News Consumers' Attitudes, Memory, and Behavioral Intentions', *New Media & Society* 18(11) (2016): 2576–94.

12. Kari Andén-Papadopoulos and Mervi Pantti, 'Re-imagining Crisis Reporting: Professional Ideology of Journalists and Citizen Eyewitness Images', *Journalism* 14(7) (2013): 960–77.

13. Linfield, 'Perpetrator Images of Atrocity and Suffering: Then and Now'.

14. Allan, *Citizen Witnessing: Revisioning Journalism in Times of Crisis*.

15. Mervi Pantti and Piet Bakker, 'Misfortunes, Memories and Sunsets: Non-professional Images in Dutch News Media', *International Journal of Cultural Studies* 12(5) (2009): 471–89.

16. Stuart Allan, 'Witnessing in Crisis: Photo-reportage of Terror Attacks in Boston and London', *Media, War & Conflict* 7(2) (2014): 133–51.

17. Andy Williams, Karin Wahl-Jorgensen and Claire Wardle, 'More Real and Less Packaged: Audience Discourse on Amateur News Content and Its Effects on Journalism Practice', *Amateur Images and Global News*, Kari Andén-Papadopoulos and Mervi Pantti, eds. (Bristol, UK: Intellect, 2011), 193–210.

18. Helen Boaden, 'The Role of Citizen Journalism in Modern Democracy', keynote speech at the e-Democracy Conference, Royal Institute of British Architects, London, Vol. 13, 2008.

19. Ibid.

20. Anthony Feinstein, Blair Audet and Elizabeth Waknine, 'Witnessing Images of Extreme Violence: A Psychological Study of Journalists in the Newsroom', *Journal of the Royal Society of Medicine* 5(8) (2014): 2054270414533323.

21. Ibid., 1.

22. Questions pertaining to user-generated content-based work included the following: (a) how often do you view violent images (daily, weekly, monthly); (b) how many hours per shift do you view violent images (1, 2, 3, 4, 5, 6, and >6h) and (c) do you find this work traumatic (rated on a simple analogue scale of 0–10, the higher numbers indicating greater emotional upset).

23. The interview data and names or the news organizations have been anonymized.

24. David E. Morrison and Howard Tumber, *Journalists at War: The Dynamics of News Reporting during the Falklands Conflict* (London: Sage Publications, 1988).

25. The Dart Center for Journalism & Trauma is a charity based at the Columbia University Graduate School of Journalism in New York. It provides support for journalists suffering from stress incurred through coverage of traumatic news stories; it also provides best practice guidelines and resources for trauma-literate reporting by promoting better understanding of issues around trauma. The author of this chapter chairs its European operations.

26. Interview with the author.

27. Graphic video footage on August 21, 2013 of children writhing in agony at what later turned out to be confirmed by UN inspectors as a chemical weapons attack in Damascus caused international outrage. Nabila Ramdani, a French-Arab journalist who had worked extensively in Syria, recounted how her contacts in the country sent her almost contemporaneously video footage of children dying from the effects of nerve agents. See Nabila Ramdani, 'Assad is a War Criminal, But an Attack Will Do

Nothing for the People of Syria', *The Observer,* August 31, 2013. Available from: http://www.theguardian.com/commentisfree/2013/aug/31/syria-assad-war-criminal.

28. In her analysis of affect and television, Misha Kavka refers to the screen as a "join" across which affective forces can flow. See Misha Kavka, *Reality Television, Affect and Intimacy: Reality Matters* (London: Palgrave Macmillan, 2008), 37.

29. Karin Knor Cetina and Urs Bruegger, 'Traders' Engagement with Markets: A Postsocial Relationship', *Theory, Culture & Society* 19(5–6) (2002): 161–85.

30. Ibid., 162.

31. The U.S. freelance journalist James Foley was abducted in November 2012 in Northern Syria and beheaded by ISIS in August 2014 after U.S. airstrikes in Syria. A video of his beheading was posted on YouTube.

32. Feinstein, *Witnessing Images of Extreme Violence,* 4.

33. Working with Traumatic Imagery. See https://dartcenter.org/content/working-with-traumatic-imagery.

34. This can involve applying a temporary mask or matte to part of the screen, avoiding the loop play function when editing video and developing workarounds.

16

Emotions, Social Media Communication and TV Debates

Morgane Kimmich

THIS CHAPTER INVESTIGATES the role of emotions in social media communication in the 2012 American and 2010 British televised leader debates. More specifically, it looks at how Twitter users reacted to the emotions displayed by politicians during the debates and by journalists covering the debates. Regarding their growing popularity and multifaceted aspects, TV debates can be considered as a microcosm of politics and media and have become cornerstones of election campaigns in many countries such as Canada, France, Germany, Australia, the Netherlands, and most recently the United Kingdom.[1]

TV debates have impacted politics but also the journalistic coverage of political campaigns[2] and are intrinsically linked to emotions.[3] The presence of emotions in TV debates can be seen as symptoms or attempts to grasp what scholars describe as the "emotionalisation of society".[4,5,6,7,8,9,10] The emotionalisation of society puts emotions and emotional expressivity at the centre of society, with a special focus on the management and process of personal reflection linked to emotions in everyday life—in institutions at a state or organisational level—as well as communications in the public sphere—what Richards calls the "therapeutic".[11]

In order to examine how Twitter users reacted to the debates and their coverage, this chapter is guided by the following research question: how did Twitter users react to the emotions and emotionality used by candidates and journalists in the 2012 American and 2010 British televised debates? This chapter goes beyond previous research on emotional contagion by arguing that non-linear emotional chains exist between politicians, journalists and Twitter users all reacting to each other's emotions during and around live political debates. Specifically, Twitter users responded negatively to the emotions displayed by politicians and journalists. This chapter concludes that emotions are not a straightforward means for politicians and journalists to reach out to voters and news consumers who have become highly sceptical of journalistic and political matters.

Methodology

In order to analyse how Twitter users reacted to the debates and their coverage, a sample of 10 per cent of the total population of American and British tweets were coded: 30,000 in the American case, and 3,000 in the British one. This approach is consistent with previous studies analysing such a large amount of tweets.[12] These samples were acquired through simple random sampling, which randomly chooses elements in the population of data giving each element (in this case tweets) the same probability of being chosen and therefore avoids all possible influence of researchers over their data. To respect the anonymity of private users, tweets were rendered anonymous throughout the study.

A content analysis was applied to all tweets contained in the samples. For this purpose, each tweet was read several times in order to identify the type of tweet (original tweet, retweet, mention or reply, hashtag), the type of Twitter user (individual users, politicians, journalists, experts or PR people), the hyperlinks shared (news website, political website, expert website, image, video, broken link, other websites), the emotions and emotional references contained (emotions, humour, references to family, friends or anecdotes) along with the context of each tweet (e.g. debates in general, a particular candidate, topic or issue). Notes regarding the language used, focus of each tweet and other elements that could help answer the research question were also taken into account. To code elements in emotional (tweets containing emotions, humour, references to family, friends or anecdotes) or non-emotional (tweets not containing any emotions, humour, references to family, friends or anecdotes) codes, the types of words (e.g. adjectives, pronouns, verbs) as well as on the definitions of each emotion were also considered.

Before presenting the findings, it is vital to mention the understanding of emotions used throughout this study. Emotion is conceived as an umbrella term including feelings and their specific thoughts, with their own psychological, cultural and biological states and tendencies to act.[13] More specifically, this chapter follows the framework of emotions as understood by

Richards and Brown, who claim that the concept of emotionalisation is not linked to any specific psychological theory of affect, but rather to a broad range of mental states, which can generically be termed affects, feelings, moods, passions, or sentiments.[14] This analysis does not limit itself to emotions such as anger or love but also includes other attitudes or behaviours that can elicit an emotion such as references to family, friends and anecdotes. This chapter also takes a closer look at humour, which, although not an emotion itself, is closely related to emotions. As Freud puts it:

> There is no doubt that the essence of humour is that one spares oneself the affects to which the situation would naturally give rise and dismisses the possibility of such expressions of emotion with a jest.[15]

Findings

Social Media, Emotions and TV Debates

This first sub-section looks at how Twitter users reacted to politicians using emotions during the 2012 American and 2010 British TV debates. A preliminary analysis revealed that American candidates, Obama and Romney, mainly displayed mixed emotions (empathy, anger, pride, happiness and frustration), while British candidates were more specific (mixed emotions for Cameron and Clegg, negative emotions for Brown). All candidates also referred to their families, friends and anecdotes. Table 16.1 indicates that Twitter users mainly responded negatively to politicians both in the United Kingdom and United States using emotions during the debates.

In the American case, the most tallied coded elements are humour, anger, frustration and enthusiasm. Interestingly, although humour cannot be classed as a positive or negative emotion, its use was mainly negative as Twitter users displayed humour to mock or criticise politicians' use of emotions. For example:

> #MittRomney just said his sons are a bunch of liars. I wonder where they learned that from. #debates

Although enthusiasm was coded a significant number of times, this positive emotion remains overshadowed by negative ones such as anger or frustration. The least coded emotions of this analysis are shame and anxiety. The following tweets illustrate Twitter users' anger and frustration at candidates, here Obama, using and manipulating emotions during the debates:

Wtf was that @BarackObama we don't give a Hoover damn about your relationship. #Debates

#Obamaplaybook: interrupt. lie. deceive. mock. sidestep. talk in platitudes. emotionally manipulate and stumble. #debates #fail

In the British case, the most coded elements of the analysis are similar to the American ones with humour, frustration, enthusiasm and disappointment. Twitter users marginally displayed sadness and shame, pride, anxiety and hate regarding British candidates using emotions. The following British tweets illustrate the frustration and anger of Twitter users regarding British candidates using emotionality during the debates:

I think at the next two Leaders' Debates, it would be wise not to use the phrase "the other day" unless it actually was.

That's the 3rd time in the debates that Cameron has looked straight into camera and exploited the death of his child.

Like the American results, humour in British tweets was mainly negative as it was used by Twitter users to mock or criticise Brown, Cameron and

TABLE 16.1
Percentage of Emotions and Humour Displayed by Twitter Users
Regarding Candidates' Use of Emotions

	Obama	Romney	Brown	Cameron	Clegg
Admiration	7.5	4.4	7.8	3.5	13.9
Anger	23.8	21.5	7.8	14.2	4.1
Anxiety	0.1	0.1	1.1	2.7	1.6
Disappointment	7.9	3.9	6.7	13.3	7.4
Empathy	0.2	0.2	0.0	0.0	0.0
Enthusiasm	11.2	6.2	13.3	8.0	23.8
Fear	1.0	1.3	3.3	3.5	4.9
Frustration	13.9	16.1	18.9	18.6	15.6
Happiness	0.7	0.3	2.2	0.9	6.6
Hate	1.8	1.3	3.3	2.7	0.8
Hope	1.0	0.5	3.3	3.5	4.9
Humour	28.0	42.2	30.0	24.8	9.8
Love	1.2	1.1	2.2	3.5	3.3
Pride	0.9	0.4	0.0	0.0	2.5
Sadness	0.6	0.6	0.0	0.0	0.8
Shame	0.1	0.1	0.0	0.9	0.0
Total	100.0	100.0	100.0	100.0	100.0

Source: The Author.

Clegg using emotionality during the debates. For example, the following tweets display humour to express more negative emotions such as anger and frustration:

> @rozicollier yeah, they joked about that tonight. i got bored of the debates, has davey met any more black people yet?

> Is the man in the middle a Sheffield MP? One never knew. He has only mentioned it 50 times over the last few debates.

However, these British results are more revealing than the American ones when it comes to each candidate. Indeed, from table 16.1, it can be seen that most negative emotions were coded for candidates Brown and Cameron with most references to humour, frustration, anger and disappointment. Only 13.3 percent of references to enthusiasm were coded for Brown and 8 percent for Cameron. Reversely, most positive emotions (23.8 percent of references to enthusiasm, 13.9 percent to admiration) were coded for Clegg. The same emotions (anxiety, sadness, pride, shame, hate and happiness) were the least coded for each candidate. Thus, although enthusiasm is one of the most coded emotions, it was predominantly directed towards Clegg.

All in all, although all American and British candidates tried to manipulate emotions and emotionality during the debates, this failed its purpose as Twitter users mainly responded negatively (using negative emotions, especially frustration, anger and humour) to mock and/or criticise this manipulation of emotions. Positive emotions were either marginal or coded for specific candidates (e.g. Clegg).

Social Media, Emotions and Journalistic Coverage of TV Debates

After analysing what emotions Twitter users displayed in relation to candidates using emotions, this second sub-section turns to Twitter users' reactions regarding journalists using emotions. A preliminary analysis revealed that American and British journalists mainly used humour and negative emotions (anger, fear, frustration, disappointment, anxiety) during their coverage of the debates. Table 16.2 indicates that the coverage of the debates in both the United States and United Kingdom triggered mainly negative emotions, especially anger, frustration, hate and disappointment.

In the American case, the most coded elements of this second analysis are humour, frustration, enthusiasm and anger. Twitter users only marginally (0.9 percent or less) associated shame, nostalgia, happiness, sadness, pride,

TABLE 16.2
Percentages of Emotions and Humour Displayed by Twitter Users
Regarding the Coverage of the American and British debates

	American press coverage	British press coverage
Admiration	0.6	2.1
Anger	14.9	11.5
Anxiety	0.0	2.1
Disappointment	8.1	15.6
Enthusiasm	16.8	16.7
Fear	0.6	0.0
Frustration	23.3	24.0
Happiness	0.3	1.0
Hate	0.9	0.0
Hope	0.9	1.0
Humour	30.7	22.9
Love	0.9	3.1
Nostalgia	0.3	0.0
Pride	0.6	0.0
Sadness	0.6	0.0
Shame	0.3	0.0
Total	100.0	100.0

Source: The Author.

fear, admiration, hope, love and hate to the journalistic coverage of the debates. Twitter users more often mocked, criticised and expressed more negative emotions regarding the media coverage of the debates by using humour in their tweets. Furthermore, many Twitter users displayed both humour and enthusiasm to share their excitement about the upcoming coverage of satirical shows such as *The Daily Show with Jon Stewart* or *Saturday Night Live* (29.6 percent). Furthermore, users also displayed enthusiasm towards new reporting techniques, such as news media publishing GIFs mocking the debates (3.7 percent), specific news commentators giving their opinions about the debates (9.3 percent) or enthusiastically telling what channel or medium they were following (14.8 percent). In total, only 42.6 percent of references were identified to enthusiastically congratulate journalists on their coverage of the debates, making this emotion marginal compared to frustration or anger. In addition to expressing negative emotions regarding the tone of the media, Twitter users were also disappointed, frustrated and angered by what journalists chose to cover, namely trivia, emotions and emotionality. For example:

> media will largely ignore any substantial points made and focus on big bird and happy anniversary comments . . . #debates @sadbuttrue

Love how all the media cares about in the #debates are the marketing aspect of the candidates. Let's talk policy for once.

Similar elements were coded in the British case with most references coded for frustration, humour, enthusiasm, disappointment and anger. Twitter users only marginally displayed happiness, hope, admiration, anxiety and love regarding the journalistic coverage of the British debates (3.1 per cent of references or less for each). Enthusiasm corresponded to Twitter users either looking forward to some journalists' analysis, or congratulating some journalists or news programmes. For example, the following users shared their excitement at the coverage of the debates:

Looking forward to the next two debates now. The analysis on question time should be excellent

Looking forward to seeing round two of the great leaders' debates tonight . . . wonder who will be gracing the front pages tomorrow?!

While others congratulated some journalists and news programmes:

RT @richardpbacon: Michael Cockerill's "How To Win The TV Debate" (the story of leaders' TV debates) was a propa TV gem last night.

Two nights ago "The Daily Show" did a brilliantly funny review of the British election, including its debates and television coverage.

Despite this relative enthusiasm, the press coverage in both countries was rather seen as biased, unfair and manipulated. For example, the following tweet illustrates anger regarding the American journalistic coverage of the debates:

If all these "journalists" want so badly to insert their views into the Presidential debates, they should run for office. Otherwise, STFU.

Furthermore, some Twitter users urged other social media users not to follow press coverage. For example, the following tweet recommends not following the British coverage of the debates:

Great thing about debates: YOU the people saw & heard them & will not be told what to think by polls, spinning politicians or the newspapers

All in all, Twitter users displayed mainly negative emotions regarding the American and British news media coverage of the debates, especially frustration, anger and disappointment. The coverage in both countries was perceived as biased, manipulated and unfair and triggered feelings of powerlessness in social media users. Many references to humour and enthusiasm were also coded; however, these mocked or expressed excitement towards upcoming satirical news programmes, the analysis of some pundits or alternative reporting techniques. Lastly, Twitter users not only felt strongly against the tone of the media, they also expressed negative emotions regarding what journalists chose to cover: mainly trivia, emotions and emotionality, according to Twitter users.

Discussion: Emotional Chains

While previous scholars have conducted empirical research indicating that emotional contagion is possible on text-only communications, social media and indirect communications media,[16,17,18,19] the results presented here indicate that politicians (during the debates), journalists (through their articles), and Twitter users (through their tweets) were emotionally connected during the debates' period forming an "emotional chain". However, while an emotional chain of responses from politicians to Twitter users via journalists has been identified in this work, it does not work in a predictable, uniform or straightforward way. In other words, politicians, journalists and Twitter users all emotionally reacted, using mainly negative emotions, to what the initial emotions were. However, this was not simply linear as although politicians tried to manipulate emotions and emotionality during the debates, this failed as Twitter users mainly responded by using negative emotions in relation to these attempts to influence emotions. Similarly, although journalists tried to manipulate emotions to fit their narrative and present their favourite candidate in the best possible way, Twitter users mainly expressed negative emotions regarding the coverage of the debates. These results therefore contradict the findings of Coviello et al. and Ferrara and Yang, who reported that mainly positive emotions were identified during emotional contagion.[16,17]

These differences can partly be explained by methodological differences. Firstly, previous studies mostly relied on sentiment analyses,[16,17,18,19] while the results presented here were obtained following content analysis. Secondly, contrary to Kramer,[18] the results presented in this chapter were observational, associational and empirical and did not rely on data manipulation or interaction with users. Lastly, the chapter presents a study of emotional contagion across media (television, newspapers and Twitter) and thus does not focus on social media platforms only. These differences therefore beg the question as to whether emotional contagion is context-dependent, especially when it comes to specific media or events and issues.

Conclusions

Before turning to the conclusions of this study, it is worth mentioning that our findings from the debates in the United Kingdom and United States were similar, overall, notwithstanding differences in proportions of coded emotional responses. We found that Twitter users displayed mainly negative emotions (frustration, anger, and disappointment, used in conjunction with humour) regarding candidates using emotions and references to family, friends and anecdotes. As well, mainly negative emotions prevailed in Twitter users regarding journalistic coverage of the debates, both in the UK and US. Humour was the most coded element of both analyses and was rather negative in its use, as Twitter users displayed humour mainly to mock, criticise, and/or to express negative emotions regarding a candidate, the debates or their coverage.

The consequences of these negative emotions were similar in both case studies. Firstly, the use of emotions and references to family, friends and anecdotes in debates by candidates backfired and turned into mockery, support for opposite candidates and an increasing scepticism and scrutiny on Twitter. Secondly, the coverage of the debates in both countries was perceived as biased, manipulated and unfair, and triggered powerlessness in social media users who urged others not to follow the news media to make up their minds. Users not only criticised the tone of the media, they also displayed negative emotions in relation to what journalists chose to cover, namely trivia, emotions and emotionality according to Twitter users. Thus, these results suggest that emotions are not a straightforward means for politicians and journalists to convince voters and news consumers. Further, and to the extent that Twitter users are representative of news-consuming citizens of both countries, it would appear that they have lost interest in, and become, increasingly distrustful of politics and journalism, respectively.

Notes

1. Stephen Cushion, *The Democratic Value of News: Why Public Service Media Matter* (Basingstoke, UK: Palgrave Macmillan, 2012).

2. Cushion, *The Democratic Value of News*, 2012.

3. James S. Newton, Roger D. Masters, Gregory J. McHugo and Denis G. Sullivan, 'Making up Our Minds: Effects of Network Coverage on Viewer Impressions of Leaders', *Polity* 20(2) (1987): 226–46.

4. Barry Richards, *Emotional Governance: Politics, Media and Terror* (Basingstoke, UK: Palgrave MacMillan, 2007).

5. Jonathan H. Turner, 'The Sociology of Emotions: Basic Theoretical Arguments', *Emotion Review* 1(4) (2009): 340–54.

6. Mick Hume, *Televictims: Emotional Correctness in the Media AD (after Diana)* (London: InformInc, 1998).

7. Frank Furedi, *Therapy Culture: Cultivating Vulnerability in an Uncertain Age* (London: Routledge, 2003).

8. Barry Richards and Joanne Brown, 'The Therapeutic Culture Hypothesis', in *Lifestyle, Desire and Politics: Contemporary Identities*, Thomas Johansson and Ove Sernhede, eds. (Goteborg, Sweden: Daidalos, 2002).

9. Darren Lilleker, *Key Concepts in Political Communication* (London: Sage, 2006).

10. Darren Lilleker and Mick Temple, 'Reporting Politics: Enlightening Citizens or Undermining Democracy?', In *Journalism: New Challenges*, Karen Fowler-Watt and Stuart Allan, eds. (Bournemouth, UK: Centre for Journalism and Communication Research, Bournemouth University, 2013).

11. Richards, *Emotional Governance*, 2007.

12. Zizi Papacharissi and Maria de Fatima Oliveira, 'Affective News and Networked Publics: The Rhythms of News Storytelling on #Egypt', *Journal of Communication* 62(2) (2012): 266–82.

13. Jörn Bollow, 'Anticipation of Public Emotions in TV Debates', In *Emotions in Dialogic Interaction: Advances in the Complex*, Edda Weigand, ed. (Amsterdam: John Benjamins Publishing, 2004).

14. Richards and Brown, 'The Therapeutic Culture Hypothesis', 2002.

15. Sigmund Freud, 'Humour (translated by Joane Riviere)', *The International Journal of Psychoanalysis* 9(1) (1927): 2.

16. Lorenzo Coviello, Yunkyu Sohn, Adam D.I. Kramer, Cameron Marlow, Massimo Franceschetti, Nicholas A. Christakis and James H. Fowler, 'Detecting Emotional Contagion in Massive Social Networks', *PLOS ONE* 9(3) (2014), http://journals.plos.org/plosone/article?id = 10.1371/journal.pone.0090315#s1.

17. Emilio Ferrara and Zeyao Yang, 'Measuring Emotional Contagion in Social Media', *PLOS ONE* 10(11) (2015), http://journals.plos.org/plosone/article?id = . 10.1371/journal.pone.0142390#sec001

18. Adam D. I. Kramer, 'The Spread of Emotion via Facebook', *Proceedings of the SIGCHI Conference on Human Factors in Computing Systems* (2012): 767–70.

19. Adam D. I. Kramer, Jamie E. Guillory and Jeffrey T. Hancock, 'Experimental Evidence of Massive-scale Emotional Contagion through Social Networks', *PNAS* 111(24) (2014): 8788–90.

17

The Failed Utopias of Walden and Walden Two

Robert Wright

THE BEHAVIOURAL PSYCHOLOGIST B. F. Skinner published in 1948 a fictional vision of a modern utopia titled *Walden Two*.[1] The foundation upon which this envisioned world was to be built on was the knowledge base that Skinner and his contemporaries were developing in their newly emerging science of behaviour. It was Skinner's fundamental belief that behaviourism could one day free people from their trivial material concerns and ultimately enable them to pursue pure self-actualization. His utopia was influenced by the American philosopher Henry David Thoreau who, almost a hundred years earlier, also envisaged a utopia (known as *Walden*[2]) whereby "man" could be similarly liberated. However, whereas Thoreau's vision was based on radical individualism or absolute autonomy, the divergent structure adopted by Skinner could be described as radical behaviorism. *Walden Two's* most striking difference from *Walden* was that it required an empowered elite to govern; a point Skinner viewed as an unfortunate practical reality, but a prospect which Thoreau would have vehemently disapproved.

Rather than elected, this elite group of technocratic planners would be selected entirely on their capability to fulfill the role as determined by a managerial pseudo-class.[3] These planners, informed by the science of behaviorism, would tweak how society functioned, in order to ensure maximum peace and contentment amongst the citizenry. The reasoning for this particular arrangement, according to Skinner, was that democratic governments were plodding in nature, rendering them slow to adapt to the immediate needs of their populations.[4] This adaptability is of particular importance in making Skinner's vision a success as it is crucial to his behavoural utopia that citizens *feel* as though they are happy and free. This would be ultimately achieved by the proactive and reactive monitoring and modifying of the living environment, so as to produce these positive feelings optimally.

One of the specific ways this was approached in Skinner's science was by taking advantage of what he termed "operant conditioning". This concept explains that behaviours are learnt as a result of feedback, be it positive feedback where desirable behaviours are rewarded (Skinner's preferred method), or negative feedback where "incorrect" behaviours are punished. Skinner's utopia primarily hinged on the idea that if we could comprehensively understand and control how behaviours are learnt in society we could reshape human actions for the better.

A vocal critic of this future "utopia" was the sociologist and philosopher of technology Lewis Mumford, who regarded Skinner's idea as dystopic. Directly expressing such concerns in regards to *Walden Two* he stated:

> Skinner has an ingenious way of making a system of highly compulsive organisations seem as though it were a very humane one. . . . You make people do exactly what you want with some form of sugar-coated drug or candy which will make them think they are actually enjoying every moment of it. This is the most dangerous of all systems of compulsion. That's why I regard Skinner's utopia as another name for Hell. And it would be a worse hell because we wouldn't realize we were there. We would imagine we were still in Heaven.[5]

Despite this warning, such behavioural "utopias" are indeed possible today, and have become particularly prolific within cyberspace. As follows, what I call here Walden Three succeeds by hiding the superstructure of power by giving us the false impression of existing in a direct and communal democratic paradise. By seemingly bridging the conceptual gap that exists between the utopian visions presented by both Thoreau and Skinner, these environments give us the feeling that we possess autonomous freedom while, in fact, we operate within a restrictive landscape matrix, designed explicitly for behavioural manipulation. Take as evidence, for example, the much maligned "Facebook research" into triggering emotional contagion in which the social feeds of users were algorithmically manipulated to observe whether the expressed emotional state of individuals could be modified. A 2014 study found that "features of emotional contagion" were present in their subjects' online behaviour and could be manipulated in relation to whether the content presented in their news-feeds had a structural bias towards being mostly positive or negative in tone.[6]

It is argued in this chapter that the remarkable potency of social media is that there exists within it a two-tier behaviour modification system. In the first tier, we actively participate and sustain ourselves via affective quantified interactions—in a mode which has been previously described as lateral surveillance, participatory surveillance or social surveillance—which I describe, in its behavioural mode, as reflexive surveillance (or the reflexive panopticon).[7] The other level, and perhaps the more potent tier of behavioural management, is enacted technocratically by those who own the platforms. Somewhat akin to Skinner's technocratic elite, the actors operating in Walden Three—rather than being put in place openly by society—have rather "earned" their positions via capitalistic determinism.

We relate this structure of social media then as being somewhat similar to Jeremy Bentham's Panopticon. A theoretical prison design, Bentham's panopticon of 1798 appears to be a seemingly simple looking circular structure with an observation tower placed within the centre. The uniqueness of this design is that those incarcerated within are unable to gauge whether or not they are being observed by the guards in the tower. Resultantly, prisoners behave in-line with the ruling norm without the need for traditional coercion.

Foucault's later analysis of the panopticon in his 1975 work *Discipline and Punish* adopts this plan as a metaphor through which to analyze the power structure of contemporary surveillance societies. He suggests that the underlining principles of the panopticon are also applicable to many other social environments, such as schools and work-places that are sculpted around the same basic idea. In architectures such as these, he notes we are directed to essentially internalize the role of watchman and become 'the principle of [our] own subjection'.[8]

Social media is described here then as being a two-tier peer-run cybernetic panopticon where the tower and the real prison guards (that is to say the people and algorithms running a given social network) are, by design, cognitively disavowed by the users of the system. Our gaze is instead lead to focus on our fellow observing inmates who, as well as policing internally, now collectively externalize the role of watchman across the network. The tower, however, remains and transforms us into "objects of information" that can be manipulated for financial or political gain while we are distracted by the self-policing capillaries of power that flow amongst and between our fellow entranced user-prisoners within echo chambers seeded by our own actions in the cybernetic environment.

Before looking further at the two levels of behavioural control in action, within social media (or Walden Three), we first address why behavioural psychology has grown in interest and relevance in today's world.

Nudge Economics and the Appeal
of Behavioural Psychology

It was Skinner's positive view that his science could lead to the creation of planned environments in which the psychological needs of all would be satisfactorily met, while not appearing to impose change. It was specifically through this latter characteristic that behavioural psychology has, on one hand, influenced politics, and on the other, fed into the practical considerations of online entrepreneurs wishing to effectively monetize big data. This development has subsequently led to what could be described as "behavioural capitalism", whereby political strategists and corporate social media make use of digital technologies that game and correlate human affective tendencies in order to help generate tangible outcomes and profits.

To understand why politicians today—and subsequently technologists and entrepreneurs—have embraced behaviorism, we note the sea-change in politics which began with the rise of Thatcher and Reagan. What crucially united these two conservative figures was that much of their rhetoric played to the assumed desire of humans to be autonomous individuals. Thatcher effectively utilized this for her political agenda in promising to strip away the "nanny-state" which she framed as overtly restricting an individual's behaviour. She further tried to separate this illusion of individual freedom from notions of social collectivity, by famously stating that 'there is no such thing as society'.[9]

However, this inherent faith in individual freedom has subsequently wavered amongst political classes to whom the concept, on a practical level, is no longer seen as entirely convenient as a tactical tool through which to maintain either hegemonic or economic power. A new widely embraced political idea has emerged which allows the public to retain their belief in Thatcher-style deregulated freedom, while also allowing those in power to once again attempt to actively change behaviour without garnering accusations of direct manipulation.

In more recent times then focus has shifted back to societal manipulation via so-called "Libertarian Paternalism" and wider nudge theory.[10] These both set out that it is politically legitimate and practically possible for governmental or corporate organizations to attempt to manipulate mass behaviour while respecting contemporary and often commercially based notions of individual freedom. One clear and relatively early political adoption of this can be observed in former British PM David Cameron's creation of the now-privatized research body known originally as the Behavioural Insights Team.

Formed to give advice on how to best implement behavioural-based policies, the body promoted a new strategic style of political influence in stating:

> We are interested in the soft touch of policy rather than its heavy hand: going with the grain of human nature, rather than rubbing us up the wrong way. . . . This shifts the focus of attention away from facts and information, and towards altering the context within which people act.[11]

This statement shares much with the ideas that underpinned Skinner's utopia. Crucially however, it also points to the fundamental structural design of social media, with this specific style of behavioural control being not only enacted by the platform owners, but also amongst users themselves. The key to success for these systems, in a world steeped in the rhetoric of individualized freedom, is the key requirement that behavioural manipulation is hidden and disavowed, for people would not knowingly want to ordinarily enter such a system of external coercion. As discussed below, if these services are not thoughtfully designed, people will simply not engage or perhaps even reject such behavioural constructs when they are consciously recognized.

Fear and Loathing in Silicon Valley: People against Peeple

In late September 2015, Silicon Valley based entrepreneurs Julia Cordray and Nicole McCullough announced to the world—to much confusion, mockery and even outrage—their plans for a new app called *Peeple*. Promoted by what was meant to be a positive epithet, they sold their idea by stating "Character is Destiny".[12] It was this very concept, and in particular the way in which it was both foregrounded and structurally weaved into their product, which became part of the vitriolic backlash Peeple subsequently received.

Their core concept, framed as "Yelp for People",[13] was that individuals (whether they were using the service or not) would be given a rating out of five stars. These ratings were to be applied to people by their peers in three distinct categories: professional, personal and romantic. The idea was to give individuals confidence in strangers, via the aggregation of peer submitted feedback data, in a way similar to how confidence is built in online commerce. In a later promotional video the developers expressed this goal by stating: 'We believe that your character can be a new form of social currency'.[14]

The design of the app was intended to openly and explicitly quantify human relationships and regulate behaviour through the creation of an overt peer-run reflexive panopticon. After an initial backlash, safeguards were put in place to try and minimize potential abuse and to ease some of the privacy concerns that were being expressed. However, the damage was irrevocable and despite what was in essence a techno-utopian solution to trust building, the app could not escape what it fundamentally was: an explicit environment for behavioural control. Interestingly, many of the concerns expressed about *Peeple* had been, one year previously, parodied in an episode of the American sitcom *Community*, in which two software developers beta test a new people rating app at a college.[15] Operating in a similar, but stripped down manner to *Peeple*, their *Meow Meow Beanz* app gave the students the opportunity to rate each other out of 0 to 5 cats. One of the characters in the episode, Abed, describes this app as being 'addictively affective' and explains that the supposed appeal of the service is that it 'takes everything that's subjective and unspoken about human interaction and reduces it to explicit and objective numbers'.[16] Later on, a cynical world-weary teacher instantly recognizes the more negative side of the app and states:

'When you get older your [sic] gonna see the warning signs; Mark Zuckerberg is Fidel Castro in flip flops. *Meow Meow Beanz* is gonna make East Berlin look like Woodstock, you take my word for that'.[17]

In the episode we observe how the characters actively change their behaviour in order to achieve a higher rating from their peers, with one going as far as to pretend to have a limp after noticing he was getting higher ratings out of sympathy, while another achieves a high rating by simply smearing mustard on her face (an action she later repeat to gain more attention). The overall farcical outcome is that the college transforms itself into a camp sci-fi dystopia, where a new technologically mediated and peer-maintained class system emerges, giving certain individuals greater privileges over others based on their in-app ranking. What the episode does then, for comic effect, is exaggerate the latent features of already-existing social media platforms by foregrounding it in a fictional app similar to how *Peeple* would have fundamentally operated.

Two Levels of the Invisible Tower

The behavioural system in social media is essentially panoptic. However, this central tower in the underlying power structures of social media is, by design, disavowed since we are encouraged to focus our gaze on fellow users who surround us in echo chambers within the greater power structure. While we do this, the platforms' owners are free to tinker with the environment (often for payment) so as to encourage certain behaviours without our noticing.

This is a process that occurs on two levels. In the first level of behavioural tinkering, users apply to each other via the use of likes, "hearting buttons", up-votes and other similar quantified interactions. These structurally embedded tools allow us, in essence, to positively reward favourable behaviours within the network. When we receive these kinds of rewards, we get a small buzz of pleasure which grows in intensity in correlation to the number of positive reinforcements received. As social media researcher Lauren Sherman argues, when our posts go positively viral, we feel ecstatic.[18] The ultimate outcome of this reward feedback loop is the encouragement to post similar content again. These interactions act similarly to how the food pellet did in Skinner's early experiments into operant conditioning in pigeons, except that, rather than being obtained from a single observable master, these behavioural rewards are distributed by everyone within the network.[19] We all become both experimenter and subject, and it appears as though hierarchical power has been eliminated, for we all have a say in what environmental variables are being reinforced (at least within our respective echo chambers).[20]

However, despite this seemingly utopian outcome, the negative effects of this first level of behavioural tinkering has been illustrated by Das and Kramer, Marwick and Boyd and Marder and colleagues, who have demonstrated how users constrain themselves based on the expectations of their social media peers.[21] For example, Marder et al. conclude that: 'Overall . . . [social networking sites] are not necessarily liberating, but rather they have the potential to be somewhat oppressive, as users normalize their behavior (or behavioral intention) both online and offline'.[22]

While then we are entranced by this peer-panoptic process, we find ourselves, often unknowingly, generating data which is valuable to those who operate the second layer of technocratic behavioural control. We could describe the nature of the operations taking place at this level as perhaps being the "invisible hand of behavioural tinkering". With this in mind, an influential 2015 study into personality and metadata argued that with just 150 Facebook likes, their analytical model of human behaviour could predict a user's personality better than an individual's friends could, and with 300 likes it could outperform a spouse![23] Using this kind of behavioural data analysis, companies can and do alter digital environments in order to further influence behaviour.

An example of behavioural data analysis can be observed in the 2016 US presidential election in which the Donald Trump campaign made use of the big data communications company Cambridge Analytica. Their CEO and President Alexander Nix has claimed that his company works with over 5000 unique data points and have profiled the personality of every adult in the

United States of America (around 220 million individuals).[24] As a result, Cambridge Analytica claims to be able to target anyone in the United States for specific messaging via a process they call "Behavioral Microtargeting".[25] By utilizing the insights of Cambridge Analytica, Trump's team was able to deliver highly "personalised" communications to specific audience segments in order to provide them with differing conceptions of what Trump stood for. In other words, they could present the rational for a given policy in a multiplicity of ways so that Trump could mean different things to different people.

Commenting on this big-data derived behavoural power, Professor John Rust from Cambridge University's Psychometric Centre has strongly stated that:

> It's no exaggeration to say that minds can be changed. Behaviour can be predicted and controlled. I find it incredibly scary. I really do. Because nobody has really followed through on the possible consequences of all this. People don't know it's happening to them. Their attitudes are being changed behind their backs.[26]

Conclusion: Walden Three?

The core political and ethical issue at stake here is who ultimately possesses and utilizes this power to manipulate behaviour? In Walden Two this power was made explicit through a set of recognized people known as "the planners" who were representatives of the wider community and could be consulted. However, in what I call Walden Three, the power is always obfuscated, despite the Silicon Valley bluster about transparency, and promoted in conjunction with the utopian rhetoric of open networks. This primarily ensures that users, who would not ordinarily situate themselves in such an environment, are not wise to the existence of these underlying compulsive behavioural systems.

The widely embraced cyber-utopian view of our digital world is one in which we are supposedly liberated by networked technologies and their disruptive ability to break and undermine hierarchal power. However, I have argued in this chapter that we are in fact living in a disavowed dystopia. Through social media, in particular, we are systemically encouraged to be distracted by our peers while the core *occulted* behavioural system attempts to nudge us—via, for example clandestine marketing campaigns—toward specific quantifiable interactions, based on psychological profiling. Rather than granting us radical freedom then, our willing entry into Walden Three traps us in an illusionary utopia.

Notes

1. B. F. Skinner, *Walden Two* (London: Collier Macmillan, 1976).

2. David Henry Thoreau, *Walden* (New York: Franklin Watts, 1969).

3. Described as pseudo-class because the society depicted in Walden Two was materially equal while also aiming to be as non-hierarchical and fluid as technically possible. Anyone could theoretically be granted the opportunity to be a manager should they possess the requisite skills. However, the specifics as to how one actually gets the opportunity to enter this pseudo-class is unfortunately never fully explained in the novella.

4. Dennis G. Stevens, 'On Skinner's Politics', *Political Science Reviewer* 12(1) (1982), 255–56; Towards Tomorrow (directed by Ramsay Short; BBC One, March 14, 1968).

5. Towards Tomorrow (directed by Ramsay Short; BBC One, March 14, 1968).

6. Adam D. I. Kramer, Jamie E. Guillory and Jeffery T. Hancock, 'Experimental Evidence of Massive-Scale Emotional Contagion Through Social Networks', *Proceedings of the National Academy of Sciences* 111(24) (2014), 8788–90).

7. Mark Andrejevic, 'The Work of Watching One Another: Lateral Surveillance, Risk, and Governance', *Surveillance & Society* 2(4) (2005), 479–97); Anders Albrechtslund, 'Online Social Networking as Participatory Surveillance', *First Monday* 13(3) (2008.); Adam N. Joinson, 'Looking at, Looking up or Keeping up with People?: Motives and Use of Facebook', *Proceedings of the Twenty-Sixth Annual SIGCHI Conference on Human Factors in Computing Systems*, 2008, 1027–36; Robert S. Tokunaga, 'Social Networking site or Social Surveillance Site? Understanding the Use of Interpersonal Electronic Surveillance in Romantic Relationships', *Computers in Human Behavior* 27(2) (2011), 705–13).

8. Michael Foucault, *Discipline and Punish: The Birth of the Prison* (London: Penguin, 1991), 200.

9. Douglas Keay, 'Aids, Education and the Year 2000', *Women's Own*, October 31, 1987, 8–10.

10. Cass R. Sunstein and Richard H. Thaler, 'Libertarian Paternalism Is Not An Oxymoron', *The University of Chicago Law Review* 70(4) (2003), 1159–202); Cass R. Sunstein and Richard H. Thaler, *Nudge: Improving Decisions about Health, Wealth and Happiness* (London: Penguin, 2009), 4–6, 13–14.

11. Paul Dolan, Michael Hallsworth, David Halpern, Dominic King and Ivo Vlaev, *Mindspace: Influencing Behaviour Through Public Policy* (London: Institute for Government and Cabinet Office 2010.), 13–14.

12. Barbara Speed, 'Why the Philosophy of People-Rating App Peeple is Fundamentally Flawed', *New Statesman*, October 9, 2015.

13. Caitlin Dewey, 'Everyone You Know Will Be Able to Rate You on the Terrifying "Yelp For People"—Whether You Want Them to or Not', *The Washington Post*, September 30, 2015, https://www.washingtonpost.com/news/the-intersect/wp/2015/09/30/everyone-you-know-will-be-able-to-rate-you-on-the-terrifying-yelp-for-people-whether-you-want-them-to-or-not/.

14. Peeple, *Welcome to Peeple* (film, YouTube Video, 01:17. Posted March 5, 2016.

15. Community, App Development and Condiments (series 5, episode 8. Directed by Rob Schrab, written by Jordan Blum and Parker Deay; NBC, March 6, 2014)

16. Ibid.

17. Ibid.

18. Lauren E. Sherman et al., 'The Power of the Like in Adolescence: Effects of Peer Influence on Neural and Behavioral Responses to Social Media', *Psychological Science* 27(7) (2016), 1027–35)

19. In his experiments on pigeons, where they were placed in controlled environments eponymously called Skinner boxes, Skinner would reward his subjects with food pellets when they performed a certain desired action, for example pecking at a symbol of a cross. In doing this he was providing them with positive reinforcement in order to foster 'operant conditioning', that is to say the creation of new behaviour patterns. Later he went on to discover what he called 'Schedules of Reinforcement' in which he observed that behaviour would be more strongly reinforced, once an initial pattern had been established, when rewards were deferred. For example, making pigeons peck the cross symbol not simply once, but several times, before paying out further reinforced the behaviour; a principle that we can clearly see in addictive play exhibited at casinos and gambling more widely.

B. F. Skinner, 'Superstition in the Pigeon', *Journal of Experimental Psychology* 38 (1948) 168–72; C. B. Ferster and B. F. Skinner, *Schedules of Reinforcement* (New York: Appleton-Century-Crofts, 1957).

20. B. F. Skinner, *Beyond Freedom and Dignity* (New York; Bantam Books, 1972), 192.

21. Sauvik Das and Adam Kramer, 'Self-Censorship on Facebook', *Proceedings of the Seventh International AAAI Conference on Weblogs and Social Media*, 2013, 120–27); Alice E. Marwick and danah boyd, 'I Tweet Honestly, I Tweet Passionately: Twitter Users, Context Collapse and the Imagined Audience', *New Media and Society* 13 (1) (2010), 114–33); Ben Marder et al., 'The Extended "Chilling" Effect of Facebook: The Cold Reality of Ubiquitous Social Networking', *Computers in Human Behavior* 60 (2016), 582–92.

22. Ben Marder et al., 'The Extended "Chilling" Effect of Facebook'.

23. Wu Youyou, Michal Kosinski and David Stillwell, 'Computer-based Personality Judgements are more Accurate Than Those Made by Humans', *Proceedings of the National Academy of Sciences* 112(4) (2015), 1036–40).

24. Concordia, *The Power of Big Data and Psychographics.* (Youtube video, 11.00, September 27, 2016. Accessed June 25, 2017.) https://www.youtube.com/watch?v=n8Dd5aVXLCc.

25. Ibid

26. Carole Cadwalladr, 'The Big Data Billionaire Waging War on Mainstream Media', *The Observer,* February 26, 2017, https://www.theguardian.com/politics/2017/feb/26/robert-mercer-breitbart-war-on-media-steve-bannon-donald-trump-nigel-farage.

Co-curator Mikey Georgeson. Selfie.

Index

Author Biographies

Tony D. Sampson is Reader in digital media cultures and communication at the University of East London. His publications include *The Spam Book*, coedited with Jussi Parikka (Hampton Press, 2009), *Virality: Contagion Theory in the Age of Networks* (University of Minnesota Press, 2012) and *The Assemblage Brain: Sense Making in Neuroculture* (University of Minnesota Press, 2016). Tony is the organizer of the Affect and Social Media conferences and a co-founder of Club Critical Theory in Southend, Essex.

Sophie Bishop is a PhD Student and Associate Lecturer at the University of East London in the department of Arts, Technology and Innovation. Her research looks gender and the political economy of social media platforms, particularly focusing on YouTube and the development of the UK vlogging "industry".

Rebecca Coleman is a Reader in Sociology at Goldsmiths, University of London and Co-Director of the Methods Lab. Her research focuses on visual and sensory culture, bodies, temporality (especially presents and futures), inventive methodologies and feminist and cultural theory. Recent publications include a special issue of *Sociological Review*, "Futures in Question" (2017, edited with Richard Tutton) and a special section of *Theory, Culture and Society*, "Visualising Surfaces, Surfacing Vision" (2017, edited with Liz Oakley-Brown). Since 2018, her research focuses on a new project, "Mediating Presents: Producing 'the Now' in Contemporary Digital Culture" (funded by a Leverhulme Research Fellowship).

Zara Dinnen is Lecturer in Twentieth and Twenty-First Century Literature at Queen Mary University of London. She is author of *The Digital Banal: New Media and American Literature and Culture* (Columbia University Press, 2018), and co-editor of *The Edinburgh Companion to Contemporary Narrative Theories* (Edinburgh University Press, 2018).

Darren Ellis is a senior lecturer in Psychosocial Theory and Practice at the University of East London. His research focuses on psychosocial perspectives of emotion and affect in a variety of contexts. For example, Darren draws on stoic notions of *apathia* to conceptualise experiences of the affective atmospheres of surveillance. Darren co-authored a book entitled *Social Psychology of Emotion* (Sage, 2015) and is presently completing a book entitled *Emotion in the Digital Age*, to be published in the *Routledge Studies in Science, Technology and Society* series.

Lewis Goodings is a Senior Lecturer in Psychology at Anglia Ruskin University. His publications focus on the role of social media and the impact of introducing different social technologies into mental health communities. He is driven to understand the changing ways that people interact with new forms of technology and is interested in how social media produce subjective or collective spaces that afford complex relations of thinking, feeling and acting.

Jamie Hakim is a lecturer in media studies in the School of Art, Media and American Studies at the University of East Anglia. His research is concerned with masculinity, the body, intimacy, affect and digital media. His book *The Male Body in Digital Culture* will be published as part of Rowman & Littlefield's Radical Cultural Studies series in 2020.

Stephen Jukes is Professor of Journalism at Bournemouth University. His research focuses on objectivity and emotion in news with an emphasis on affect, trauma and conflict. A former foreign correspondent and Head of News at Reuters, he has edited a series of books on the Middle East and written extensively on journalism and trauma.

Morgane Kimmich is a visiting research fellow at the School of Arts and Creative Industries at London South Bank University. Her research focuses on the intersection of emotions, social media, politics and journalism. She is currently looking at how emotions were used in live televised political debates by politicians interacting in debates, by newspaper journalists covering debates and by Twitter users following debates and reacting to their coverage.

Stephen Maddison is Professor of Cultural Studies and Director of Research for Arts, Technology and Innovation at the University of East London. He is a series editor of Radical Cultural Studies for RLI, a member of the Centre for Cultural Studies Research at UEL (http://culturalstudiesresearch.org/), and of the editorial board of the journal *Porn Studies*. Stephen's work on pornography, embodiment and cultural politics has appeared in several major collections, including *Mainstreaming Sex* (2009), *Porn.com: Making Sense of Online Pornography* (2010), *Hard to Swallow: Hard-core Pornography on* Screen (2011), and Transgression 2.0: Media, Culture, and the Politics of a Digital Age (2012), as well as in the journals *New Formations* and *Topia: Canadian Journal of Cultural Studies*. Stephen is the author of *Fags, Hags and Queer Sisters: Gender Dissent and Heterosocial Bonds in Gay Culture* (Palgrave, 2000).

Maurizio Mauri, PhD, PsyD, is Adjunct Professor at Università degli Studi of Milan for the class in Consumer Psychology and he has a teaching position at Università degli Studi of Bari for the class in Neuromarketing. He is co-founder (in 2010) and operative coordinator at the Behavior & Brain Lab at IULM University of Milan. His main publications include and/or research focuses on the emotional impact generated by different kind of media exposures, from social networks to advertising campaigns, by means of the simultaneous analyses of eye-tracking recordings, neuro-psychophysiological reactions and facial expressions. He was co-organizer of the "Measuring Behavior 2014" conference that related to his previous two-year experience (2005–2007) at Brain & Cognitive Sciences department at MIT (USA).

Kaitlynn Mendes is an Associate Professor in the School of Media, Communication and Sociology at the University of Leicester, UK. Kaitlynn is an expert on feminism, activism and gender issues in the media, and is the author of editor of five books including *Digital Feminist Activism* (Oxford Press, forthcoming 2018, with Jessica Ringrose and Jessalynn Keller) and *SlutWalk: Feminism, Activism and Media* (Palgrave, 2015), which was selected as Book of the Week for the *Times Higher Education* magazine. She has also published in journals such as *Feminist Media Studies; Media, Culture and Society; The International Journal of Cultural Studies,* and the *Journal of Gender Studies*. In addition to her academic research, Kaitlynn has appeared on programmes such as the BBC's Woman's Hour, and regularly writes op-eds for publications such as *The Conversation* and local newspapers.

Alyssa Niccolini researches affect and its intersections with education. Her work has been published in *Gender and Education, International Journal of Qualitative Studies in Education, Journal of Gender Studies* and *Qualitative Inquiry*.

Jussi Parikka is Professor at the Winchester School of Art (University of Southampton). In addition to his work on media archaeology, his other books include the media ecology trilogy *Digital Contagions* (2007, 2nd edition 2016), the award-winning *Insect Media* (2010) and most recently, *A Geology of Media* (2015), which addresses the environmental contexts of technical media culture. This topic was continued in the short booklet *A Slow, Contemporary Violence: Damaged Environments of Technological Culture* (2016). He is also the co-editor of *Across and Beyond:– A Transmediale Reader on Post-digital Practices, Concepts, and Institutions* (2016, co-edited with Ryan Bishop, Kristoffer Gansing and Elvia Wilk).

Helen Powell is Course Director of Creative Advertising with Marketing and Acting Head of Creative Industries at London South Bank University. She has written widely on the intersection of advertising and consumer behaviour including *Promotional Culture and Convergence* (2013) and most recently as co-editor and contributor to *The Advertising Handbook*, 4th edition (2018).

Jessica Ringrose is Professor of Sociology of Gender and Education at the UCL Institute of Education (London, UK), where she leads teaching in Social Justice and Education. Her current research explores young people's digitally networked gender and sexual cultures; and LGBTQ + and Feminist activism in Schools. Recent books include: *Post-Feminist Education? Girls and the sexual politics of schooling* (Routledge, 2013); *Deleuze and Research Methodologies* (EUP, 2013, co-edited with Rebecca Coleman); and *Children, Sexuality and Sexualisation*, co-edited with Emma Renold and Danielle Egan (Palgrave, 2015). Her latest book: *Digital Feminist Activism: Girls and Women Fight back against Rape Culture*, co-authored with Dr Kaitlynn Mendes and Dr Jessalynn Keller (Oxford University Press) will be out in 2018.

Greg Singh is Associate Professor in Media and Communications at the University of Stirling, where he is Programme Director of Digital Media. His main publications include *Film After Jung* (Routledge, 2009) and *Feeling Film: Affect and Authenticity in Popular Cinema* (Routledge, 2014). Greg is currently working on a monograph relating to ethics, connectivity and recognition theory. He has also recently published on celebrity and YouTube, lifestyle television, and Charlie Brooker's Netflix drama, *Black Mirror*. Greg is Co-Director of the RSE Life in Data Research Network.

Yiğit Soncul is a PhD candidate and Visiting Lecturer in Global Media at Winchester School of Art, University of Southampton, where he works as a member of the Archaeologies of Media and Technology (AMT) research group. His current project investigates the contemporary visual culture of the mask. Research interests include theories of visuality, materiality, technology, and network politics. Previously a visiting fellow at the University of Sydney, his work appeared in journals *Theory, Culture & Society* and *Between*.

Luke Stark is a Postdoctoral Fellow at Dartmouth College and a Fellow of the Berkman Klein Center for Internet and Society at Harvard University. His research focuses on the history of behavioral science in computing, digital privacy, and emotional expression online. Luke's work has been published in venues including *The Information Society*, the *International Journal of Communication*, and *History of the Human Sciences*; he has also organized a number of workshops dedicated to exploring ethics and values in the design of digital systems. He holds a PhD in Media, Culture, and Communication from New York University.

Ian Tucker is Reader in Social Psychology at the University of East London. He has a long standing interest in the social psychological aspects of emotion and affect, which has theoretically informed empirical work in the areas of mental distress, social media and surveillance. He has conducted research for the Mental Health Foundation and the EPSRC Communities and Culture Network +, and is currently working on projects focused on social media and peer support in mental health communities, and the material environments of forensic psychiatric settings. Ian has published numerous articles in the areas of mental health, social media, space and place and surveillance.

Robert Wright is a PhD Student in Media and Technology based within CADRE (Centre for Art, Design, Research and Experimentation) at the University of Wolverhampton. He holds an MA in Popular Culture and his current PhD project is titled: "Magic and Cybernetics in 21st Century Capitalist Cyberspace: A Theoretical Study into the Socio-Cultural Effects of Algorithms, Social Media and Big-Data".

CPSIA information can be obtained
at www.ICGtesting.com
Printed in the USA
BVHW08s2338260618
520127BV00001B/4/P